Praise for *Sisters of Influence*

"Zina, Amy, and Rose lived full lives, and Ross has captured their idiosyncratic personalities as well as their achievements and stumbles in a rich saga of thought, action and affection."

—**Patrick T. Reardon**, author of *The Loop: The "L" Tracks That Shaped and Saved Chicago* (SIU Press, 2020)

"Andrea Friederici Ross's triple biography is captivating in its detail and absorbing in its revelations of the achievements of three sisters whose social and cultural contributions, like those of many women of their era, have been under-studied and under-appreciated."

—**Charles H. Cosgrove**, author of *They Both Reached for the Gun: Beulah Annan, Maurine Watkins, and the Trial That Became* Chicago (SIU Press, 2024)

"This engaging book tells the story of a prominent family and its contributions to a changing America as it transformed from Victorian customs to progressive values. *Sisters of Influence* addresses many critical issues for women at that time, from marriage to music; public roles to voting rights; volunteerism to employment opportunities. Most importantly, it covers these issues from the perspective of three fascinating sisters whom history has overlooked—but whose collective biographies enlighten major societal transformations from the 19th to 20th centuries."

—**Greg Borzo**, author of *Chicago's Fabulous Fountains* (SIU Press, 2017)

Sisters of Influence

Sisters *of* Influence

A Biography of
Zina, Amy, and Rose Fay

Andrea Friederici Ross

Southern Illinois University Press
Carbondale

Southern Illinois University Press
siupress.com

Printed in the United States of America.

First published August 2025.

Jacket and cover illustration: Harriet Melusina Fay Peirce headshot from 1908 (left). Photo courtesy of Christopher King. Amelia Muller Fay headshot (center). Photo courtesy of Christopher King. Rose Fay Thomas headshot (right). Photo courtesy of Anti-Cruelty. A close-up of textured black fabric with a repeating gold floral pattern (cropped and inverted; background). Adobe Stock #86805660 by Vic.

Part-title illustrations: PRELUDE: Family photograph taken at the 1866 golden wedding anniversary celebration for Bishop Hopkins and his wife, Melusina. Zina is at far left; father Charles stands between the pillars on the right; Lily is at top center, below the bearded man in the background; Kate is at extreme right, next to Charles Jerome Hopkins, who is leaning on Norman; Rose stands next to Norman. Though unidentified, Laura may be in profile, leaning on a pillar in the background, and her husband, Frank, may be just before the rightmost pillar. Amy was absent. 37 Bishop Hopkins' golden wedding by G. B. Davis; The Picture Art Collection, Alamy Stock Photo. ALLEGRO AGITATO: Zina in her finest in the mid-1850s. Courtesy Tuttle Collection, Institute for Studies in Pragmaticism, Texas Tech University. SCHERZO: Official publicity photo of Amy taken by the Scherer Studio in 1901. Courtesy Christopher King. CONCERTO GROSSO: Rose in the early 1900s. Courtesy Anti-Cruelty. FUGUE: Family members enjoying the beach at Fishers Island, where Sister Kate's summer home was a site of frequent family gatherings in the early 1900s. Courtesy Christopher King. SHEET MUSIC IN BACKGROUND ON PART-TITLE PAGES: Musical scores penned by Theodore Thomas, from the collection of the Newberry Library. Photos by the author.

ISBN 978-0-8093-3978-5 (paperback)
ISBN 978-0-8093-3979-2 (cloth)
ISBN 978-0-8093-3980-8 (ebook)

Printed on recycled paper ♲

SIU
Southern Illinois University System

To my own siblings,
Claudia and Peter,
With much love and admiration.

Contents

Illustrations

IMAGES

GALLERIES

FAY FAMILY TREE

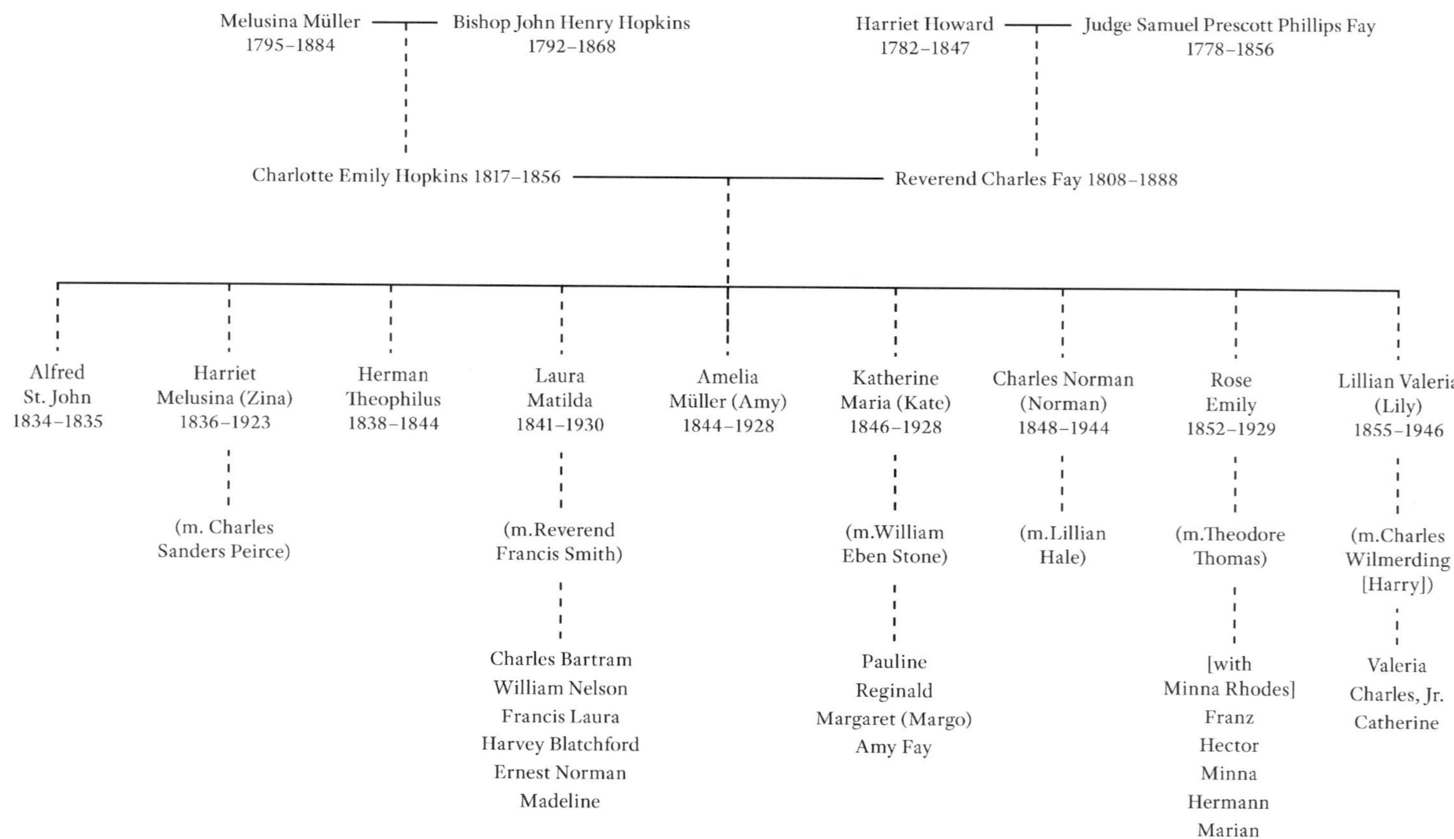

Preface

GENERALLY, HOARDING IS NOT A good thing. But sometimes it can lead to surprising treasures. In the 1970s, writer Sylvia Wright Mitarachi, digging through her ancestors' belongings in a cluttered attic, came across a couple of trunks that brought the past to life. Her grandmother Kate's trunk, smelling of violets, contained the usual assortment of lacy dresses, layers of undergarments, hats, family photos, and knickknacks—no big surprises there. But her great-aunt Zina's trunks overflowed with thousands of yellowing slips of paper, fraying at the edges: a lifetime's worth of family letters and newspaper articles, neatly clipped and dated, many authored by her. People keep what they value. Zina valued ideas.

Sylvia, a novelist and an editor and essayist for *Harper's Bazaar*, spent years with these materials, sorting through them and researching the issues of the day. She eventually landed a National Endowment for the Humanities grant to write a manuscript about Zina. Though Sylvia died before completing her book, a draft remains, as do the original materials—now, thanks to Sylvia, neatly organized and archived at the Schlesinger Library in Cambridge, Massachusetts.

Sylvia fixated on Zina—a fascinating character, to be sure. A women's reformer in the mid-1800s, she challenged established beliefs about a woman's role and advocated for cooperative housekeeping, improved education for women, and a women's parliament to run alongside the men's houses of government. Zina is the subject of numerous dissertations and essays; that she married logician Charles Sanders Peirce, one of the greatest minds of the century, just added to her mystique.

But I came at this project from a different direction, through Zina's sister Rose. Because of my volunteer work at an animal rescue organization, I knew Rose Fay Thomas as the founder of the Anti-Cruelty Society. That she was also the wife of Chicago Symphony Orchestra conductor and musical legend Theodore Thomas increased my interest. As I dug a little deeper, I discovered another sister, Amy (rhymes with Sammy), who studied with composer Franz Liszt and became a professional musician. They called to mind the sisters in *Little Women*, writing, performing music, and exploring the edges of their restricted female world. That their father was a clergyman and that they suffered a heartbreaking death within their family, forcing them to ponder the purpose of a woman's life, only strengthened the ties to the Louisa May Alcott classic.

Zina's trunks, after gathering dust for decades, opened a door into a forgotten world. Out marched all seven Fay siblings—Zina, Laura, Amy, Kate, Norman, Rose, and Lily—and their parents and spouses, to tell their stories of what life was like in the mid-nineteenth century.

To be clear, these were not children of privilege. Their father, the Reverend Charles Fay, moved the family from parish to parish for years before finally settling into the community of St. Albans, Vermont, not far from the Canadian border. Mother Emily managed the household, which included a small dormitory to house boarding students who attended the private classical school Charles ran to bring in more income. They struggled financially. Everyone pitched in with cleaning, teaching, cooking, and sewing. Emily grew depressed and died at the age of thirty-nine; family lore held that it was because of overwork. Her abbreviated life galvanized her daughters, particularly Zina, to want more for women than the daily drudgery of housework.

What was the role of a middle-class White woman in the second half of the nineteenth century, coming out of the Civil War and through Reconstruction? Zina brazenly tried to redefine their role; Amy sought to broaden the opportunities for women in music; Rose worked within the acceptable confines of the women's sphere but headed clubs and associations that brought women together and strengthened their sisterhood. And siblings Laura, Kate, and Lily, who chose the traditional roles of wife and mother, provided interesting contrast and occasional argument. Along the way, they navigated complicated issues such as slavery, suffrage, temperance, and education for women. The Fay women are a perfect case study in women's history during a time when the rules and traditions were changing.

Of the assorted things I have done in my life, raising two children is, without question, my proudest accomplishment. Therefore, it pained me to relegate Laura, Kate, and Lily to being merely supporting characters for this book, as I so highly value their efforts as mothers. I view motherhood as both a vitally important job and the most undervalued in our society. But in terms of what constitutes the unusual, the interesting, the book-worthiness of a life, it was clear that Zina, Amy, and Rose were the key players. Given the plethora of materials available documenting the lives of White men, I had no hesitation about casting Norman as a minor character.

As the sisters were growing up, their feminine role was closely defined. They were supposed to confine themselves to running a household and raising a family, their involvement in the greater community restricted primarily to church activities. The public sector was for the men. But throughout their lives, Zina, Amy, and Rose nudged at those limitations. Mostly, they did it in ways that did not challenge the men. They built up social capital and cultural power behind the scenes, with a smile and in the safe company of other women. In their clubs and activities, they worked in an undefined zone between the spheres that had been delineated for men and women. Their work bridged the gap between Victorian domesticity and Progressive reform.

All operated in areas and manners true to their interests and personalities. One was outspoken and brash, another winsome but persistent, and the third gentle yet determined. None of the three were suffragists. Honestly, part of me wishes they had been among those early firebrands. But there was far more to the argument than just being pro- or antisuffrage. Women's reform was much broader than just the vote. The Fay women represented a tremendous swath of women, the vast majority of whom, in fact, initially did not believe they belonged in the election booth. It takes time to reshape the status quo.

The extensive family correspondence, other personal materials such as poems and journals, and the numerous works the siblings authored give us a close-up look at their lives in their own words. Wherever possible, I have tried to let them speak for themselves.

Rather than juggle multiple life stories simultaneously, I chose to break the book into sections, one covering each of the three sisters. Because Zina, the eldest daughter, did the bulk of her reform work relatively early in her life, and Rose, as one of the youngest siblings, did not find her stride until many years later, there is a natural chronological flow to the story, with Amy fitting nicely in between. Furthermore, because they worked together on certain projects, there are areas that neatly overlap. The organization is not perfect, though, and on occasion, the narrative circles back around to provide updates on what the other family members were doing.

Family dynamics are a curious thing. It is interesting to observe how the Fays reacted to their siblings' successes and failures, sometimes becoming proud or resentful, and stretched away from each other only to eventually grow close again. Because of financial instability, some of the sisters lived together at various points in their lives or ran boardinghouses together to make ends meet. And despite differences in opinion or hurt feelings, the siblings were there to help each other through the uncertainties of life and indignities of old age.

Change is not tidy. Change does not occur in a straight line nor at a steady pace. These three sisters remind us that it often takes many different voices and assorted strategies to gain traction. By the end of their lives, all three had moved their movements forward significantly, mirroring nationwide gains in rights for women. We might do well to ask ourselves who is playing these roles for women today.

This story stretches from the East Coast of the United States to Germany to Chicago and then back east again. It details the beginnings of the Anti-Cruelty Society of Chicago, the Chicago Symphony Orchestra, and the creation of Orchestra Hall, though it is not intended to be a thorough history of these organizations. It involves the Fireside Poets, the academic elite of Cambridge, and several of the world's greatest scientists and musicians. But really, it is the story of three sisters who tried to make the world a bit better, in their own various imperfect ways.

Sisters of Influence

Prelude
Childhood

Charles and Emily

1832–1837

LIKE MANY TALES, THIS ONE starts with a love story. In Cambridge, Massachusetts, in 1832, fifteen-year-old Charlotte Emily Hopkins, known as Emily, had fallen for a handsome Harvard grad. One of fourteen children born to Episcopal priest John Henry Hopkins and his wife, Melusina Müller Hopkins, blue-eyed Emily was bright and tremendously gifted musically and artistically. Her own formal education had been completed the previous year, when her father declared, "You know enough for a woman."[1]

The object of Emily's affection? Charles Fay, twenty-four years old, tall, slender, and, according to various family accounts, quite dashing.[2] Charles had graduated second in his Harvard class of 1829, where the competition had been fierce; many of his fellow graduates went on to fame, including physician and writer Oliver Wendell Holmes, mathematician Benjamin Peirce, Supreme Court Justice Benjamin R. Curtis, and Samuel Francis Smith, author of "America" ("My Country, 'Tis of Thee"). Charles was the third generation of Fay men to attend Harvard. His father, Samuel Prescott Phillips Fay, was a prominent judge with strong ties throughout the community. The Fays were well regarded in Cambridge and considered true patriots: Charles's ancestors included a Midnight Rider, a Boston Tea Party participant, and going further back, Anne Hutchinson, the Puritan religious dissident. His mother, Harriet Howard, had grown up next door to Paul Revere.

Though Charles had intended to study law, John Henry Hopkins's sermons drew the young scholar in and convinced him that he should study theology instead, to the disappointment of his father, the judge. In Charles, Emily saw an intelligent, kind, pious young man. Years later, Charles and Emily's daughter Laura described her father as "the gentlest and most compassionate of men." She wrote, "Though I do not think that he was in love with Emily Hopkins, he admired her beauty and her extraordinary intelligence, especially as regard [*sic*] her musical genius, and so he allowed himself to be engaged to her."[3]

It is ironic that the relationship started with Emily's passion and Charles's reluctance, for that balance reversed in the years to come. But it was a start. After marrying in September 1833, the young couple settled in with the Hopkins family. John Henry Hopkins had recently been appointed bishop of Vermont, and the entire family, including the young newlyweds, moved to Burlington. Surely the union pleased the bishop, as he desired that his sons become men of the cloth and his daughters marry clergymen.[4]

The bishop was a commanding figure, supremely self-confident and considered by his family to be "as close to God as a human could get."[5] In addition to his duties as bishop, he preached at St. Paul's Church in Burlington, taught, published dozens of pamphlets and books, painted landscapes, composed music, played violin and viola, and designed churches. His children learned to paint by copying his artwork. The bishop's great-great-granddaughter quipped, "He was the type of nineteenth century ancestor guaranteed to make his descendants feel that things and they have gone downhill."[6]

Charles and Emily assisted at St. Paul's and helped at the school the Hopkinses ran to bring in additional income. In its heyday, the school had eighty male students divided into six classrooms. Inspired by growing enrollment, Bishop Hopkins had undertaken a considerable enlargement of the school (later called the Vermont Episcopal Institute at Rock Point), clearing additional land, planting an orchard, building a dining facility and a hall of fine arts, and establishing an orchestra, improvements with which the whole family assisted. This overly optimistic growth later spelled financial disaster for the family.

As Emily was the oldest child and her parents kept having more children, the generational line between aunts and uncles and cousins blurred. In 1834, for instance, both Emily and her mother were pregnant. The first child of the new generation, Charles and Emily's son Alfred St. John, arrived that year.

Tragedy struck the Hopkins household in December 1834 in the form of typhoid fever. Seven family members, one servant, and six boarding students contracted the disease. The bishop prayed that if anyone should die, it would be one of his own children, so as not to cast doubt on his care for other people's children. His fervent prayer was granted; all recovered except for Emily's merry-hearted little sister Melusina, age eleven.

The day after Melusina's funeral, Emily, Charles, and baby Alfred, who had not been among the ill, moved to the town of Vergennes, Vermont, about twenty miles south, where Charles had been appointed rector. Though they would return to Burlington to assist the bishop, it marked their first sojourn to a new parish.

In Vergennes, the couple enjoyed their fresh marriage, a new congregation, and a little son. But in December 1835, with Emily seven months pregnant, seventeen-month-old Alfred died. The cause remains unknown, but it seems to have happened quickly. Emily recorded the event in poem form, as was her style, describing a vivid dream in which both she and her little boy were bedridden, feverish, failing. Angels appeared to escort little Alfred to heaven, leaving Emily behind.[7]

Alfred was interred in Elmwood Cemetery in Burlington. While the 1830 child mortality rate for White males under the age of five was roughly 44 percent, and many families suffered such losses, Alfred's death broke Emily's spirit.[8] From this moment on, she began to idealize death, writing, "Death is the one bright spot." She also wrote other poems about the relief, joy, and exaltation she believed death would bring. Emily was now but eighteen years old.[9]

Their second child, a daughter, arrived two months after Alfred's death, on February 24, 1836: Harriet Melusina, named after her two grandmothers as well as her recently deceased aunt, and called Zina. Emily's pen was silent on Zina's birth; her next poem, "Musings on Sickness, etc. etc.," written a few months later, made no mention of the new baby:

> Another week has lapsed its weary course
> Unmarked by good or ill; save with dull pain

> Piercing h'invisible nerves, & tracing out
> Precisely accurate, the weeks, the days,
> The hours, aye even the minutes of my time.
> On the increasing weakness of my frame.[10]

Though its source remains mysterious, this physical strain—the dull pain, the nerves, the weakness—took its toll on Emily. Five feet, three inches tall, Emily was broad-shouldered and stocky, but all her children later wrote about her fragility. For Emily, after Alfred's death, life was a trial to be endured.

Family historian and writer Sylvia Wright Mitarachi summed up Zina's fate: "Thus Zina was born in the northern Vermont winter, in a winter world of sharp blacks and whites, despair and joy, pain and bliss, enough space for grandeur but too chilled a world to support the warmth of spontaneous pleasure—or a natural joie de vivre. She had now by death been established as the oldest child, the one who would be most weighted with her parents' lives, whose spirit would limp bearing them."[11]

That "chilled" black-and-white world would shape all the Fay children.

Churches and Children

1838–1852

After Zina's birth, the little family began a long stretch of relocations and additions. As a young priest, Charles faced frequent reassignments to different parishes. Emily and Zina found themselves uprooted time and again. Each reassignment meant difficult travel, a new home, different communities, and sometimes challenging circumstances. The Episcopal Church strove to keep up as the country's population grew and spread westward, adding new parishes and schools.

For each new town, also a new child. First on the itinerary: Highgate, Vermont, a border city north of Burlington, where son Herman Theophilus was born on December 14, 1837. Charles likely assisted at St. John's Episcopal Church, which had been consecrated by his father-in-law, Bishop Hopkins, four years earlier.

Next up, in what must have resulted in some culture shock for the Fays, they traveled far south to the hamlet of Montpelier, Georgia. Charles served as principal of the Montpelier Institute, a school founded by Bishop Stephen Elliott Jr. on an eight-hundred-acre campus that included a working farm staffed by enslaved people. It was one of the first schools in the state to admit girls, who were instructed in Lamar Hall; boys were in Chase Hall, one mile away. Faculty was recruited from England. Bishop Elliott felt the farm setting was ideal for a school, not only for the agricultural education students could absorb but also because they would "be trained in the best mode of performing their duties as the owners of enslaved people and the masters of human beings for whose souls they must give an account." Whatever Charles may have felt about that mission, the bishop was pleased with his work, stating that the schools had succeeded "beyond our most sanguine expectation."[1]

Montpelier lay just a few miles east of Milledgeville, then the capital of Georgia. The cotton boom caused exponential growth in this region; enslaved people made up more than 50 percent of the county's population. Milledgeville had a college, an asylum, and a central square, where the Fays likely encountered auctions of enslaved people. Here another new Episcopal church, St. Stephens, was built in 1841, the year second daughter, Laura Matilda, was born (April 21).

While the first years of the school seemed a success, it was short-lived. Just as Bishop Hopkins had overstepped in his expansion of his Vermont school, so, too, did Bishop Elliott, who was ultimately forced to sell all his personal land and property, including his workforce of enslaved people. In 1850, the school was sold at a sheriff's sale. In stepped Charles's brother, Uncle Joseph Storey Fay (called Storey), a wealthy cotton plantation owner in Savannah, to purchase it.[2]

By that point, however, the Fay family had already moved on to Bayou Goula, Louisiana, to run a small boarding school for the girls of the wealthy sugar plantation owners. It was here that daughter Amelia Müller (called Amy, which rhymed with Sammy) was born on May 21, 1844.[3] Louisiana was then on the western frontier; Texas did not become a state until 1845. The economy of Louisiana was powered by "white gold"; over a quarter of the world's cane sugar resources came from the state. Sugar mills ran twenty-four seven, with enslaved children and adults working amid scalding boilers, unforgiving rollers, and open furnaces.[4] Bayou Goula was an important port town on the shores of the Mississippi River, even offering a couple of nice hotels.

The Fays lived in a small frame house right on the river. Charles grew disheartened by the miserable living conditions as well as the lackadaisical attitudes toward education and self-improvement. He offered church services to enslaved people from nearby plantations, reporting that they attended his evening services in great numbers. Often the Fays were the only White people present.

In letters home to his parents, Charles initially expressed high hopes about bringing the gospel to the Black populations but then wrote of steadily increasing despair. His sermons addressed morality and salvation, offering hope and education, which seem to have been gratefully accepted, but he also "impressed upon them the faithful observance of their duties to their earthly master, without which they could not expect the blessing of their heavenly master."[5] Whether he said that merely to reassure his parents and mollify the plantation owners or truly believed it is unclear. A variety of opinions about slavery existed among the Fays. While some of Charles's siblings favored abolition, his brother Storey enslaved workers on his properties.

The Bayou Goula plantation owners may have harbored concerns over Charles's educational efforts. Blaming the "miserable Creoles" who "wished to keep their slaves upon a level with the brutes," Charles complained, "Louisiana takes the stand that the souls of the slaves must be destroyed and their minds kept in brutal ignorance in order that their bodies may be kept in bondage."[6] This was rebellious language from a member of the clergy who had been instructed to provide religious instruction to keep the plantation workers docile and obedient. Like the Georgian Bishop Elliott, Leonidas Polk, the bishop of Louisiana, owned several plantations and four hundred enslaved people,[7] later shedding his frock and donning a Confederate major general's uniform.

The family's difficult time in Louisiana became all the more painful when, just four months after Amy's birth, six-year-old Herman died of "congestive fever" (likely malaria). He was laid to rest on the Dunboyne sugar plantation.[8] Again, Emily immortalized the moment with a poem, "Thoughts written after Herman's death; & of both my sons," in which she described little Herman asking her, "Ma, if I should die, would you love me, & remember me still, as you do Alfred?" To which Emily replied, "Surely I would, how could I help it. It would be the greatest pleasure left to me."[9] Although Emily had three young girls to raise, she fixated on her lost sons.

Reassigned yet again, the Fays may have been pleased to leave Bayou Goula behind, heading farther south to New Orleans to tend an Episcopal church and run a school for girls. Here daughter Katherine (Kate) Maria was born on July 6, 1846. The young family was on the move, burgeoning, bustling.

New Orleans suited Emily, with Laura later reminiscing, "In New Orleans my mother had what we call the time of her life. The warm air of the South, the luxuriant flowers, the tropical fruits, the frank kindliness and hospitality of the people, so different from the frigid reserve she had been accustomed to in Vermont society, all charmed her, and she would have been glad to remain there permanently. There was some opportunity in New Orleans also for social pleasure and for music, which had been denied my parents for years."[10]

Emily, aside from her skills as a poet, also excelled at painting, calligraphy, and particularly music. She possessed perfect pitch and played the piano, organ, harp, flute, and violin.[11] Though she had little time to indulge in these talents, aside from playing the organ at church, she and Charles valued the arts and ensured their children were well versed in them.

The Fay children were raised on a bracing diet of religion, hard work, and music. Daily private prayer was a cornerstone of their childhood and, for most, continued for their entire lives. Idleness was not tolerated; any free time after the many chores were completed was to be filled with art or music. All the children learned to play the piano and grew to deeply appreciate music. Zina played the melodeon, a type of accordion, and led church hymns from an early age.[12]

In New Orleans, Emily recruited a few piano students, using the opportunity to make a little money. She explained to her mother, "I have five music scholars engaged, & . . . this puts me in much better spirits, as I can at least pay my own expenses, & need feel humiliated at my dependence on Charles & his family no longer: a matter which is no trifle to my happiness."[13] The fact that Emily felt "humiliated" over being dependent on her husband financially is remarkable for the time, and her hustle resurfaced in some of her daughters in years to come. Her comments also reflected a reluctance to accept support from Charles's side of the family, which was far more financially stable than the Hopkins clan.

New Orleans in the 1840s was the nation's third-largest city, its port one of the busiest in the world thanks to its prime location at the juncture of the Mississippi River and the Gulf of Mexico. Most of the people disembarking from the arriving ships were destined for a brutal life of enslavement. Swamplike conditions, mosquitoes, humidity, and a lack of sanitary procedures led to outbreaks of cholera, malaria, and yellow fever among the population of more than a hundred thousand. The Fays suffered through many of these maladies. Emily had a severe attack of yellow fever and nearly died under the prescribed treatment of calomel and leeches.[14]

Losing faith in modern-day medicine, which included bloodletting, mercury in the form of calomel, and mustard plasters, Emily turned to homeopathy and became an able practitioner, using these skills on family members, neighbors, and parishioners for many years to come. Homeopathy was popular in the mid- to late nineteenth century, before allopathic medicine standardized its education and procedures. This pharmacological approach to medicine used small doses of natural remedies (bark, fungi, leaves, herbs) to ward off disease and included dietary recommendations as well as an assessment of the patient's overall physical and emotional well-being. Emily may have purchased one of the popular ready-made kits containing dozens of numbered vials filled with pills and liquids, along with a brief guide explaining their usage.[15] Son Norman remembered, "She set up a case of Homeopathic medicine, pills and tinctures, and we children were brought up on them, dosed and nursed by her exclusively, through measles, scarlet fever, croup, whooping-cough, and mumps: all of which I can recall in our childhood."[16] Emily administered diluted doses of smallpox to the children as vaccination. Laura reported that people came from miles around for treatment from Emily.[17]

In both her homeopathic practice and her piano lessons, Emily challenged the script she had been given. As a middle-class White woman in antebellum America, she found her role restricted to her home and family. But whether because of a streak of independence or the family's involvement in community through their churches, Emily was more public than most women. Their tight economic circumstances provided both an excuse and an opportunity.

Something in fertile, verdant, fetid New Orleans spoke to maudlin Emily, as evidenced by her poem "To the Crescent City during epidemic," in which she celebrated the city's "death, disease, bereavement, agony and distress":

I spurn the sordid, soar beyond the vain —
Yet oh! My city, still I love thee well!
Thou hast a charm, one only charm for me
And tis a charm eternal, tis thy woe![18]

Dark love aside, in August 1848, the Fays left New Orleans. The year marked the start of the gold rush, the end of the Mexican-American War, and the first women's rights convention, in Seneca Falls, New York. But to the Fays, it was the year they came home.

Likely Charles had once again been reassigned, but Laura believed they had relocated because he was so disgusted by the frequent illnesses.[19] The family packed up again, with an extremely pregnant Emily, traveling over fifteen hundred miles from the southwestern corner of the country practically to the northern border aboard a Mississippi River steamboat, bumpy stagecoaches, jolting trains, and finally a boat across Lake Champlain. Eldest daughter, Zina, was twelve; Laura, seven; Amy, four; youngest daughter, Kate, only two.

The travelers stopped in Burlington to stay with family for a few months, where son Charles Norman (called Norman) was born on August 13, 1848. Then they continued north to St. Albans, Vermont, where Charles had been assigned to the Union Episcopal Church. Nestled between glittering Lake Champlain on the west and the Green Mountains on the east, St. Albans was just twelve miles from what would become the Canadian border. Despite Emily's fondness for New Orleans, after more than a decade of fending for themselves in far-flung parishes, the Fays must have taken comfort from being back in familiar territory.

In St. Albans, they stayed first in a brick home on eleven acres before finally settling into a large white home on a four-acre lot on South Main Street, purchased by Judge Fay for them to use. A stream ran nearby, and mature maples studded the lot, providing a name: Mapleshade.

The Fays arrived in St. Albans at the same time as the railroad; easy access to the town caused its population to double from thirty-five hundred in 1850 to seven thousand twenty years later. More residents translated to more parishioners. However, many of these arrivals were Catholics, recent immigrants from Ireland.[20] The changing demographics provided both challenges and opportunities for Charles.

Family legend has it that Charles, concerned about the burgeoning size of his family, stopped having sex with his wife, whereupon Emily approached her father, Bishop Hopkins, and implored him to talk with her husband about fulfilling his marital duties.[21] For women of Emily's background, more children meant more blessings. Sex for enjoyment was likely not on her radar. The nationwide marital fertility rate had dropped from 7 children in 1800 to 5.4 in 1850, but Emily was not part of that trend.[22] That she was already fatigued by her existing children did not seem to dampen her desire for more, though she likely hoped for boys.

However it happened, on September 4, 1852, the family welcomed another daughter, Rose Emily Fay, named for the flowers a friend had sent Emily. "Do you know I have named my baby after your flowers on purpose to commemorate your kindness?" she wrote. "This flower, the rose, has had so much to do, more than you can ever guess, or know, with my inner life: it is like a breath of Paradise over me, whenever I receive it once more; and I so needed it today."[23] Whether Rose ever knew the reason for her name is unknown, but it proved an apt appellation, for she spent her life giving comfort, spreading kindness, and promoting the therapeutic value of gardens.

Mapleshade

1852–1854

LIFE AT MAPLESHADE WAS NOT easy. Winters in St. Albans were brutal and long, especially for people accustomed to the Southern climate. Later, eldest daughter Zina wrote, "I cannot . . . look back upon my childhood, and find in it one single ray of youthful pleasure from beginning to end."[1]

Emily did her best to preside over the busy household, but she still suffered from poor health and frequently spent weeks or months resting, dictating chores and orders from her bed. In the mid- to late 1800s, women were often diagnosed with neurasthenia, an all-encompassing term that could include persistent fatigue, headaches, anxiety, irritability, and trouble sleeping. Fay family correspondence never uses this term; perhaps Emily refused standard medical treatment and thus avoided the diagnosis. Surely depression played a part as well.

Years later, daughter Laura wrote that "a cough that [Emily] had contracted in Georgia through sleeping in a room the plastering of which had not been perfectly dried out fixed itself permanently upon her in the sharp, cold air of the Vermont winters."[2] The older siblings helped clean, mend, cook, tend the garden, and raise the younger children. In a letter to a sister, Emily confessed that it was due only to Amy's vigilance that Kate, then quite young, avoided being scalded in the kitchen and falling out of an upstairs window.[3]

In addition to suffering from her physical ailments, Emily still grieved the death of two sons. According to Norman, she was "always so busy and concentrated on it that she seemed to have no glance or smile for us all around her. . . . In consequence, and because she was a stern disciplinarian . . . like the Bishop, we were all rather afraid of her."[4] Family lore indicates that Emily used to hit the children's hands with knitting needles when they made mistakes at the piano.[5] Laura wrote of Emily's "bitter loneliness," concluding that "her unending battle with poverty and ill health warped her spirit and made her more austere and arbitrary than she would naturally have been."[6] Charles, by nature both quiet and uncomplaining, did little to change the tenor Emily set for the home environment. Over the years, he struggled with depression as well.

Money was tight. Charles's annual salary amounted to a meager $800. His father and siblings (his mother, Harriet Howard Fay, had died in 1847) were all better off financially and worried about him. A letter from Judge Fay to Charles's brother Storey illustrates the family's concern: "Charles had a parishioner who took a great interest in them, and provided Emily and the children with clothes and in fact supplied most of the deficiencies in the household." The letter goes on to say the parishioner offered to provide for the family in his will. The judge took comfort in the promise "that Charles, who is so good may have a friend in need. Charles says he could spend a large income very agreeably, but situated as he is, he can live on very little and if Emily had good health they would be very comfortable."[7]

Sundays found Charles in the pulpit at Union Church and Emily at the organ. With a rapidly growing congregation, the duties kept Charles busy: homilies, baptisms, confirmations, visits, weddings, burials. In addition, Charles ran a private coeducational school, the St. Albans Classical Preparatory School, to supplement his income. A rear addition to the house served as a dormitory where the students could live, paying $300 per year for tuition and board.[8] The school was just over a small creek named Stevens Brook. As a Harvard graduate and a clergyman, Charles attracted pupils from the Eastern Seaboard, southern Canada, as far west as Chicago, and from the Southern communities where the Fays had previously lived. There is some indication, though unconfirmed, that Charles may also have served as the county's superintendent of schools for a few years.

The school offered a classical curriculum, including languages (Latin, Greek, German, and French), Cicero's orations and Virgil's epic poems, and Euclid's theorems. A young man, Charles Farrar, taught the latest in arithmetic by fellow Vermonter Benjamin Greenleaf. Students absorbed mechanics, astronomy, and basic physics from *Comstock's Philosophy.* Music and drawing were vital components as well, and studies of the Roman antiquities served as art history. All students were expected to have drawing supplies, a dictionary, and a slate.[9]

While these programs were designed with primarily young men in mind, the Fay children participated in the classes from an early age, providing the daughters with much richer educations than most girls received at the time.[10] Amy confessed, "School is desperate hard work and we have to study in earnest."[11]

At the time, White middle- and upper-class American girls received only enough education to be able to instruct their own children successfully or, at the very most, to become teachers. Higher education for women was essentially nonexistent before the Civil War. Girls born to poor or Black families frequently had no formal education at all. The Fay family were outliers, with scholarly Charles invoking a love of learning and a belief that girls should be taught alongside boys. The Fay girls studied Latin and the same mathematics as the male students.[12] Charles's emphasis on education ultimately provided the Fay daughters with a pathway out of what Norman considered the "family-poverty" conditions of their childhood.[13] It was certainly a more progressive option than simply marrying off his daughters at a young age to more prosperous families.

The boarding school added to the family's workload. The twelve to fifteen young students (primarily boys but an occasional girl) needed to be fed and kept in clean clothing. Classes had to be taught, services and music for church programs prepared, and the house and school cleaned. Parishioners often stopped by unannounced, necessitating not only a clean house at all times but also the ability to set work aside to politely host the visitors. Emily taught composition, drawing, and music, with her older daughters pinch-hitting during her times of sickness. The children helped in the classroom from a remarkably young age; Emily wrote to her mother that Amy appeared to be "a capital teacher, & perfectly able to keep order in the schoolroom," though this seems unlikely for a ten-year-old among older students.[14]

Charles's account book indicates they took the students on excursions: horseback riding, fishing, viewing fireworks, and sailing (once each summer), as well as on other outings. They celebrated Thanksgiving and Christmas with nice dinners. Charles or Emily ensured that the boarders made it to the barber, dentist, and doctor if their parents so requested. Charles meticulously documented every penny spent on each student in the bills to their families. The invoices also included line items for an allowance and donations to the church plate, the Union Church thereby benefiting in at least this small way from the school.[15]

Sewing became an intolerable task for Emily. The pile from the boarders plus her own children never seemed to diminish, with hemming and letting out, mending, sewing new dresses, and turning old ones inside out so they would look fresh. While Emily decried idleness, her letters indicate that she felt overwhelmed by her work. When the church's ladies' sewing circle, the Tabitha, stepped in to help, Emily explained to her mother, in equal measures of glee and shame, "There was more cordial pleasure & industry manifested over my children's aprons, stockings & petticoats, & Charles' shirts, than I have ever seen over nick-knacks & nonsense. One lady 'rejoiced that the minister had a family to help.'" The ladies emphasized that they wished to provide Emily with more time for her music lessons and organ practice. Emily quickly reassured her mother she would divert the Tabitha's assistance to people more in need, but the idea that help might be at her disposal seems to have been a revelation.[16]

The constant onslaught of sewing needs was a regular refrain in Emily's life. One of the few remaining family stories about little Herman exists in the form of a letter from Emily to her mother. Two-year-old Herman, sticking up for his older sister Zina, whom he called Ninie, declared, "Ninie, don't you know you ought to be good. Mama, Ninie wants to be good she-self. She does, Ma. Ninie will love to sew and then you won't scold her any more, Ma, will you?" Zina later copied down his words and kept them in her wallet for the rest of her life as a remembrance of her lost little brother.[17]

Emily also wrote to her mother about an incident in which two-year-old Kate unraveled half of Emily's knitting and bent her needles, drawing attention when she cried out in frustration, "They so hard & naughty, I declare I can't break 'em." Kate's punishment for her behavior was a whipping.[18] It seems Emily had made her hatred of needlework apparent even to a two-year-old. In later years, Zina wrote of her mother, "Nailed to her chair, the swift needle went in and out—went, as it often seemed to her, through her delicate lungs as well as through the cloth."[19]

While Emily described little Kate as mischievous and staunchly independent ("Never mind Ma, never mind . . . Katie can take care of Herselt"),[20] she sang the highest praises of Zina, her conscientious eldest daughter and chief helpmate in household responsibilities. "I sometimes feel as if Zina were too good for this world," she wrote, "for certainly nothing earthly that I have ever seen comes up to her peculiar character, and the expression of her face is as superior to others, as the cultivation of her mind & heart. There is an expression almost heavenly about her & what one feels as if it were no sin to term angelic."[21]

Laura, next in line in terms of age, did not figure as prominently in Emily's letters and forever lived in Zina's shadow. She suffered from frequent headaches that led to depressive episodes, though, ever dutiful, she performed her daily chores as best she could.

Amy, the pet of the family, had spirit and exuberance that carried her easily through life, with only occasional bruises from the outside world. Emily recalled an incident when Amy dashed home to collect homeopathic remedies for a friend suffering from croup, then rushed back only to witness the girl's death. Emily, forever fascinated with death, reported, "Amy never saw death before & it has made her half-glorious with a grave elevation all afternoon. I never saw such a sublime child as she is in my life. Oh! How I hope to see her healthy and happy in perfect womanhood, for she is a host in herself."[22] Amy did, in fact, have special gifts, though not the kind her mother implied. From a very young age, Amy displayed musical talent, playing by ear and even composing tunes at four years old.[23]

It is not entirely surprising that Emily doted on Norman, her sole remaining son, explaining the concern she felt over an early illness of his: "I cannot help loving him as I never loved anything else; from his birth I have felt as if he were a little seraph on the wing; and although his health is so poor, his mind appears to be precocious beyond his age or strength."[24]

Rose received scarce mention in Emily's letters, perhaps because by this point her time and energy to tend to young children had been steadily decreasing. The care of the youngest siblings fell largely to Rose's older sisters Zina and Laura, both by then able surrogate mothers.

Separation

1854–1856

It must have been hard on Emily when, in late 1854, eighteen-year-old Zina went to visit relatives, leaving home for the first time. This incredibly tight-knit family relied on each other to keep the home and school running. Zina, as Emily's second in command, was a linchpin. Emily's first letter to her daughter reported, "We felt your going very severely. Amy & Katie cried themselves nearly ill the whole afternoon & evening: & nothing can induce Amy to go near your room, or to touch anything of yours. Katie on the other hand goes & lingers over everything, & seems to feel better after so doing. Laura too shows the deepest feeling for you."[1]

To Emily's credit, in her long letters to Zina, she seemed to be trying to ensure that her daughter did not follow her example of marrying young and immediately being faced with the responsibilities of children and running a household. Emily urged Zina, "Do whatever presents itself and study society & human nature."[2] She specified, "You should do so while you are young, & not drudge away your first bloom in a corner till old & faded like your luckless mama. . . . My cares are heavy, my lot is fixed, & is inalterable, & it is a very good lot. You, on the other hand, have all before you."[3]

Zina went first to Rochester, New York, to visit one of her aunts, Harriet Fay Greenough, Charles's sister. Aunt Harriet had an agenda, trying to talk Zina into taking a teaching job in Rochester and, ideally, to lure the entire family to town, as the local church had an opening for a clergyman. Charles, however, preferred to minister in a smaller town.

There was consternation in the Fay family about Charles, not only in terms of his financial struggles but also concerning his ability to withstand the burdens of Emily's ill health, the workload at Mapleshade, and his own deepening melancholy. While his sister Harriet advocated for moving the family to Rochester, his brother Richard invited him to Boston for the express purpose of cheering him up. While there, Richard encouraged Charles to expand his school and suggested advertising in Boston, Montreal, and New York papers for more students. And Judge Fay offered to transfer the deed for Mapleshade to Charles's name, an outright gift of the house.[4]

Emily's letters to Zina during this separation provide a lasting record of her beliefs, such as her statement that "God never made woman for the life of a student."[5] Much as her father, Bishop Hopkins, had curtailed Emily's education at age fourteen, she believed in educating her daughters only to the extent that they were equipped to teach in their family school. Women should never become so educated as to intimidate men. As teaching was one of the few acceptable professions for women, Emily hoped to expand their own school with help from her daughters.

But for Zina, the trip proved eye-opening, changing the trajectory of her own life as well as that of her entire family. She had the opportunity to see Niagara Falls, traveled on to visit family in New York City, and finally went to Cambridge, Massachusetts. Zina stayed with her grandfather Judge Fay and his one remaining unmarried daughter, Maria Fay, a charming, happy hostess. Fay House, at 10 Garden Street, just off the Cambridge Commons, was "the center of fun and frolic" for the Harvard crowd.[6] The judge, exceedingly well connected in the community, ruled at the Probate Court of Middlesex County and served as a member of the governor's council. A Harvard graduate, he sat on the university's board of overseers. On most evenings, Fay House was filled with music, impromptu theater, unannounced visitors, and spirited discourse.

Coming from Mapleshade, where the mood was solemn and the duties heavy, Zina marveled at the easy, joyful atmosphere of Fay House. Harvard classics professor Evangelinos Apostolides Sophocles kept his chickens in the basement, poet James Russell Lowell (who had married Maria's cousin) frequently bypassed the door in favor of climbing through a window, Henry Wadsworth Longfellow stopped by for evening charades, and brothers Henry and William James were regular guests. In 1836, Charles's brother-in-law Samuel Gilman penned the fight song "Fair Harvard" while staying at Fay House for Harvard's two hundredth anniversary.[7] What the Charles Fay branch of the family lacked in financial resources, it made up for in social connections.

Zina sent home gleeful stories about going to the theater, playing blindman's bluff, and posing on a tabletop as statuary. Emily grew concerned, replying, "Nothing in my whole life ever tempted me to such extremes of levity, & it is hard for me to realize how you are surrounded, for of yourself I'm sure. You could not be desirous of such things."[8] Emily had been thoroughly indoctrinated into the Cult of True Womanhood prevalent in the Victorian era, socialized to believe that a woman was to be pious, pure, submissive, and entirely domestic. The sort of frivolity Zina described fell far outside the comfortable realm of religion and home life and likely made Emily fear for her daughter's soul.[9]

Emily's letters continued to center around illnesses and the interminable sewing pile. Now perhaps aware that life need not always be filled with joyless toil, Zina suggested to Emily that they purchase a sewing machine, recently made more affordable and accessible through the efforts of inventors Elias Howe and Isaac Singer. Emily replied, "I sympathized with your feelings about the sewing machine very keenly: because every day I am easy till I begin to sew, & as soon as I sew the remorseless pain of my chest begins & increases so that I can't help believing the sewing to be the one main cause of my sufferings."[10]

It was likely during this visit that Zina first encountered a promising fifteen-year-old with slick black hair and flashing dark eyes, Charles Sanders Peirce (pronounced purse), Harvard professor Benjamin Peirce's brilliant son who was soon to start studying at the college himself. Family members called him Charley or Charlie (their correspondence uses both spellings; I have chosen to use Charley throughout the book for consistency). Unlike any young man Zina had ever met, brash Charley brimmed with confidence, ready to take the world by storm. At parties, he would recite Edgar Allan Poe's "The Raven" in full voice, captivating the room.[11]

Zina came to embody traits of both families—the cosmopolitan, intelligent, yet merry Fays and the duty-bound, righteous, and hard-working Hopkinses—as she moved forward in life. In March 1855, her request for additional time in Cambridge having been denied by her mother, Zina returned to the responsibilities and patterns of home in Mapleshade with a sewing machine in tow.[12]

Back home, there was more than ever to be done, for Emily had become pregnant again, a fact she had not shared in her letters to Zina. Youngest daughter Lillian Valeria arrived on July 10, 1855, and the family was finally complete at six daughters and one son, having lost two boys.

Emily grew ever feebler, taking to her bed for weeks at a time as she battled tuberculosis, then known as consumption. How the family isolated her to prevent the highly contagious disease from spreading to other family members is unknown. She would have required considerable care, with the disease causing prolonged coughing fits, chills, and fever. Most of the work around the home fell to the older girls. For Zina, having seen the lighter side of life in Cambridge, it must have been a grim return. She wrote to an uncle, "I do nothing but work from morning till night to the very limits of my strength. Mama is very unwell all the time, and I am hopeless of her ever getting well again."[13]

In what was to be her final poem, Emily wrote again about her sons' death:

> But yet, what comfort 'tis to know in my distressed estate,
> That the precious souls are safe in Heaven and there my
> coming wait.[14]

Just days after writing that poem, at the age of thirty-nine, Emily died. The official cause of death was determined to be consumption and disease of the heart. All her children claimed that she died of overwork, however. In Norman's words, she was "worn out by incessant drain."[15] For Emily, who had lived each day looking forward to being reunited with her dead sons, it may have been a relief. Laura recalled a vivid rapture in her expression, and Zina described a look of "freedom and exaltation."[16] Zina's next words became her life's mission: "I resolved to remember the woe and earthly wreck of her thwarted nature, and never to cease until I saw some better way for women than this which can so horribly waste and abuse their finest powers."[17]

Rose, only four when her mother died, managed to maintain a more optimistic image of her mother, later remembering her as a beautiful woman unable to pursue her gifts in music, painting, and poetry:

> But she and her husband were very poor as long as she lived, and she had a large family of children to take care of, and so she had to give up all the things she liked to do, + instead she had to sew, mend, teach, sweep + dust, take care of babies, and in short do nothing but the very things she most disliked, as long as she lived. She did not murmur or complain, however, but kept right on working for others till at last she broke down completely and died when she was still quite young.[18]

As for the youngest, Lily, she grew up telling people she had no mother.[19]

Zina took a harder view, blaming the men in Emily's life for not allowing her to pursue her genius: "She was never idle a moment; but, alas! neither father nor husband nor one of all her twelve brothers and brothers-in-law saw that it would be better economy to give the genius they were all so proud of, a musical or an artistic or a medical education, that she might pay with her earnings some commoner mortal to make clothes for her little ones, than to let her do it herself with the painful toil of the needed."[20]

Emily's hardscrabble life and early death galvanized her daughters to want something better for themselves.

Scattering

1856–1860

IT FELL TO CHARLES, AS rector, to coordinate the funeral of his wife. On September 21, 1856, Emily's father, Bishop John Henry Hopkins, presided at the ceremony.[1] Charles buried Charlotte Emily Hopkins Fay in Greenwood Cemetery, just down the street from their home. Years later, her remains were moved to Rock Point in Burlington to be near the graves of other family members.[2]

Charles's flock at the Episcopal church regarded him highly. A church brochure written many years later described him thus: "A gentleman of scholarship, refinement, and high social culture, he possessed unusual gentleness and kindness. In his thoughtfulness and sympathy for the poor he was remarkable."[3] During his time as rector, due in part to the rapid growth of the town, the number of communicants doubled, and he confirmed over one hundred people.[4] Harvard University bestowed an honorary doctorate in divinity on Charles for his community work.[5]

But this scholarly, gentle man struggled after Emily's death. He had seven children depending on him, including a daughter scarcely a year old, a church over which to preside, and a boarding school to run. The Fays had one longtime servant, Irish immigrant Catherine "Cat" Stevens, and occasionally were able to hire additional help for work around the house, but it was not enough.

The household duties were considerable, particularly with the school and boarders, and all the family members worked hard.

Laundry alone was staggering. Bedsheet linens, towels, shirts, pants, dresses, petticoats, and other underclothes needed to be soaked, boiled, rubbed against the washboards, wrung and rinsed repeatedly, and then hung on the line. Starching and ironing followed, a tedious ordeal consisting of at least two flatirons heated on a stove or in the fire, used alternately as the other cooled. Both endeavors were time-consuming and tough on the hands.

Like sewing and laundry, cooking was considered woman's work. Feeding nearly twenty people each day was a considerable undertaking before the days of refrigeration and other conveniences, often involving going to the market, baking bread, cutting up whole chickens, boning fish, peeling potatoes, tending the stove fires, and making cider. Afterward, the cleanup necessitated boiling hot water for the dishes, emptying the slop bucket, polishing the silver, and setting up for the next morning. And there was always the need to shovel fireplace ashes, tote water from the nearby stream, haul wood, fill kerosene lamps, and hem and mend clothing. The soot from the stove and lamps coated every surface with grime, requiring regular washing of the ceilings, walls, floors, and furniture. The sisters did it all while wearing corsets, stockings, and crinolines in the hot summer months as well as the long Vermont winters.

Despite his helpful children, Charles's grief and responsibilities overwhelmed him. Perhaps to lighten his load, Charles sent four-year-old Rose to live at the Rochester, New York, home of Judge Samuel Lee Selden. A former student of Bishop Hopkins, Selden served as an early director for Western Union Telegraph Company and a justice of the New York Supreme Court. Samuel and Susan Selden had two boys, one of whom died young. The other, Henry, studied briefly with Charles at Mapleshade in 1857.[6] Then in 1858, twelve-year-old Henry went to Irondequoit Bay with his father to learn how to swim. In a fluke accident, the boy drowned right before his father's eyes, despite frantic rescue efforts.[7]

It is possible that Charles sent cheerful Rose to the Seldens' quiet home to help them recover from this tragedy. She appeared on the 1860 census both in St. Albans and, as Rosa Fay Selden, in Rochester.[8] Charles's sister Harriet lived in Rochester as well, providing family nearby.

Whereas Samuel Selden's two children had died, his brother, Henry Rogers Selden, lived nearby with his family. Henry's son George attended the Fays' school in St. Albans while Rose lived with the Seldens, a curious trade.[9]

During Rose's stay in Rochester, Henry Rogers Selden played a vital role in a key moment of history. A lawyer like his brother, Henry strongly opposed slavery. In 1859, following the capture of John Brown after the Harpers Ferry raid, Henry was aboard a train headed home from Philadelphia when he overheard a federal marshal planning to arrest abolitionist Frederick Douglass for suspected involvement in planning the raid. Disembarking in Rochester, Henry raced to Douglass's house to warn him and lent him a horse for his getaway. Thanks to Henry Selden, Douglass escaped safely to Canada. The identity of the person who alerted Douglass remained publicly unknown, however, until after Henry's death in 1885.[10]

Little Rose had gone from living with her sheltered Vermont family to residing with a family active in the most contentious issues of the day. In the mid-1800s, Rochester was thriving, a midsize metropolis with easy access to the West and to Canada, providing well-oiled connections for freedom seekers on the Underground Railroad. It was also a hotbed of suffrage activity, home of Susan B. Anthony and host of the nation's second women's rights gathering, just two weeks after the 1848 Seneca Falls Convention.

But for Rose, at only four years old, it must have been bewildering to be the only child sent away. Even baby Lily stayed at St. Albans. Rose never wrote about this great upheaval in her life. She spent four years with the Seldens, returning home only in the summers.[11]

MEANWHILE, IN 1856, ZINA, PERHAPS emboldened by her time in Cambridge, wrote to Transcendentalist essayist Ralph Waldo Emerson, having just read his *English Traits* and finding it bereft of any trace of Christianity. Her letter ran to fifteen hundred words, and she eventually apologized, "I do not know why I have written all of this to you—so great & admired & distinguished a man. . . . I was reading a little in your book to-day, & I suddenly felt a burning impulse to write just what you have read, & so I have done it." She explained at the end, "My father is an Episcopalian clergyman (don't sneer) & my Grandfather is the bishop of Vermont. My Mother died two weeks ago, & left seven children, of whom I am the eldest, & I am twenty. We have besides in the house twelve pupils—boys & girls of different ages, so you may suppose that my time is so much taken up that I have very little leisure for reading & study, so I am very ignorant, I frankly confess, to what I should like to be."[12]

Remarkably, Emerson wrote back. Thus began a correspondence that lasted several years and changed the course of Zina's life. Why he nurtured this relationship is unknown. Perhaps he was touched by her circumstances or impressed by her gumption, or maybe he knew the Fay name, as they were so prominent in Cambridge. In any case, Emerson took an interest in Zina and faithfully continued writing for three years, during which he urged her to further her education.

It appears Zina invited Emerson to visit Mapleshade, but the naturalist demurred, blaming infirmity in his feet. Instead, he prodded Zina to leave home and attend school:

> I wish I could come to St. Albans, but cannot yet reach my own orchard. Yes, by all means, come to Cambridge, if that is made easy to you. My two daughters in succession have attended & have now left the school. Ellen, the eldest, thought it had every advantage for those who would learn. . . . I have called my wife & Ellen to counsel, & they would fain urge you to come to the Concord school. But in Concord or in Cambridge, I shall not fail to see you, & you will come to visit me, & shall see my wife & children, & I can show you in my neighborhood one or two rare persons whom a good soul would not willingly leave unseen. Your friend, R. W. Emerson.[13]

Given the choice between attending Emerson's school run by his governess Sophia Foord in Concord and one in Cambridge, Zina opted for the familiar, though her grandfather Judge Fay had died in the meantime, and her aunt had temporarily rented out Fay House. Leaving St. Albans in November 1859 at age twenty-three, after sewing little Lily a complete wardrobe with room for growth, Zina took a room in a boardinghouse on Ash Street.[14] She enrolled at the Agassiz School for Young Ladies, where she remained for two years. It is unknown whether father Charles was able to afford the $150 annual tuition or they received financial assistance from someone.[15]

Decades later, perhaps to assuage some residual guilt, Zina explained to her sister Kate, on whom some of the Mapleshade responsibilities fell after Zina's departure, "I shouldered and carried the burden for three years and probably would not have stopped then only I felt that if I must teach I must go to school and learn much more than I knew. So I went to school to Mr. Agassiz in Cambridge and from that came my marriage to a Cambridge man and my home in Cambridge."[16]

The next-oldest daughter, eighteen-year-old Laura, took over running the household, with able help from Amy, fifteen, and Kate, thirteen. Laura lacked the authority and devotion to duty that Zina had inherited from Emily, and it is clear the household had a cheerier feel with her in charge. The letters from the sisters at home to Zina in Cambridge no longer sounded grim. While the sisters reported that the onerous cleaning and sewing continued—"a drudging treadmill of care"—and their cooking and breadmaking were improving, they also described ice-skating parties, sleigh rides, socials, and young men coming to visit.[17] This type of merriment had been scarce under the watch of Emily and Zina.

Father Charles was distracted. While he was kind and well-intentioned, his many responsibilities precluded him from paying close attention to his children. Furthermore, that was woman's work. To add to this came more physical absences. He found himself increasingly called away, sometimes for months at a time, to serve as a guest rector in various churches.

In addition to his other duties, Charles oversaw the construction of a new church in St. Albans to be built on the site of the old one, which, ironically, had caught fire during a meeting to discuss a new building. With architectural sketches from Bishop Hopkins in his pocket, Charles traveled to New York City to engage architect J. Coleman Hart for technical plans. Bishop Hopkins consecrated the new building, renamed St. Luke's Episcopal Church, in 1861, assisted by the Right Reverend Lord Bishop of Montreal and fifteen priests from nearby parishes. In Emily's memory, the Fay family donated a spectacular stained-glass window depicting nine scenes from the life of Christ, from the annunciation to the resurrection. Designed by noted artist Owen Doremus, it held the place of honor behind the altar, the visual focal point of the building. Charles's sister Maria Fay donated a baptismal font, with help from the St. Albans Sunday school class.[18]

Charles ran the St. Albans Classical Preparatory School until the new church was built and paid for. On behalf of the family, he had pledged $500, plus an additional $500 for the window in commemoration of his beloved Emily. School tuitions were critical in helping cover that astronomical cost. But continuing to run the school proved too difficult without Emily's and Zina's help, and Charles stopped as soon as he was financially able. He sent Norman, twelve, to the local high school for geometry lessons. Laura told Zina she debated between running the household and moving south to find a teaching job that could help provide more income.[19] Zina had done so briefly before going to the Agassiz School, spending a few unhappy months in Pass Christian, Mississippi, where she taught piano at a girls' boarding school.[20] According to her grandmother Hopkins, Zina returned from the South "completely disgusted with every place and everybody and now values her sweet New England home more highly than ever!"[21] Without Emily, the family began to scatter.

It speaks volumes about Charles's commitment to education that he allowed his eldest daughter (and most vital home assistant) to leave the family. An 1860 letter from Charles to Zina indicates that she had his backing in her Cambridge lessons:

> I rejoice to hear that you are achieving such exploits in science, though I perceive the usual wail ascends up from the depth of your soul, that is the sad experience of all explorers in the boundless realms of knowledge, viz., the more you study & the greater the attainments you make, the more you realize how very limited is the scope of the human intellect.
>
> I think, however, you have well merited the enjoyment you are now taking in your studies & your other pursuits. You have always faithfully availed yourself of all the advantages which you possessed at home: you have been a devoted daughter & sister, you have labored very hard in the discharge of your manifold duties, & you have a fair right for attending to your self

> improvement, & I hope you will derive all the benefit you anticipate from your present sojourn in Cambridge. If I had the means I should like to send you to Europe for two or three years, as I know no one who would more profit by it than you.[22]

The Agassiz School for Young Ladies, on Quincy Street across from the Harvard gates, was begun by Elizabeth Cary Agassiz and her stepchildren to raise additional income for their family. Alex and Ida helped teach, while youngest daughter, Pauline, was a student. Elizabeth served as the driving force behind the school, while her husband's name and reputation made it a runaway success.[23]

Swiss naturalist Louis Agassiz was a titan, one of the best-known scientists in the world, who crossed specialties with ease: Harvard's professor of zoology and geology, founder of the Museum of Comparative Zoology, a legendary ichthyologist, and a glacial theorist who first suggested that the earth had experienced an ice age. He was a prominent voice in the scientific debates, and he took issue with Charles Darwin's recently published theory of evolution. An opportunity for a young woman to be educated by Louis Agassiz enabled Zina to learn traditionally masculine subjects such as science and mathematics.

In later years, Zina described her time at the Agassiz School, using the third person: "Her education previously had been almost wholly a home education, and the limited means of a country pastor's family had compelled her to mingle teaching with household duties from an early age. The intellectual horizons that opened upon her from the lectures of Professor Agassiz & the lessons & lectures of his assistants, most of whom were Harvard professors like himself, were a revelation."[24]

A very different firsthand account of the Agassiz School was written by Zina's cousin Lillie Greenough. A free-spirited daughter of Charles's sister Harriet, Lillie attended the school a couple of years before Zina. Her lightheartedness and lack of true interest in education often riled her more serious cousin. Lillie Greenough later charmed her way into the court of Napoleon III and married the Danish minister to the United States. From her book *In the Courts of Memory* comes this delightful description of the school:

> To begin with, Professor Agassiz gives us lectures on zoology, geology, and all other ologies, and draws pictures on the blackboard of trilobites and different fossils, which is very amusing. We call him "Father Nature," and we all adore him and try to imitate his funny Swiss accent.
>
> Professor Peirce, who is, you know, the greatest mathematician in the world, teaches us mathematics and has an awful time of it; we must be very stupid, for the more he explains, the less we seem to understand, and when he gets on the rule of three we almost faint from dizziness. . . .
>
> We learn history and mythology from Professor Felton, who is very near-sighted, wears broad-brimmed spectacles, and shakes his curly locks at us when he thinks we are frivolous.[25]

Zina, on the other hand, was hungry for knowledge and absorbed all the school had to offer. Several years older than most of her classmates, she cared little for popularity but appreciated the intellectual intensity around her.[26] The atmosphere bristled with energy, the highlight being Louis Agassiz's lessons, with up to seventy people, including neighbors, crowding into the house to hear his daily lectures. The abundant physical specimens of flora and fauna that Agassiz collected added to the busyness; it was not uncommon to find snakes in the cabinets or a bathtub filled with turtles.[27]

Zina spent occasional weekends in Concord with Emerson's daughters Ellen and Edith. There she likely would have come in contact with members of their inner circle, such as Louisa May Alcott and Henry David Thoreau. Zina reported being happier than she could have expected.[28]

THE 1860 ELECTION, WITH ABRAHAM Lincoln as victor, threw the entire country into disarray. Two states that the Fays had once called home were among the seven that immediately seceded from the Union to establish the separate Confederate States of America. Four more soon followed. The issue of slavery was debated not only on a nationwide basis but also within the Fay family's circles.

At a time when their opinions would still have been largely shaped by the influential adults in their lives, the Fay siblings heard disparate views on slavery. The loudest voice they heard most likely would have been their father's. Most of the children had been too young during the family's time in the South to remember their experiences in congregations filled with enslaved people hoping for better lives. But the church record in St. Albans indicates that Charles performed baptisms and burial rites for a number of people of color throughout his time as rector, though their status was unknown. St. Luke's historical records show that the church "made a definite statement in the years leading to the Civil War as the Parish provid[ed] the Sacraments to a number of Afro-Americans who were using the Underground Railroad to attain freedom in Canada."[29]

In 1849, Charles baptized nine Black children at once, an unusual occurrence certainly, only outdone by the fact that Zina, thirteen at the time, served as one of their sponsors.[30] It appears that Fay family members may have stepped up as sponsors for individuals who otherwise lacked church support. Providing religious guidance to people of color carried potential risk, and as rector, Charles would have had to be somewhat clandestine. Though Vermont was the first state to abolish slavery, that was but the first of many steps in a long—and ongoing—journey toward equality. A large percentage of the population still presumed White superiority; racial prejudice was widespread, and it is therefore unlikely that Charles ever would have publicly addressed the issue, nor do we truly know what he believed. Of the thirty-five hundred people living in St. Albans in 1850, only sixty-seven people identified as Black.[31]

In one clear incident, Charles, in "passive resistance against wrong," baptized a woman who had formerly been enslaved. The woman, Diana, resided in a house just down the street from the Fays and was accompanied by a member of the White family who owned the home, a stop along the Underground Railroad. The dwelling had three tunnels leading in and out of the basement and a hidden room in the front parlor with space to hide five adults.[32] Several houses in St. Albans served as part of the Underground Railroad network. Freedom in Canada was just a short distance away over land or across Lake Champlain.[33] There is no evidence that Mapleshade ever operated in this manner, however.

On the other hand, their Uncle Storey had previously enslaved people, though he abandoned his Georgia plantation and moved north during the war. Like many Southern landowners, he viewed slavery as an economic necessity. And in what stirred up a hornet's nest, their grandfather Bishop Hopkins wrote in a widely distributed pamphlet, *The Bible View of Slavery,* as well as in two books, that nowhere in the Bible was slavery condemned.[34] He also represented Black people as an inferior race, prone to savagery if not efficiently kept occupied and managed. Bishop Hopkins declared that the question should be left to the Southern states to decide, but his writings, as the presiding bishop, lent credence to the standpoint that the Episcopal Church supported the institution.

Most of the Fay's Cambridge connections, including Charles's sister Maria, became involved in the antislavery movement. Friends Henry Wadsworth Longfellow and James Russell Lowell were outspoken abolitionists, and Longfellow's best friend, Massachusetts Senator Charles Sumner, served as one of the nation's foremost opponents of slavery. As for Zina's primary teacher, Louis Agassiz, he believed in polygenism, that White people and Black people had biologically distinct origins, but he ultimately came down in favor of granting Black men the right to vote.[35]

It was a cacophony of opinions. For now, the Fay children listened.

"I Do"

1860–1862

FAMILY CORRESPONDENCE FROM THE EARLY 1860s makes little mention of the Civil War, which tore the country apart. Instead, the letters among the sisters focused on the young men who came to call. Mapleshade was, after all, the home of three vibrant young ladies of courting age: nineteen-year-old Laura, sixteen-year-old Amy, and fourteen-year-old Kate. With father Charles largely distracted and often out of town, this energetic trio, bursting with wit and serious musical and literary gifts, not to mention hormones, attracted considerable attention from the opposite sex. Laura's letters to Zina included a long list of young men who dropped by unannounced, causing the siblings to abandon their chores in favor of entertaining their visitors. The retinue included a young priest, Francis (Frank) Wyman Smith, who assisted Charles at St. Luke's Church and had set his eye on Laura.

Zina had her own beau, a Cambridge man, no less. Charles Sanders Peirce, who had graduated from Harvard in 1859, was a man of considerable promise—though with a dismal school record, including terrible attendance, sloppy work, and insolence toward his professors. The Peirces lived on Quincy Street, near the Agassiz house, and Charley studied natural history with Louis Agassiz privately. Charley was a supremely confident man, full of grand ideas and certain of his own success—all traits likely irresistible to provincial Zina.[1]

His family doted on him and believed him to be a genius. Charley's brother Herbert recalled that as a boy, Charley was "forever digging into encyclopedias and other books in search of knowledge upon abstruse subjects, while discussions with his learned father upon profound questions of science, especially mathematics and philosophy, were common matters of astonishment, not only to his brothers and sister, but to his parents as well."[2] Today Charles Sanders Peirce ranks among our nation's most original thinkers in the field of scientific philosophy.

The collegiate bond ran strong throughout Charley's family. He was the son of Sarah and Benjamin Peirce, Charles Fay's former Harvard classmate and current professor of mathematics and astronomy at the college; grandson of another Benjamin Peirce, who had been the Harvard librarian; and younger brother of James Mills Peirce, who graduated from the Harvard divinity school (also 1859) and eventually assumed his father's old position. Surely everyone expected that Charley, undeniably brilliant, would follow suit. But his path took some unexpected twists, and as it turned out, Zina accompanied him for part of that ride.

Charley had unlimited promise but some personal shortcomings. Though he could be charming and witty, he was notoriously spoiled, conceited, and short of temper. Philosopher and psychologist William James, who later became his most loyal friend, wrote in 1861, "In last year's [class] there is a son of Prof. Peirce, whom I suspect to be a very 'smart' fellow with a great deal of character, pretty independent and violent though."[3] Charley suffered from facial neuralgia (now called trigeminal neuralgia), which could cause excruciating pain. His reactions to these neuralgic episodes ranged from sullen withdrawal to depression to violent outbursts.[4]

Charley's 1861 pocket diary recorded that on January 19, he "called on Miss Zina Fay for the 1st time."[5] The visit must have gone well, for just four days later he returned. Thus began their courtship, one based not so much on physical attraction as on cerebral interest. While Charley confessed to falling in love easily and often (beginning at age five, according to him), Zina's interest appears to have been largely in Charley's ideas.[6] They debated John Stuart Mill's *On Liberty*, Sir William Hamilton's writings, and Charley's own philosophies. One letter Charley wrote to Zina is titled "Introductory to

Metaphysics." In Zina, Charley met a woman who dared to approach him intellectually. It is perhaps noteworthy that in his pocket diary, Charley's lesson of the year 1861, written in his own hand, was this: "A man who makes a friend of a woman, however sympathetic, true & good—is a nincompoop."[7]

Also preserved among his writings is this brief poem to Zina:

> Nor wintry sky, nor chilly air,
> Nor frost, nor sleet nor snow,
> Congeals my truest love for thee—
> I laugh at 5° below.[8]

For some unknown reason, that spring, Zina had to abruptly leave the Agassiz School—and her fledgling romance—three months early, presumably to help at home. She graduated in June 1861 and was awarded the honor of presenting the class oration.[9] No record exists of this speech, but it marked Zina's first public address. There would be many more.

Zina brought Charley to meet her family at Mapleshade, where he basked in the attention of all the sisters, who called him Professor and asked to be taught. But while Laura, Amy, and Kate were flexing their feminine wiles, Zina won the long game by appealing to his intellectual side.[10]

For Zina, another Charles figured prominently: Charles Jerome Hopkins, technically the Fays' uncle on Emily's side but just two months older than Zina, was a frequent visitor and correspondent. While he studied chemistry at University of Vermont, his real talent lay in music composition and performance. He became a popular performer and a champion of American music, helping promote contemporaries such as classical-creole innovator Louis Moreau Gottschalk and composing hymns supporting the Union cause during the war, including "God Save Our Fatherland."

Zina and Charles Jerome had been best friends since childhood. In an early artist profile he wrote about himself for a concert program, Hopkins mentioned one of their escapades: "His first musical performance was the deliberate smashing of window panes, at the early age of three years, at which time he was discovered by one of the servants in the garret, in company with a favorite niece of about the same age, each with a stick alternately breaking a window pane and then following the clear ring of the falling fragments by a merry laugh of delight. His first flogging dates from this period, as might well be expected!"[11]

In their teenage years, their friendship took on romantic overtones, despite their family ties. In his journal, Hopkins wrote of his love: "I never wanted to marry her, how could I? She was my niece. I only thought that she was the purest, holiest, and most enchanting of her sex. She certainly was to me.... Oh Zina! The pain you caused me!"[12] While Hopkins pined for Zina, she dismissed the idea of love entirely, writing to him in her late teens, "You need not trouble yourself to love me. I hate & despise the very name of love between a man & a woman, & I believe there is *no such thing.* It is a *delusion* of the imagination and I don't care whether you 'love' me or not."[13]

Zina may have picked up this attitude toward love from her mother, Emily, who, despite her youthful idealistic notions, later came to believe that "wretchedness in marriage is God's will" and that "married life is, even in its best aspect, miserable."[14] After witnessing her mother's unhappiness and premature death, Zina likely dismissed the idea of romance in favor of a partnership that offered intellectual and social advancement instead.

By March 1862, Zina and Charley were engaged. A jealous, petulant Charles Jerome Hopkins complained, "I took that seemingly stupid Mr. Peirce on a walk this morning from the purest sense of duty and for fear Zina might not like it if I did not show him some attention. He is not very demonstrative, is rather taciturn, has a crooked nose, smokes segars, has a rather affected sort of pronunciation and smacks horribly at table, besides which, he did not place his teaspoon in his cup after breakfast."[15]

After Charley finished his master's degree from Harvard in July 1862, all hurdles were cleared for the couple to marry. But first Zina erected one more, insisting that Charley, whose family was Unitarian, convert to Episcopalianism. He did so under Bishop Hopkins at the Vermont Episcopalian Institute in Burlington, with Zina, father Charles, and other family members looking on.[16] All reports indicate that lovestruck Charley pushed for the wedding, with Zina more reserved and perhaps focused on pragmatic advantages of the union.

The Peirce family felt pleased that Charley had found such an ideal bride. His father, Benjamin, wrote to a friend, "What do you say to Charley Peirce's having fallen in love with a young lady of Vermont, daughter of my old friend and chum in College, Rev. Charles S. Fay of your church, and grand-daughter of Bishop Hopkins. Of course she is as poor as the crows and ravens who fed the prophet in the wilderness. But then she is very full of knowledge and really a person of great mind—and although far from a beauty, Charles is quite in love with her."[17]

In a later letter, the mathematics professor added that the Agassizes "seem to regard her as a wonder of intellectual ability combined with the most sterling qualities which go to make a good and useful woman, and they also regard [her] as quite pretty."[18] While Zina's apple cheeks and careful dress conveyed the appearance of a demure young lady, her piercing blue eyes flashed with intelligence, never missing a beat.

Zina and Charley may have eloped during the summer of 1862, before their official wedding that October 16 in St. Albans, where father Charles officiated. Though no record of the earlier ceremony exists, Hopkins recalled happening upon the pair on a train car to Keene in July and expressing surprise at this mysterious trip. A year later, in June 1863, he recorded, "A letter came from Amy from which for the first time, I learned about Zina's clandestine marriage at Brattleboro previous to the grand wedding and second ceremony at St. Albans, a year ago I guess! I am amazed!"[19]

Had the couple eloped? Could Zina have been pregnant? What seems most likely is that Amy deliberately and perhaps playfully deceived Hopkins to diminish his ardor. But with the information currently at hand, there is no way to know for sure.

The newlyweds hoped to open a school together one day. Charley worked for the U.S. Coast Survey in what he intended to be a temporary measure. The first scientific agency within the federal government, the Coast Survey employed some of the nation's most preeminent scientists, including Benjamin Peirce (who soon became the director), Louis Agassiz, and naturalist John Muir. The department created detailed mapping of the country's coastal regions, nautical charts, and tidal predictions. Charley's work for the agency involved primarily swinging pendulums to make incredibly specific measurements of the intensity of the earth's gravitational fields for mapping purposes. It was tedious, physical work that had little to do with his desire for deep thoughts. Furthermore, it required frequent travel, often to remote locations.

It is unfortunate that Charles Jerome Hopkins was in New York City and unable to (or perhaps chose not to) attend the wedding ceremony, for it would have been helpful to read his description of the event, but his bleak journal entry is telling: "Thoughts and love of Zina fill my being. Dear pure angel! Ah! She will die I believe she must ere long. Women so intellectually brilliant and of her peculiarities were meant for something less common and better than child-bearing."[20] Even five years later, shortly before his own wedding, Hopkins continued to profess his love for Zina.[21]

But Zina charged ahead. The newlyweds moved in with Zina's in-laws on Quincy Street in Cambridge, with father Benjamin Peirce enthusing, "Mrs. Charles S. Peirce is come to stay with us and she is the most charming acquisition to the family circle."[22]

Sadly, for Zina, there was not to be a happily ever after.

New Horizons

1862–1864

MEANWHILE, IN ROCHESTER, THINGS HAD not been going well for Rose. After four years of living with Samuel and Susan Selden, Rose watched Mrs. Selden suffer from consumption, as her own mother, Emily, had. Susan Ward Selden died on April 11, 1862. According to Norman, Rose remained close to the extended Selden family.[1] The Seldens were active in key issues of the day. At such a young age, Rose likely did not absorb much of the content, but it would have raised her awareness in later years, as the Seldens repeatedly made news.

Their nephew George Selden, six years older than Rose, became St. Albans Classical Preparatory School's most famous student. In 1878, George filed a patent for the first gasoline-powered automobile engine, predating Henry Ford's efforts. However, because of a slight difference in engine technology, he ultimately lost a court battle with Ford for royalties.[2] That minor mechanical detail meant the difference between fame and fortune and relative obscurity.

His father, Henry Selden, who had assisted Frederick Douglass, was at the forefront of the women's suffrage movement when he defended Susan B. Anthony. Having boldly cast a ballot in the 1872 election based on the wording of the Fourteenth Amendment, which gave all "citizens" the right to vote, Susan B. Anthony actually hoped to be jailed because that might have triggered a legal technicality allowing her to appeal to the Supreme Court. But Henry Selden, who had represented her pro bono, was too uncomfortable with the notion of seeing a woman he so respected in jail and bailed her out, dashing her hopes. Ironically, he may have botched an early opportunity to get women's suffrage before the Supreme Court. It took nearly fifty more years before women were granted the right to vote.[3]

Despite his noble principles in supporting abolition and suffrage, it seems that Henry Selden was a strict and domineering father. According to one biographer, Selden subjected his son George to a "steady stream of hostility and ridicule," lending no assistance to his automobile endeavor.[4] It is unknown whether his brother Samuel was cut from the same cloth or what Rose had experienced.

After Susan Selden's death, Rose returned to Mapleshade to rejoin her family.[5] Father Charles had stopped taking on students, and in 1863, he retired as rector of St. Luke's, leaving him with more time to devote to his family.

When Zina and Charley managed to save up enough money to move out of the Peirce family home, they first moved into a boardinghouse and then finally purchased their own place at 2 Arrow Street in Cambridge.[6] Zina quickly opened her home to her siblings. The younger siblings rotated between St. Albans and Cambridge for the next few years, with occasional visits to their grandparents and cousins in Burlington, Vermont. Whether Charley was bothered by the comings and goings of his wife's younger siblings is unknown. Perhaps Zina felt their presence might offer her some protection from Charley's darker tendencies.

Rose, about twelve, benefited the most from this arrangement. An opportunity arose to attend school in poet Henry Wadsworth Longfellow's home on Brattle Street, a historic building that had been used as General George Washington's headquarters during part of the Revolutionary War. Hannah Davie, Longfellow's governess, was teaching his three daughters, Edith, Alice, and Annie, and invited a handful of neighborhood children to attend, Rose among them.

Every weekday from 9 a.m. to 1 p.m., the schoolgirls took their lessons on the second floor in what had been General Washington's bedchamber. Henry Wadsworth Longfellow—a warm, loving man—welcomed Rose into his household, becoming a second (or third) father figure to her. His daughter Edith and Rose became lifelong friends.

Longfellow was the nation's most beloved poet. In a time before radio, poetry inhabited the space popular music does today, with people memorizing verses and stanzas to entertain others. Longfellow's poems, with their bouncing cadences and easily accessible language, became instant hits.

His famous poem "The Midnight Ride of Paul Revere" is a perfect example. Longfellow wrote this verse to bolster a sense of patriotism at a time when the nation seemed to be falling apart. Certainly, the poem increased awareness of a key moment in American history, the frantic 1775 ride to Concord to alert the colonists that the British were coming to raid their arsenals. However, by conflating three riders—Paul Revere, William Dawes, and Samuel Prescott—into one figure, Longfellow inadvertently propelled Revere alone into the history books. Of the three riders, only Dr. Samuel Prescott actually made it to Concord, but thanks to Longfellow's poem, Paul Revere forever earned the credit.

In fact, Samuel Prescott was a Fay relative. His sister Lucy married Jonathan Fay, Rose's great-grandfather. It is unknown whether Rose or Longfellow knew of this historical connection. "The Midnight Ride of Paul Revere" first appeared in book form in 1863, published as "The Landlord's Tale" in a collection of poems titled *Tales of a Wayside Inn*, while Rose studied in the Longfellow house.

There Rose would have been privy to the comings and goings of the literary elite and otherwise famous local personages. Every Wednesday evening brought meetings of the Dante Club, where luminaries such as physician and poet Oliver Wendell Holmes Sr., poet and critic James Russell Lowell, poet and professor Charles Eliot Norton, and author and editor William Dean Howells gathered to translate *The Divine Comedy* into English. Sunday dinners usually included Longfellow's best friend, Massachusetts Senator Charles Sumner.[7]

A sense of the school's liveliness can be gained from a literary journal the students produced for several years, *The Secret*. The schoolgirls filled the pages with short stories, poems, rebuses, and puzzles. Rose contributed an essay that ran over several issues, titled "The Pathway Towards the Light." It concerned two sisters on a journey through woods, rivers, and other dangers, culminating in an angelic vision rewarding them for their bravery. The religious overtones in the essay are unmistakable, indicating that Rose still adhered tightly to the values imbued during her early childhood at Mapleshade. Historically, her essay can be seen as a lovely metaphor for her own journey through tough times to a more joyful place, as well as realizing the importance of sisterhood.[8]

One of the other schoolgirls, Henrietta Dana Skinner, who had grown up next door to the Longfellow house (and whose brother Richard Jr. married Edith Longfellow), wrote a charming description of the "easy-going and happy-go-lucky" school in her book *An Echo from Parnassus.* The curriculum leaned heavily on books and languages (including Latin), though the students also learned history and math and attempted occasional homemade science experiments. Unlike Zina's experience in the Agassiz house, which had science at its core, the Longfellow lessons stressed literacy and had other elements of the traditional girls' schools, including sitting through lessons with beanbags on their heads for good posture.[9]

Before and after classes, the girls climbed trees and played for hours in the large yard, including games such as I spy and prisoner's base, archery, badminton, and gymnastics. A favorite activity involved acting out scenes from the books they had read. Henrietta Skinner recalled, "With grace-sticks for swords and croquet mallets for battle-axes we slashed blood-thirstily at bushes and trees, in fierce encounter with dragons."[10]

Between Rose's experiences with the Seldens and in the Longfellow house and Zina's time at the Agassiz School and with the Peirces, the Fay family's circle expanded rapidly. No longer confined to the small world of St. Albans, they found their intellectual and social horizons widening.

Cambridge

1864–1865

DESPITE THE FUN AND GAMES at the Longfellow house, it was not a carefree time. Military funerals parading down Brattle Street toward Mount Auburn Cemetery, accompanied by fife and drum corps, became regular occurrences during those school days. Many of the young women in the neighborhood belonged to a local sewing group, the Banks Brigade (the Bee, for short), to aid the Union army. They met every Friday afternoon, when they would knit blue socks with red-and-white borders and sew shirts, quilts, and later, bedding and towels for the new hospital down Mount Auburn Street. Though Rose does not appear in the official records of the Bee, she is identified as a member in occasional newspaper accounts and family letters.

While plenty of friends were among those who enlisted in the war, including over fifty men from St. Albans and Longfellow's eighteen-year-old son, Charlie, who ran off to join the Union army, the Fay men remained exempt. Father Charles was too old to be drafted, and only son, Norman, was too young.[1] Charley, eventually excused by virtue of his job with the U.S. Coast Survey, exclaimed, "I perfectly dread going, I should feel that I was ended & thrown away for nothing."[2]

Following the Enrollment Act of 1863, in which men of draft age could opt out only if they paid a $300 fee or found a substitute, Zina offered to step up for her uncle Charles Jerome Hopkins. He journaled, "Dear Zina last week wrote me a most overwhelmingly affectionate letter and offering me as a loan or gift (which last she would prefer) the money wherewith to pay my exemption fee from the draft! Is there any girl equal to this darling on the face of this corrupt and depraved earth? God bless her ten thousand years!"[3] How Zina could offer this large sum is puzzling, as Charley's yearly salary at the Coast Survey totaled only $1,500, but it demonstrates that she maintained affection for her uncle.

Meanwhile, the Fays' old Vermont hometown of St. Albans was the scene of the northernmost Civil War activity in October 1864. Approximately two dozen Confederate soldiers who had traveled in from Canada robbed three banks, killing one man, Elinus J. Morrison, the building contractor who had constructed St. Luke's Church. The raiders herded the townsfolk into the village green, in front of the church, to contain them while they gathered $208,000 from the banks and stole horses for their getaway. They had intended to set the town ablaze, but these efforts failed. About one hundred hardy townsfolk chased the attackers off, and they fled back to Canada, where most were arrested by Canadian authorities. The Canadian government reimbursed the St. Albans banks to the tune of $88,000, making the raid a significant financial success for the Confederates.[4]

Eight years had passed since Emily's death, and the family dynamics had substantially changed. In May 1864, while Ulysses S. Grant's forces battled Robert E. Lee's army in Virginia's Battle of the Wilderness, father Charles traveled to Rock Island, Illinois, to marry Sophronia Babbit Adams White. Sophronia's first husband, William Warner White, a prominent lawyer and state senator, had passed away a couple of years earlier. The Whites were active Episcopalians in St. Albans and lived just down Main Street from the Fays. Sophronia had inherited the house, all its belongings, their pew at St. Luke's, and $10,000 when her husband died.[5] In addition, Sophronia's father bequeathed her Forest Hill Farm on Grand Isle, Vermont, in Lake Champlain. She and Charles spent their summer months here in the years to come.

While the Fay siblings visited Grand Isle for long stretches, they never entirely warmed up to Sophronia. This was perhaps in part because she was eighteen years younger than the fifty-six-year-old

Charles, whose brown hair had receded and gone entirely gray, with bushy sideburns framing his ruddy face. Surely the union must have finally eased Charles's financial worries, though Amy postulated that the marriage contributed to his larger plan to make himself as miserable as possible.[6] (In the sisters' correspondence, they occasionally made mention of Charles's tendency to depression.) Granddaughter Madeline Smith wrote that Sophronia was "cordially disliked" by her stepdaughters, adding, "Poor 'Auntie Fay' who wouldn't allow her step-grandchildren to call her 'Grandmother'—but one delightful habit she had when visiting our family was, at leave taking, to present each child with a five dollar gold piece! That was truly a red letter day for us."[7]

Wedding bells also rang out for Laura. In September 1865, she married the Reverend Frank Smith, later described by their daughter as a "reserved and serious Vermonter twelve years her senior," who had assisted Charles at the pulpit for several years.[8] Laura fell into the mold cast by her mother, helping her clergyman husband and immediately having children, though she had her first child at twenty-five, much older than the sixteen-year-old Emily.

Zina, having benefited from her time in the Agassiz School, took it upon herself to ensure that her younger siblings obtained a good education. In Norman's case, the path seemed fairly straightforward. After a short stint at St. Albans High School, he moved to New York City under the watchful eye of Charles Jerome Hopkins, who complained, "Norman Fay is now my roommate. He is an innocent boy of 13 but so meddlesome, curious, garrulous and self-confident that I ANTICIPATE a good deal of annoyance from him, besides he snores at night, and that is enough to rob me of my equanimity for the next day at least."[9] Norman worked for a few months at an engine repair shop. Then Zina lured him to Cambridge, where he briefly attended Cambridge High School and studied privately before taking his inevitable seat at Harvard.

For the sisters, who had no standardized higher education routes in place, their paths were forged according to their interests. Zina urged Laura to study singing and art in New York, which she managed to do only briefly before marrying Frank and settling down. The youngest, Lily, spent most of her time with Charles and Sophronia in St. Albans and on Grand Isle; it is unknown whether she enrolled in any local schools. Lily's greatest educational opportunity still lay ahead. For Kate, there is no documentation indicating further education nor whether this was because she was deemed most likely to marry young or lacked interest in advanced intellectual pursuits. She showed considerable musical talent but was overshadowed by Amy at the piano.

Kate may well have been jealous of Amy, who received a first-rate musical education, starting with Bohemian pianist Jan Pychowski in Geneseo, New York. Then Zina, through her connections, arranged for Amy to come to Cambridge to take private lessons from famed Harvard music professor and composer John Knowles Paine. She was also granted permission to sit in on classes with Otto Dresel at the New England Conservatory of Music. These opportunities soon opened up a new world for Amy.

With so many siblings at the table, Zina and Charley's budget was stretched thin. Amy taught piano and worked as a governess to help bring in some money. Zina urged Charles Jerome Hopkins to assist his fellow family musician financially, but he resisted. He journaled, "[Zina] wants Amy to be made a public pianist and rather abuses me for not adopting her and helping her father to support his large family! My God! Who does she take me for! Because I have tried to be a little attentive to her to the tune of more money than I ever spent on myself in so short a time, Zina talks as if my own hard times were over and as if it were not even yet hard work for me to make a living!"[10]

Hopkins continued to blur the lines between uncle and boyfriend, flirting with Amy, though he complained, "Amy has proven ungrateful too and I do not believe she loves me disinterestedly."[11] Amy was a bit of a flirt. Self-confident and vivacious, Amy playfully referred to herself as "darling Amy" or "Am-Am." With a welcoming smile, flashing blue eyes, curly blonde hair, and an aquiline nose, Amy had no shortage of suitors. Her first beau had been a boarder at the Fay school, George Cogswell, who went off to fight and, a few months later, died in the Civil War with a lock of Amy's hair in his pocket.[12] After introducing Amy to composer Louis Moreau Gottschalk, Hopkins worried that Gottschalk was overly attentive to her and that she would fall in love with him.[13]

Amy's reputation as a pianist grew steadily, and she began playing recitals at local venues, such as Lyceum Hall in Cambridge, and teaching the piano, including at the Longfellow school. A charming letter written in Henry Wadsworth Longfellow's hand provides proof of these music lessons, as well as a sense of the playfulness inherent in the house: "We the undersigned, citizens of Cambridge, County of Middlesex in the State of Massachusetts, humbly petition that Miss Fay will give us a Holiday on Saturday, May 5th, it being the Anniversary of Napoleon's death!" The request is signed by four of Rose's classmates.[14] Amy became a favorite with Longfellow, as much for her engaging personality as for her skill at the piano.

IN 1865, THE LONG, BLOODY Civil War finally came to an end, but it was followed closely by the assassination of President Abraham Lincoln. Young Rose and her friends at Longfellow's school, upon hearing of the president's death, acted it out, as they did with most things that captured their interest. Classmate Henrietta Dana Skinner recalled being assigned the role of John Wilkes Booth: "The other girls, led by Trudie Horsford and Rose Fay, were the sheriff's posse, hot on my tracks, but delayed as they dashed wildly about the grounds by stopping to search every thicket of shrubs, or climb every tree where I might possibly have tried to conceal myself. Even 'Trap,' Mr. Longfellow's small fat Skye terrier, was enlisted in the search party, representing a brace of man-hunting bloodhounds."[15]

Americans mourned for their president and his unexpected death, as well as for the staggering losses of the war. The nation still bore deep divisions, and the task of reunification loomed large. Piecing the Union back together, but with new parameters, would involve heated debate, careful compromise, and controversial legislation.

It fell to Bishop John Henry Hopkins, who was now, by virtue of being the senior-most bishop in the United States, the presiding bishop of the Episcopalian Church, to preside over the reunification of the church. Though there were some hiccups along the way, he successfully negotiated a return to the fold of the Southern delegations who had broken away to form their own Protestant Episcopal Church in the Confederate states during the war. However, his refusal to condemn the institution of slavery scarred his reputation historically.

One year later, in June 1866, thirty-seven members of the Hopkins clan gathered in Burlington to celebrate the fiftieth wedding anniversary of Melusina and John Henry. Much of the family correspondence leading up to the event concerned gifts (all were to be gold), dresses, and entertainment. Zina's mother-in-law, Sarah Peirce, observed that the gold presents were "rather hard upon poor people like the Fays!"[16] Everyone attended except for Amy, who had to cancel at the last minute.

Upon her arrival, Zina declared herself in charge of the ladies' hairstyles, as reported by her aunt Alice: "Zina was threatened by one of her sad headaches, but succeeded in throwing it off. She was anxious to do my hair in some super-fashionable style with rolls and frizzes, and I put myself willingly under her hands . . . with her hot slate pencils."[17]

Kate and Charles Jerome Hopkins played a piano duet composed by the bishop, Zina sang one of his songs, and Rose and the others danced.[18] Although it was a rainy day, following the reception, a rainbow appeared—some reports indicate a triple rainbow, and son John Henry Hopkins Jr. claimed to have seen a quintuple rainbow. Everyone saw it as a good omen.[19]

Reverend Charles Fay in a photo professionally taken at a Boston studio (undated). Courtesy Christopher King.

Landscape titled *View Above High Bridge, Burlington, Vermont*, painted by Emily in the early 1850s. Courtesy David Fay Smith.

Mapleshade in St. Albans. The family lived in the front portion, while the boarding students occupied a dormitory in the rear. Courtesy Bill and Kathy Connolly.

Charles Norman Fay at graduation and again later in life (ca. 1889–94). Norman's images were included in a photographic series of Harvard's class of 1869. Rijksmuseum, Amsterdam.

Zina's husband, Charles Sanders Peirce, posing in 1872. Courtesy Tuttle Collection, Institute for Studies in Pragmaticism, Texas Tech University.

Harriet Melusina Fay Peirce in 1908. Even in her later years, Zina maintained her clear-eyed and determined countenance. Courtesy Christopher King.

Fay House in the 1890s, now part of the Radcliffe Institute.
Courtesy Schlesinger Library, Harvard Radcliffe institute.

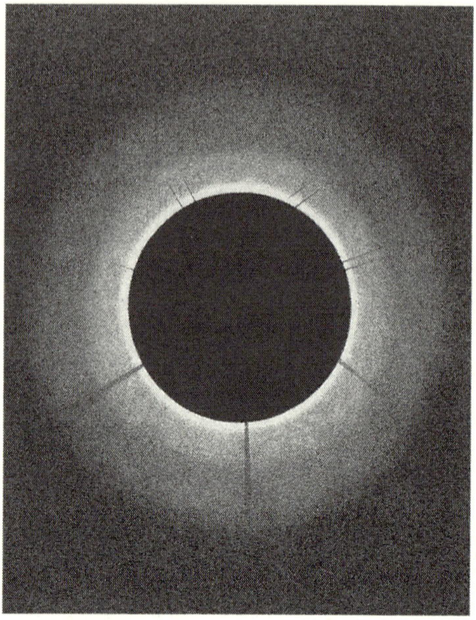

Zina's sketch of the corona during the 1870 total solar eclipse, included in the official report from the U.S. Coast Survey. Courtesy Universidad de Navarra.

Amelia Müller Fay. This publicity shot of Amy was taken by the Scherer Studio in 1901. Courtesy Christopher King.

Amy spent hours every day at the piano.
Courtesy Tuttle Collection, Institute for Studies
in Pragmaticism, Texas Tech University.

Amy's book *Music-Study in Germany*, edited by Zina. The book became very popular, with over twenty printings and several translations. Photo by author.

The house on Bellevue Place in Chicago, shared by Zina, Amy, Rose, Norman, and Lily. Photo by author.

Allegro Agitato

Zina

Reform

1865–1869

ZINA WAS FRUSTRATED. AFTER TWO years of marriage, the banality of her daily existence was becoming evident. Not that she had been starry-eyed going in. Years of running the household at Mapleshade had taught her the domestic duties all too well, and she was fully aware of her feminine role as keeper of the home. Though she and Charley had talked about opening their own school, this was looking less and less likely. Charley was in demand, working at the Coast Survey, guest lecturing at Harvard on the logic of science, and debating the latest theories with his fellow scientists. While he was ruminating, Zina was starching collars, ironing cuffs, mopping the floor, feeding her husband and younger siblings, and of course, sewing. Her naive expectations of an intellectual partnership were fraying. Yes, she could play the part of a homemaker, but after her years of mental stimulation in the Agassiz School, she yearned for better.

It didn't help that Charley's neuralgia brought blinding headaches and crippling pain, leaving him irritable and devoid of energy. He used ether and opium to combat the pain. Zina wrote to his brother Ben, "I am almost discouraged about his neuralgia, it hangs on so long & keeps him weak and languid even when it does not pain him, so that he gets through but little work, and even if he does get better, a breath of air will give it to him again as badly as ever."[1] Charley had little energy or enthusiasm left for a marital relationship.

The frictions between them were many. Family lore held that Zina became a good cook out of desperation, as Charley would storm out of the house, declaring the food not worth eating, and buy a pricey dinner in town.[2] Such expenses troubled his wife. When it came to budgetary issues, Zina, raised on a shoestring, often butted heads with the more spoiled Charley.

In addition to dealing with a cantankerous husband, Zina housed Rose and Amy, and she also hosted Kate, Lily, and Norman on their frequent visits. All the unmarried children split their time among Cambridge, Grand Isle, and St. Albans. There were always mouths to feed and, as had been the case with their mother Emily, cleaning and sewing to be done. In her social circle, it would have been considered unseemly not to have at least one servant, and Zina was usually able to employ one, or sometimes two during periods of relative financial comfort, to help with the household duties, but she found the chores onerous nonetheless.[3]

Surely, Zina thought, there had to be a better way. The lessons learned from Emily's, and now her own, daily drudgery forced her to consider alternatives. She wrote a letter to *The New York World*, given front-page space on July 11, 1864, making her frustration clear: "She who makes the most garments for her children during the year—above all, if she trims her own bonnet and fits her own dresses—is the best woman, and the one upheld by mothers to their daughters as the safest and most admirable model."[4] Zina argued that being bound to, and judged by their skill at, unpaid menial tasks like sewing while men ran the businesses amounted to the labor of enslaved people.

An entry from Charles Jerome Hopkins's journal in May 1863 gives insight into Zina's mindset: "Yesterday a most extraordinary letter from Zina, announcing her intention to become a political speaker to unite this country again! Well! I shall not dissuade her since she may be intended for it, but goodness! Is the girl crazy?"[5] His comment serves as a reminder that in the mid-1800s, for a woman to speak publicly was not only unusual but often considered unladylike and unbecoming. Women lecturing in public, particularly to mixed audiences, had been pelted with eggs and hymn books and drowned out by insults, leading them to flee the stage.[6] But with the country struggling to redefine itself after the Civil War, as it reintegrated the Confederate states, grappled with racial issues and voting rights, and rebuilt cities and areas that had been devastated, Zina saw an opportunity to look afresh at a woman's role.

While academia was debating the theories of natural selection and survival of the fittest after the 1859 publication of Charles Darwin's *On the Origin of Species*, Zina questioned the evolution of domesticity.[7] She was hardly the only one. Many middle- and upper-class women in the United States considered what they wanted their roles to be moving forward. Rather than just accept the status quo, as dictated by a society in which men made and enforced the laws, women began to question the ground rules, and there were many. Should women vote? Have access to higher education? Enjoy property rights? Be in positions of influence in the community? Work outside the home? Be able to pursue interests and talents as authors, musicians, actors, artists? Many people, both men and women, feared that granting women greater freedoms and rights would presage the downfall of the family.

The Industrial Revolution had taken men off the family farm and out of the home, leaving women to handle all the household labor by themselves. "Housework" first appeared in the American edition of the *Oxford English Dictionary* in 1871; before then, the word was redundant, as most work, with some exceptions, had been done at home.[8] The sexes had been separated into two different spheres, with gender roles clearly defined for the middle class: The women's sphere consisted of the home and family, with men responsible for the public sphere of government and business. However, the Civil War demonstrated that this system could be dismantled.

Elizabeth Cady Stanton, Lucretia Mott, Lucy Stone, and Susan B. Anthony were demanding voting rights for women. This became a frustratingly long and difficult fight. Women, powerless, had to persuade men to grant them this right, and do so nicely. Antagonizing the decision-makers would lead nowhere. Many men preferred to have women remain exclusively in the home, shielded from the temptations and interests of the outside world, tending full-time to family life. Nor were the women unanimously on board. Millions of women were initially ambivalent or even resistant to the idea of voting, so certain were they that their roles were solely domestic. Frankly, even questioning the boundaries of the women's sphere was considered unladylike. Wanting more, demanding anything, or causing a ruckus did not fit the serene, demure, complacent demeanor women had been taught to present.

Zina took a different tack. She maintained that, rather than asking men for anything, women should be their own champions and decide for themselves what their sphere would contain. Shortly after the publication of her *New York World* letter, Zina may have crossed paths with one of the most prominent voices in the debate over women's roles, Catharine Beecher. In 1866, seeking relief from unspecified physical pains, Zina briefly attended Dr. Diocletian Lewis's Gymnasium in Lexington, Massachusetts, where Beecher was a lecturer.[9] Beecher's 1841 *Treatise on Domestic Economy* had become a bible for simplified household practices and advocated for greater acknowledgment of the woman's position as the moral head of the household. While Zina agreed with many of Beecher's premises, she veered off in directions the older reformer did not endorse.

Emboldened by positive feedback from her article, Zina followed it up with a five-part series for *The Atlantic Monthly* (now *The Atlantic*), a progressive literary journal begun ten years earlier by James Russell Lowell, Ralph Waldo Emerson, Henry Wadsworth Longfellow, Oliver Wendell Holmes, and others in Zina's immediate circle. *The Atlantic Monthly* had published Julia Ward Howe's patriotic song, "Battle Hymn of the Republic," in 1862 and an enslaved person narrative by William Parker in 1866, reflecting the magazine's strong abolitionist stance. Running in 1868 and 1869, Zina's series suggested a cooperative model for domestic chores, including cooking, laundry, sewing, and purchasing. This was partly to allow for greater efficiency and economy in running a household. Women working together could accomplish the work faster. And if they purchased en masse from a wholesaler, prices dropped as well.

She was not the first to suggest a cooperative kitchen. In fact, she was following in the footsteps of a great-aunt on the Fay side, Caroline Howard Gilman, a well-known author and weekly magazine editor writing under the pen name Mrs. Clarissa Packard. As early as 1834, Gilman wrote about sharing cooking responsibilities: "What a desideratum is a cooking establishment, where families can be provided with prepared food, and a still greater to have our meals brought to us."[10]

In 1844, a small group of weavers in Rochdale, England, outside Manchester, had started a cooperative store to obtain their groceries more cheaply. The group expanded quickly, and soon similar efforts were undertaken in dozens of other towns in England and even in the United States, particularly in lower-class rural communities with large immigrant populations. Co-ops were not a new concept. But Zina was taking things a step further by suggesting not only a store but a housekeeping movement.[11]

The Beecher sisters concurred, almost. Coinciding with Zina's articles, Catharine Beecher and her more famous sister, Harriet Beecher Stowe, author of *Uncle Tom's Cabin*, published *The American Woman's Home*. The Beecher sisters continued to advocate for women's traditional roles as head of the home and zealous homemaker, and they too felt a communal neighborhood laundry would be desirable. In Stowe's 1868 article "A Model Village," written for Susan B. Anthony's prosuffrage newspaper *The Revolution*, she considered the benefits of a modern village that included communal laundries, bakeries, and cook shops.[12]

However, Zina parted ways with the other domestic reformers and raised eyebrows when she suggested that women get paid for this work. In a cooperative housekeeping system, neighborhood families would pay to be part of the community, enabling the women to earn wages. Frustrated that some intelligent, middle-class women were unproductively frittering their time away while paying servants to do subpar work, Zina found roles for everyone. She declared that "there must be some work in the world for educated women" and suggested that "ladies" would be supervisors, while young, unmarried women, former servants, and lower-class women would be the worker bees. It would eliminate the need for household servants, who, Zina argued, were notoriously unreliable, unskilled, and disloyal. Moving the bulk of the work out of the primary house would make for a peaceful, undisturbed home.[13]

Domestic technology was on the rise, but it would not come to full fruition until the electrical age. While the first patents for dishwashers and clothes washers were issued in the 1850s, the machines were hand powered, of poor quality, and too expensive for private homes. But in a community laundry, the latest machinery would be affordable and make the work more efficient.

The sewing establishment would, of course, feature the latest in sewing machines. Fabric was pricey, but bought in bulk, it became far more reasonable. The clothing house would be headed by women with particular strengths in fashion, the field thus far having been dominated by men. A member of the cooperative could be measured, fitted, and have the benefit of a sympathetic and creative "costume-artist" who could recommend the best styles and fabrics for that particular individual. Zina enthused that "a perfect co-operative clothing-house should be one wherein a woman might enter, so far as dress was concerned, a fright, and come out a beauty."[14]

Zina agreed that the women's sphere was the home. However, it was time for women to claim the entirety of the cooking, clothing, and cleaning realms, even the public-facing aspects, like retail clothing. She argued, "Let the women do women's work. Give us the yard-stick, heroes, and let us relieve you behind the counter, that you may go behind the plough and be off to those fields where truest glory is to be won in wrestling from Dame Nature her treasures of golden grain and sweet-smelling hay. Thus, each in a fitting sphere, shall we make a good fight for the world."[15] If women did two things, Zina argued—organize among themselves and demand to be paid for their work—they could become greater contributors to society and to their own households.[16]

Zina was also offering an alternative life path for women like her mother. She believed the sewing needle had claimed Emily's life. Bitter that her mother's talent had been squandered, Zina suggested that cooperative housekeeping could provide a path of liberation for women with other skills. One of her *Atlantic Monthly* essays described a woman, surely meant to be Emily, who was gifted in many disciplines but unable to pursue her passions because of her household workload. In her description of this talented woman, who died at age thirty-nine, Zina directed blame at her grandfather Bishop Hopkins, who had died a few months before Zina's first essay was published: "If a daughter wishes to go out into the world from the narrow duties and stifling air of her father's house, and earn a living there by some talent for which she is remarkable, he 'will not forbid her,' perhaps, but still he thinks her unnatural, discontented, ambitious, unfeminine. Her relatives take their tone from him; nobody gives her a helping hand; so that if she accomplish[es] anything it is against the pressure—to her gigantic—of all that constitutes her world."[17]

Zina envisioned a communal building that housed an industrial kitchen, a laundry, a cooperative store, and rooms designated for consultations and dress fittings. In addition, she wanted to create an ideal work environment, beautiful and cheerful, that included a dining area, reading room, and gymnasium (such as she had experienced at Dr. Dio Lewis's). She even ventured into clothing reform, suggesting that workers needed to dress comfortably, trading in the long skirt and corset for more functional calf-length skirts with trousers beneath. Elizabeth Cady Stanton and her neighbor, Amelia Bloomer, had unsuccessfully attempted to introduce these pantaloons, designed by Stanton's cousin Elizabeth Smith Miller in the 1850s. Though she was not radical enough to be a Bloomerite in public, Zina argued that these were far more practical than long skirts.[18] Cooperative housekeeping would be, Zina suggested, a "WORLD OF OUR OWN" (written in all caps), a "grand and perfect sisterhood" in which they could make the rules and set the tone, rather than have everything dictated to them by men.

In her fifth and final installment, Zina went further out on her limb. She argued vociferously that women were well suited to many different careers. Referring again to the person surely meant to be Emily, Zina maintained that she would have been an excellent physician had she been given proper training. And why, after all, should men be attending to women's ills? Similarly, it was unfair that women brought before a court were tried before male attorneys, judges, and jurors. Where was their jury "of peers"? Zina identified medicine, law, journalism, education, art, architecture, horticulture, and music as some of the fields in which a female influence would make a measurable difference.[19] These suggestions would have placed women squarely in the public arena, which many people felt would upset the natural order.[20]

The New York Times offered an editorial on Zina's ideas. It cast doubt on the idea of a communal kitchen, being dubious that multiple households could agree on what to have for dinner, but supported the concept of a neighborhood laundry.[21] Zina received fan mail from around the country. Harvard professor of modern languages and poet Elbridge Jefferson Cutler enthused, "[Zina] has taken her seat in the very front rank of writers of English."[22] She kept the letters for the rest of her life, including a letter from editor James Russell Lowell that concluded it was a manifest success: "Bravissima! . . . It is solid, serious, & entertaining, three excellent qualities too often replaced in actual life by heavy, solemn, & yet flippant!"[23]

Zina's career as a reformer had begun.

Cooperation

1869–1870

HAVING OUTLINED HER PLANS FOR cooperative housekeeping in great detail in *The Atlantic Monthly* series, Zina set to work trying it out. She was well positioned to do so. Who better to attempt a theoretical restructuring of domesticity than the intellectual elite of Harvard? On May 6, 1869, just weeks after the last installment ran, fourteen people gathered in the home of Zina's in-laws on Quincy Street to kick off the Cambridge Co-operative Housekeeping Society. Nearly half were affiliated with Harvard in some way; others included novelist Nathaniel Hawthorne's sister-in-law Mary Peabody Mann and editor William Dean Howells.

By June, her reputation and confidence growing, Zina presented her ideas to a group of nearly one hundred women. They met in a back room of the post office, more socially acceptable than a woman speaking publicly on stage. Her goals were to establish a communal kitchen and bakery (which would include delivery of breakfast and dinner), a laundry, and a retail store. To gather the necessary capital required a minimum of fifty subscribers. Zina's speech was printed as a leaflet, which was distributed widely, and published on the front page of the Cambridge newspaper.[1] Periodicals in Boston, New York, and London picked up the story.

Almost overnight, Zina's articles catapulted her into the world of reform. Domestic historian Susan Strasser described her, over a century later, as an "obscure visionary."[2] In July 1869, she received an invitation from Jane Cunningham Croly to speak at a meeting in New York City to discuss the idea of a women's parliament. Croly, one of the nation's first syndicated woman columnists, had founded Sorosis, a club to bring women together. Women's clubs were a new concept. Sorosis and the New England Women's Club were two of the first in the country. While church groups, sewing and quilting bees, and benevolent or missionary groups had been around for decades, the idea of women gathering to discuss ideas, educate themselves, and form friendships was new and uncomfortable for many. Among the middle and upper class, it was considered more acceptable to work on behalf of those less fortunate than to spend valuable time away from family to improve oneself in some fashion. Sorosis challenged these assumptions and provided a regular opportunity for women to step out of the home and broaden their horizons. Croly's focus was on increased cultural education for women. Like Zina, she believed that women needed to organize and collaborate to move their interests forward.

In October 1869, Zina and Croly presented a proposal for a separate women's parliament, running parallel to the men's houses of Congress. They envisioned elected representatives concerned with topics related to the feminine sphere—education, sanitation, health, household reform—leaving public issues to the men. Still not in favor of granting full voting rights to women, Zina and Croly believed this separate political organization would enable women to grasp the reins in territories traditionally considered feminine. Croly dreamed of "an institution as permanent as Congress itself, serving as a center for a 'great united womanhood' with branches all over the country, electing their own representatives and sending delegates to annual gatherings in New York. . . . She argued that a Woman's Parliament would offer them the privilege of the vote, without the humiliation of asking for it from those who had no right to withhold it."[3]

The year 1869 was a tumultuous one in terms of suffrage. In February, the passing of the Fifteenth Amendment, the last of the three Reconstruction amendments ensuring Black men the right to vote, reignited the issue of women's suffrage. Though the issue had been launched in 1848 at the Seneca Falls convention, the upheaval of the Civil War and subsequent efforts at Reconstruction had forced the issue to the back burner. In May 1869, Stanton and Anthony founded the National Woman Suffrage Association (NWSA), which opposed the Fifteenth Amendment and advocated for a woman's vote. A few months later, Stone, Howe, and others founded the American Woman Suffrage Association (AWSA) in Boston, taking a more moderate view of voting rights for all. While the NWSA fought for an amendment to the U.S. Constitution, the AWSA argued that suffrage stood its best chance of success through state-by-state campaigns. The competing organizations had the effect of splitting suffragists into two separate—and thereby weaker—groups.

Zina did not think the vote was the answer, arguing that "the fundamental difference between the sexes is not that men have 'rights' and women have none. It is that men are organized among themselves while women are not, and the very fact that we are begging them for rights show that they are not rights at all, but favors." She believed collaboration and education were the keys to greater parity, saying that "compared with education, the vote is a trifle indeed."[4] Women needed to step forward, lift each other up, claim their rightful place, and manage and expand their own domestic realms. Then they could match men as equals.

The relationship between Zina and Croly soon soured, perhaps because, while they had much in common, Croly did not share Zina's passion for higher education for women, viewing it as impractical. In a letter to Zina, Amy referred to a quarrel of some sort. Or perhaps the combination of these two strong-minded individuals was like oil and water. Croly once said, "I am not an amiable woman."[5] Zina, always assured of her convictions, had a similar tendency to alienate those who disagreed with her.

Another reason for Zina to be in New York City was to see off sister Amy, who had a rare opportunity to further her piano studies. Encouraged by her Cambridge piano professor John Knowles Paine to study under piano virtuoso Karl Tausig, twenty-five-year-old Amy boarded the *Silesia* steamer, bound for Germany. Zina had arranged for Uncle Storey to underwrite this extravagance, which was intended to last for several months.[6]

With the exception of Laura, who remained with her husband in St. Albans, the family had relocated to Marquette, Michigan. Uncle Storey, having given up his Southern business during the war, had become an owner of the Champion Iron Mine Company on

Michigan's Upper Peninsula, and most of the family eventually followed. The area was undergoing a boom: It had been found to be rich in iron ore, and with the 1855 construction of the locks at Sault Ste. Marie, which connected Lake Superior and Lake Huron, transportation of materials became markedly easier. Mining companies descended on the area. Father Charles took a position preaching at the Episcopal church in Marquette, bringing along Sophronia, Kate, Rose, and Lily. Norman, having recently graduated from Harvard, found a job at the First National Bank. Even Charley Peirce's brother Ben was nearby, working for Champion as an engineer.

Charley, meanwhile, had been sent to Europe by the Coast Survey to select a prime observational site for an upcoming total solar eclipse, accompanied by his brother James. He broke away for a three-week stay in Germany with Amy, who reported to Zina, "Charlie is as well as possible, & I have never seen him so free of nervousness & in such good condition. I think he was right to take this relaxation, even if it does plunge him into debt." She concluded, "Charlie seems to be more desperately in love with you than ever," a reminder that Charley had always been the passionate one, whereas Zina was more reserved, with an air of detached practicality.[7]

When Zina returned from New York, alone in her house with no husband or siblings to tend to, she had time to undertake her Cambridge Co-operative Housekeeping experiment, which swiftly made significant progress. An organizing committee established bylaws, and a society based on membership was formed in late 1869, with a board of women at the helm. Anna C. L. Mills, Charley's aunt, was appointed president, and Zina became treasurer. But Zina involved the men too, straddling a tenuous line between expanding women's opportunities and avoiding the appearance of fomenting rebellion. To provide guidance and legitimacy, she assembled a Council of Gentlemen, led by inventor and Arrow Street neighbor Gordon McKay. Furthermore, Zina stressed that any participating woman must obtain her husband's permission. Susan B. Anthony's prosuffrage newspaper, *The Revolution*, called her out on it, saying this was "licking the male boot."[8] Zina later regretted having given the Council of Gentlemen so much influence in her plan.

Moving quickly, in March 1870, the board rented a house on Bow Street, a straight shot from the Peirce house on Arrow, and began fitting it up. The plan was to start with just the laundry, but in a flurry of excitement, the board went ahead and purchased equipment for the kitchen as well. The laundry opened on May 1, with a paid superintendent and several hired workers. Unfortunately, the supervisory task proved harder than anticipated, as the inexperienced workers required constant oversight, and the first three superintendents quit within the initial nine weeks. Zina, determined to make her vision work, stepped into the breach, doing the superintendent job without pay.

A few weeks later, the bakery opened as well, ahead of schedule. Zina had described the ideal kitchen: "In my imagination I see it as one universal shine of white floors and tables, of polished tin, copper, and brass. A dozen young ladies in short dresses and white aprons standing at the long, snowy table under the direction of the head cook, would be a very pretty and pleasant sight, and they would, no doubt, enjoy it quite as much as they ever did any class in their lives."[9]

Struggling to manage the steaming laundry and fledgling bakery, the board wanted to hold off on the store. But the Council of Gentlemen and a vote of the full society overruled this, and the store opened on July 2. Buying wholesale in Boston, the board felt it got excellent quality foods at good value for the money. But again supervisory issues occurred, and often items had to be hastily purchased from Harvard Square grocers at less favorable rates.

Mistakes were made. Many of them. In the board's enthusiasm to get started, it had neglected to factor in the absence of many subscribers during the summer months, as they vacationed in Cape Cod and other cooler places. Income dropped without the subscriptions, necessitating the postponement of the horse and cart intended for deliveries. A group of women optimistically undertook a large baking, but the products grew stale without a means of delivery. The organizers soon found that their space was far too large, with expensive rent and stoves four times bigger than they required.

Furthermore, Zina seemed to be the only one truly dedicated to the success of the organization. She ended up doing much of the labor herself, later writing, in third person, "The treasurer spent her entire time in the laundry for half a year, excepting the two afternoons a week in which she did the buying for the little store."[10] The upper-middle-class women of the cooperative had never experienced the desperate hard work Zina had in her childhood. Living in their comfortable households with servants, these well-meaning educated women had no real stake in the outcome.[11] They may have liked the theory, but only Zina fully understood the practice. Ironically, Zina's pilot program might have done better in a less economically robust community.

With her husband and family gone, Zina was left to fend for herself through the summer of 1870, worn thin by working in the stifling heat of the laundry with virtually no assistance. But she had never been inclined to give up easily. Amy expressed her concern: "It really seems shocking to me that you should have to be entirely devoted to the care of other people's dirty clothes. It must be a terrible undertaking, but I hope that before many weeks you will find a way of making the thing easier."[12]

Recall that Zina's impetus to undertake such drudgery was the memory of her mother, staggering under the weight of the interminable sewing, washing, and mending of clothes. And as with her mother, Zina's health began to fail. According to family correspondence, she had suffered periods of illness since 1866, though the cause remains unclear.

Amy and Charley, worried, wrote repeatedly from Europe, urging Zina to join them. Finally, Charley provided a carrot Zina couldn't refuse: an offer to join the American Eclipse Expedition in an official capacity alongside the Coast Survey's scientific observers.

Her resignation was a defeat that could not have been easy for this determined woman to acknowledge. She wrote, "By the 1st of October, 1870, your Treasurer was unable any longer to bear unassisted the physical fatigue of the roles of head laundress and superintendent in one, and convinced of the hopelessness of making the Laundry pay expenses unless the ladies themselves would superintend it, she advised the closing of that department, and, resigning her office, called a general meeting of the society to appoint a successor."[13]

Only four people attended Zina's meeting, a reflection of the general indifference of the members of the society. It seemed everyone recognized the potential benefits of cooperative housekeeping, but no one wanted to do the work. Furthermore, Zina believed that many of the men involved merely gave lip service to the idea, quietly hoping for failure, as the project had the potential to disrupt their status quo.[14]

Ultimately, the society rented out the laundry for a few months, but that backfired when the renters did not pay reliably and ultimately left a debt for plumbing repairs. Zina returned from Europe on April 1, determined that they needed to reorganize and focus just on the store at first. But at this one-year point, the society was formally dissolved by a two-thirds vote of its membership. Cooperative laundries attempted in the Massachusetts towns of Springfield and Winchester had similar, though even quicker, demises.[15]

In retrospect, Zina pointed to three chief mistakes: They needed four dedicated superintendents but had only one; they began with the laundry, whereas the store would have been more profitable; and they should have started with volunteers and worked up to paying salaries. The idea, she maintained, could work under the right conditions. It failed, she said, for a lack not of capital, but of cooperation.

European Interlude

1870–1871

DISHEARTENED AND EXHAUSTED, ZINA CLOSED up the house on Arrow Street and sailed for Europe to join Charley on the eclipse team in late 1870. She was granted an expedited passport through the efforts of his father, Benjamin Peirce, who traveled with her.[1] She met up with Charley, his brother James, and the rest of the Coast Survey team in Catania, Italy, shortly before the December 22 eclipse. Everybody had a specific assignment. Zina's was to sketch the corona, and as always, she took her responsibility seriously, studying drawings of older occurrences and practicing rapid sketching.

The sudden appearance of clouds and rain disrupted the viewing, leaving Zina with but a fleeting vision of the eclipse. The highlight for her was the surprise appearance of three rays bisecting the halo around the sun. Though confused, she dutifully drew what she had seen. Afterward she wrote:

> Professor Peirce thought that the observations of the dark rays was new and might be important. I mentioned it to one or two of the scientific gentlemen then in Catania, but they listened as if they thought my imagination had as much to do with my impression as the facts, and it was not until we got to London and heard about the comparison of Professor Winlock's and Mr. Brothers's photographs in regard to the position of these very rifts, that I felt sure I had seen anything worth seeing.

> Mr. [astronomer Sir Joseph Norman] Lockyer, in one of his published comments on the eclipse in *Nature*, said, I believe, that "none of the sketchers in Sicily had seen the rift." I was in the hotel with Mr. Lockyer, but he had not thought it worth while to ask me what I had observed.[2]

Zina did, however, merit a mention in Benjamin Peirce's 1871 Coast Survey report of the eclipse: "Mrs. C. S. Peirce was successful in drawing the corona, and distinctly recognized the dark rifts which have become a subject of discussion, and which were photographed by Mr. [astronomer Alfred] Brothers, of the British party, at another station."[3] One hopes Zina took some satisfaction in being included in the official scientific report.

Zina and Charley, their work done, took time to enjoy traveling, visiting Rome, Florence, Milan, Turin, Geneva, and Strasbourg. But they had to avoid Paris, under siege by the Germans. In late January, they arrived in Leipzig for a joyful reunion with Amy, who was taking piano lessons at the conservatory. Charley kept a diary of their travels, which detailed train trips, dinners, shopping, and gallery visits. Despite nasty colds, the pair clearly enjoyed taking in the sights and being together.[4]

When they reached their final stop, London, Zina had the rare opportunity to meet with like-minded reformers. The Rochdale experiment begun in 1844 had grown, and over three hundred cooperative stores were in operation. She conferred with leaders of the movement and officials at associations such as the Civil Service Supply Association. Because of the interest in cooperative movements in Britain, Zina's *Atlantic Monthly* articles had been published as a book, *Co-operative Housekeeping: Romance in Domestic Economy*, earlier in 1870 in Edinburgh by John Ross and Company, making Zina a minor celebrity in those circles. However, the editors of the book made it clear in the preface that they were printing it to present the American side of the issue and doubted that even Zina believed the practice could be fully realized in any but the most favorable circumstances and communities.[5] Given her experience in Cambridge, it had become clear that a well-to-do community was not the best option either. The frontispiece of Zina's book featured a man and a woman in a sailboat, with the woman at the helm.[6]

Education

1872

HER PUBLIC FAILURE WITH THE Cambridge Co-operative Housekeeping Society did not deter Zina from tackling other areas of concern for women. Upon her return from Europe, she turned her full attention to education.

Public high schools, a rarity until after the Civil War, had been growing in number and popularity and were often open to girls as well as boys. As for higher education for females, a number of women's seminaries and colleges—including Vassar and Wellesley—had opened in the East, though none were on par with the elite men's institutions. Zina was not a fan of the seminaries, believing they were predominantly staffed with women professors who had not attended college. Surrounded as she was by brilliant minds, as she had been during her years at the Agassiz School, Zina felt that women lacked the ability to think for themselves because they had no exposure to original thinking. She wrote, "All their teachers, without exception, are text-book teachers—teachers who have themselves received knowledge at second hand, and whose minds have never gone a step beyond what they have themselves been taught by teachers and by books. The great want of womanhood, therefore, is to have *some* women, just as there are *some*—(not all)—men, brought into contact with these great minds, so that their own may be awakened and stimulated to active and independent exertion."[1] Zina prided herself on formulating her own ideas, not merely parroting those of her husband (perhaps influenced by her early correspondent, *Self-Reliance* author Ralph Waldo Emerson).

In her *Atlantic Monthly* articles, Zina had argued that women had no right to attend Harvard or other elite colleges, as they had not done any of the work in building up those institutions. Men had done all the work in establishing them. What had women done to earn entry? She compared it to a bystander demanding half of a hard-working miner's stash of ore. Worse, actually, since "wisdom is more precious than gold."[2] She suggested that women, led by rich female benefactors, raise half a million dollars to buy entry for their sex to Harvard. But just three years after writing that, with no donors having stepped eagerly forward, she changed her tune.

In January 1872, together with a half dozen other women, including Elizabeth Cary Agassiz, Zina formed the Woman's Education Association (WEA) of Boston. The WEA aimed to promote better education of women in primary and secondary schools, as well as in higher learning. WEA leaders established four committees—Industrial, Intellectual, Moral and Physical, and Aesthetic—that would meet regularly and report to the entire body at monthly meetings.[3]

The WEA's first official report acknowledged Zina's role as a driving force: "Two ladies are especially prominent among the early members of the Association, Mrs. Charles S. Peirce and Mrs. B. F. [Charlotte Frances Buck] Brooks. They secured the co-operation of other ladies."[4] Zina had first considered launching such an association at the close of her time at the Agassiz School, together with some of her classmates, but the idea was lost in the commotion of the end-of-year ceremonies. Then in 1869, inspired by speeches she heard at the New York Sorosis World Parliament conference, she vowed to try again. But it wasn't until she began collaborating with the energetic, enthusiastic Charlotte Frances Brooks that things began taking shape. A pattern throughout Zina's life was that she fledged a plethora of grand ideas but sometimes fell short in the actual administration and follow-through, often due to disagreements with the other participants.

Zina's interest lay in higher education, and as chair of the Committee on Intellectual Education, she set her sights on the prize: Harvard. She later recalled, "I resolved . . . that as soon as I was through with the Co-operative Housekeeping Experiment which was then absorbing my energies, I would endeavor to start in Boston an Association for the promotion of the *Higher* Education of Women, whose first object should be either to induce Harvard to open its doors, or to establish a female Harvard on the Norton Estate in Cambridge."[5]

As new colleges opened in the Western states, many admitted women because it was economically more feasible than having separate institutions in areas so sparsely populated. But in the East, coeducation was still a controversial topic.[6] The commonly held belief that men and women could not concentrate on the lecture with members of the opposite sex in proximity was hard to overcome. Furthermore, there were those who feared that women's fragile constitutions could not bear the load. Retired Harvard Medical School professor Dr. Edward Clarke warned that if women poured their energy into studies, they could endanger their nervous systems and "female apparatus."[7] The WEA took the middle-ground stance that young boys and girls could be educated together at first, taught separately during adolescence, and brought back together at the college level.

But something delayed WEA's efforts: science. In the 1870s, thanks in large part to Charles Darwin, science provided a hard challenge to previously unquestioned religious beliefs. Men like Louis Agassiz and Benjamin Peirce were at the forefront of this scientific renaissance. Zina, raised by two generations of clergymen but surrounded by some of the nation's leading scientists, found herself caught between both sides of the debate. Furthermore, her living room hosted meetings of the Metaphysical Club, during which Charley and his philosophical friends William James, Oliver Wendell Holmes Jr., and others debated the theory of natural selection. Charley believed that everything was constantly evolving, on every imaginable scale, from the tiniest minutiae to the universe itself. Regular exposure to questioning, reasoning, and the notion of constant change must have affected Zina's thinking on the issues that mattered to her.

Darwin's 1871 *Descent of Man* clearly asserted men's superiority over women, not only physically but also intellectually, arguing that if lists were made of men's and women's contributions to the arts, the women's list would come up short. Darwin did not take into account that women had not enjoyed the same educational advantages. Some social Darwinists took the hypothesis even further, implying that women were primarily intended for childbearing and rearing.

Inspired by the new ideas coming out of England, Harvard championed the push for science. It is likely that the new Darwinian attitudes set the women's efforts back several years, perhaps decades. While Harvard President Thomas Hill had predicted in 1868 that his institution would admit women within twenty years, his successor, Charles W. Eliot, had different ideas. In his inaugural address as president, Eliot stated that policing the interactions between young men and women would be impossible. Furthermore, in what must have riled Zina, he had grave concerns about the "natural mental capacities" of women. Zina's interactions with Eliot were likely complicated by the fact that he and Charley had a contentious relationship.[8]

The WEA settled for a compromise: Harvard would allow women to take its college exams, with the first three women completing the tests in June 1872. Gaining admission or an actual Harvard degree based on those successful exams proved far tougher nuts to crack.

A clearly frustrated Zina wrote in *The Boston Post*, "For several years the University of London has been doing for young women what the Committee on Intellectual Education of the Women's Education Association desired five or six years ago from Harvard, viz., conferring its degrees upon those who could pass its examinations. When Oxford and Cambridge comprehend what London is doing they also will probably begin to confer degrees on women; and, last of all, when it is a perfectly established 'English' precedent Harvard will bring up the rear by copying that which she ought to have been proud to take the lead in initiating."[9]

Maintaining cordial relations with Harvard's administration was vital to the success of the WEA. The group kept quiet pressure regarding the issue and temporarily settled for a system by which women could get separate instruction from Harvard faculty. In 1879, twenty-seven female students representing the Society for the Collegiate Instruction of Women, colloquially known as the Harvard Annex, began their studies in Fay House. Six years later, the society officially bought the old family residence for $20,000. Ten years later, over two hundred women were participating in classes, and in 1894, the school was chartered as the all-women Radcliffe College, with Elizabeth Agassiz serving as president.[10]

While the WEA's battle with Harvard was far from won, at least the circumstances for women in higher education were improving, and their numbers were multiplying. In 1870, eleven thousand women attended seminaries or colleges. By 1880, that number had nearly quadrupled, and by the end of the century, it exceeded eighty-five thousand.[11]

But Zina's time with the WEA was short. She helped launch the organization in early 1872 but then, despite her passion for the work, moved to Washington, DC, later in the year, when Charley was promoted to acting assistant in charge of the Coast Survey office.[12] She left the organization in highly capable hands, giving credit to the dynamic Charlotte Frances Brooks for its success: "All of us have seen and recognized her energy, and feel that the Association, since barely its first suggestion, has been pre-eminently her work."[13] Elizabeth Agassiz, Fanny Cabot Paine, and Anna Cabot Lodge were among the determined women who made sure the important work continued. Among other relatively quick accomplishments, the WEA founded the first training school for nurses in the United States, as well as schools for domestic skills such as cooking and needlework.[14] Nursing, a nurturing role where the women were often seen as subservient to male physicians, followed teaching as a profession considered acceptable for middle-class women.[15]

The following year, Louis Agassiz died, silencing a voice that had been crucial to Zina's development. This together with a strained marriage and her continuing struggles with physical weakness made it a bumpy time in Zina's life.

Discord

1873–1876

ZINA'S TIME IN WASHINGTON, DC, was brief and miserable. For one thing, she found the city unattractive and ill-conceived. She published an article in *The Atlantic Monthly* in 1873 titled "The Externals of Washington," in which she complained about the ugliness of the capital city. The National Mall was in its infancy and studded with warehouses, train tracks, sheds, and market stalls. Construction of the Washington Monument had been halted mid-build because of funding problems. Zina compared Washington with the palaces of Europe and concluded that its oddly placed buildings and complete failure of landscape design resulted in a "draggle-tail metropolis."[1]

Her dark mood may have been influenced by her physical and marital difficulties. Zina continued to battle her mysterious ailments, either undiagnosed or tactfully unspecified in family correspondence. Charley had been assigned to do his gravitational measurements in remote areas, necessitating camping. The primitive conditions exacerbated Zina's pains. Charley's neuralgia and the couple's increasing discord added to the problems. Furthermore, surely Zina resented being pulled away from her reform work in Cambridge. Her letters do not survive, but Amy's do, and she refers to Zina's "desperately blue letters."[2]

Whatever the reason, Zina left Charley in Washington and returned to Cambridge, where her father and Sophronia had taken a house on Harvard Street for the winter. It appears Charles did this mainly to rescue his daughter. Amy wrote, "Zina in her delicate state of health has had a home all winter, where she could be properly attended to medically, & very likely it saved her life. If she had returned to Washington, feeble as she was, and as she would have to have done if you had not taken the house, we don't know what the consequences might have been."[3]

Many of the Fay family members reunited in Cambridge that winter. A few years earlier, in 1871, twenty-four-year-old Kate married William Eben Stone, a chemical engineer at Champion Iron in Marquette. In 1873, Will was appointed to the upper management of Champion Iron, which meant he could relocate to the company's Boston offices. Kate and Will found a home on Hawthorne Street in Cambridge, where their first child, Pauline, was born in 1874.

Presumably, Rose and Lily were also in the house on Harvard Street that winter when Zina took shelter. Even Laura left St. Albans to make an appearance. Amy commented that it must have been a bright spot in Laura's monotonous life.[4] By 1874, Laura had given birth to five children, of whom only three survived. In addition to her workload as busy mother and wife of a clergyman, Laura struggled with ill health and bouts of melancholy. Surely she recognized that she was following in her mother's unhappy footsteps.

The Fay family dynamic from the time Zina first moved to Cambridge—and for many, for the remainder of their lives—resembled a revolving door. Family members relocated frequently—Cambridge, Marquette, Grand Isle, New York City—shuffled and reshuffled into different housing situations with siblings and other relatives for months or years at a time. Though independent in thought and action, the Fay siblings operated as one large organism, benefiting from each other's incomes, connections, and insights. Though Amy wrote to Sophronia, "But the Fays are a queer set and have not got any of that family hang-together feeling that all the rest of mankind has. They get along just as well when they are separated at the poles of the earth," the family did, in fact, hang together, tethered, as the tides of life washed them about.[5]

Charles and Sophronia remained in Cambridge only briefly, perhaps truly just to give ailing Zina a home base, and the Harvard

Street house was soon closed up. Rose and Lily moved together to an apartment in Boston's West End, just across the Charles River from Cambridge.

Though Charley returned to Cambridge, the couple was clearly struggling. It appears Zina suspected Charley of infidelity with the wife of one of his Coast Survey colleagues, as evidenced by correspondence among other members of the Peirce family.[6] Unfaithful or not, Charley had broken Zina's trust.

A couple of years earlier, Amy had weighed in on the difficult relationship:

> As for Charlie I should always be fond of him if he would be good to you. I don't blame him if he is not in love with you, for I think love is a passion one can't command . . . but you make Charlie an excellent wife, devoted & self-sacrificing, & he ought to appreciate it & to have some sense of the duties of a husband to a wife . . . when I think he is neglecting you it makes me furious. I believe that the passion of love rarely lasts between married people, but both parties ought to respect the tie they have formed & try to get along amicably.[7]

It was likely a mental marriage, short on passion. After all, Zina did not believe in love—or marriage, really, her mother's warnings still ringing in her ears—and she saw marriage as a social construct rather than an emotional connection. Having raised most of her younger siblings after Emily's death, she knew about nurturing. Zina and Charley never had children; whether because of an inability to do so or by design is unknown. Perhaps her mysterious physical breakdowns were miscarriages. Customs of the day would have dictated that such maladies were not spelled out. It is probable Zina found her own sexuality uncomfortable; it could be hard to reconcile physical pleasure with the popular idealized "true woman" image as a vessel of innate purity.[8] Family legend recorded that Zina was repelled by nudity and images of the female body.[9]

For Zina, her partnership with Charley provided the reputation necessary to facilitate a welcome embrace by Cambridge society and the newspapers and journals that accepted her articles. She also recognized and respected her husband's tremendous intellectual potential and felt certain he was destined for something great. However, Zina soon realized that managing irresponsible, mercurial Charley was nearly impossible.[10]

The couple returned to Europe in April 1875, landing in Liverpool. Zina accompanied Charley as he went to study how the Europeans were conducting geodesic research in Britain and Germany. Zina met with Lina Morgenstern, a Berlin cooperative kitchen organizer.[11] But by August, Zina chose to stay with Amy in Germany as Charley moved on to France, and the following month, she sailed for home, leaving her husband behind.

In an extraordinary letter to Carlile Patterson, Charley's boss at the Coast Survey, Zina asked her husband's superior to look out for him:

> In your official capacity toward my darling husband as well as from your sincere and long friendship for him (I doubt not) as well as for his father—you have it now, dear sir, in your power to do him a great deal of good. . . . I have known for a long time that he has been going on in a way that could not but end in wretchedness if not in humiliation. . . . I at last took the extreme course of leaving him to himself in Europe, and returning home without him, giving him to understand that unless he changed I could not any longer live with him. This I think has at last brought him to his senses, and I think he feels now that to make duty one's *first* instead of one's last object, is not only the only safe—it is the only *happy* course and principle of action.[12]

Zina encouraged Patterson to insist that Charley file his reports on time, be responsible about recording when and where he was going, adhere to budgets, and not leave all the duties to his subordinates. To dutiful Zina, who had been doing what was expected of her all her life, watching Charley shirk his responsibilities had become unbearable. She blamed it on his parents indulging him and treating him as a genius from an early age, creating a brilliant but undisciplined mess of a man. She didn't mince words: "Charley is now at a great crisis of his life, and if the good in him is encouraged, disciplined, and called to the front, he will rise as a man to the level of his wonderful intellectual gifts, and be a shining ornament in the future to his country. . . . To no one but my sister have I said as much as I have here in strict confidence to yourself. . . . Let us tame him together, if we can. Please burn this immediately."[13]

Charley's father, Benjamin, learning of Zina's missive, sent his own letter to Patterson, discounting it as feminine nonsense: "Should Zina's letter come in your way, do not hesitate to declare that it is her own independent firework, let off in one of her fits of explosions, for the amusement of her sex."[14]

Charley remained behind in Paris. He frequently dined with novelist Henry James, who received this advice from his brother William:

> I am amused you have fallen into the arms of C. S. Peirce, whom I imagine you find a rather uncomfortable bedfellow, thorny and sinuous, but the way to treat him is after the fabled "nettle" recipe: grasp firmly, contradict, push hard, make fun of him, and he is as pleasant as anyone; but be overawed by his sententious manner and his paradoxical and obscure statements—wait upon them, as it were, for light to dawn—and you will never get a feeling of ease with him any more than I did for years, until I changed my course and treated him more or less chaffingly. I confess I like him very much in spite of all his peculiarities, for he is a man of genius, and there's always something in that to compel one's sympathy.[15]

William James was indeed a good friend to Charley. It was during this time that he wrote to Daniel Coit Gilman, the president of the newly founded Johns Hopkins University, urging him to appoint Charley as a professor of logic and stating that he considered him the greatest and most original intellect of the day.[16]

But shortly after Zina left, a depressed Charley overindulged—likely on both alcohol and drugs such as ether, opium, morphine, and cocaine—and had a mental breakdown.[17] His biographer, Joseph Brent, described a nervous collapse, including complete paralysis: "This type of attack occurred twice in 1876, once in 1877, and once in 1879. In 1880, he put himself under treatment for possible insanity, and in later years he also suffered from fugues (blackouts), three cases of which he reported to [William] James in 1904."[18]

Making the decision to separate permanently must have weighed heavily on Zina. She was one who honored her commitments, believed in the sanctity of marriage (even an unhappy one), and knew that things would be difficult financially without a spouse. Historians have speculated on the reason for the break but have no conclusive evidence. Family legend maintains Zina left Charley "so that he would have an opportunity not to sin so much," which allows for many different interpretations.[19] For Charley, who preferred to spend his time pondering evolutionary theory, logic, and universal truths, the details of daily life, budgets, and deadlines would have been major inconveniences. Zina, incapable of keeping him on track, may have chosen to walk away rather than serving as ineffective enabler. Furthermore, some Peirce biographers accuse Charley of psychological and perhaps also physical abuse.[20] There was little recourse for women who suffered from domestic violence; Massachusetts outlawed wife beating in 1871, but it was largely considered a private matter.

The following summer, Zina made one more trip to Europe, likely on Benjamin Peirce's insistence, presumably to rescue Charley. She returned with him in October, but they made their separation permanent, with Charley settling in New York and Zina returning to the Cambridge house at 6 Arrow Street (a few years earlier, they had moved here from 2 Arrow).[21] Though they did not divorce at this point, the demise of their marriage had long-lasting effects on both of them.

Opinions

1872–1877

SEPARATED FROM CHARLEY BUT EFFECTIVELY single, Zina needed income, her dreams of running a school having evaporated. Her connections at *The Atlantic Monthly* and larger literary circles enabled her to write articles for local papers. And fortunately, Zina had opinions on everything and the energy to pen essay after essay. In the fall of 1872, while convalescing in Cambridge with father Charles and Sophronia, she wrote an essay endorsing and explaining the Democratic Party, as a statement on the upcoming centennial of the country and in the hope of influencing people for the presidential election. She was moving out of the domestic realm and into the political.

Frustrated by her inability to get her essay published before the election (and disappointed in Democratic nominee Horace Greeley, who carried only six states and then abruptly died twenty-four days after Election Day), Zina read her manuscript at Wesleyan Hall in Boston in the fall of 1873. That she made political statements in a public forum is surprising. Again, she would have been unsatisfied, as the audience consisted of only twenty to thirty people, many of whom were family and friends. In a final attempt to get her words out, she printed five hundred copies in 1875 of *The Democratic Party: A Political Study, by a Political Zero* and distributed them as best she could. When making more controversial arguments, such as in this pamphlet, Zina used her initials or wrote under the gender-ambiguous pseudonym Zero. The name was fitting—after all, as a woman, she did not even have a vote. She was not the only woman hiding behind a nom de plume. The Brontë sisters, Louisa May Alcott, and many other female authors sometimes published under male pen names. Writing was primarily a male domain: Women were not to portray themselves as experts on topics outside domestic issues nor appear to desire success in such a public manner.

The Democratic Party essay is an excellent record of Zina's opinions at this point in her life. She explained why she had abandoned the Republican Party, claiming that the Democrats desired "the greatest happiness of the greatest number," but then proceeded to itemize all the errors she believed they had committed over the previous three decades. High on the list was granting citizenship to immigrants, who, she argued, were not able to make wise voting decisions because of their lack of education. Zina particularly called out the Irish Catholics, believing their loyalty was to their church, not their new country.[1] The nativist movement was strong in the mid-1800s, reflecting fears that immigrants would amass too much power and influence. These concerns were expressed openly, with no appreciation of the wrongs that had been and were still being inflicted on actual Native Americans. Coming off the ratification of the Fifteenth Amendment in 1870, which outlawed discrimination in voting, an "educated suffrage" contingent argued that educated women should be granted the vote before recent immigrants or others without schooling. In actuality, even with the new amendments in place, poll taxes and literacy tests instituted by Southern states prevented many Black Americans from voting.

Zina also argued vehemently that the Democrats had misstepped when it came to the issue of slavery. She started with compassion and indignation that an entire race was conscribed "to perpetual concubinage, to perpetual ignorance, and to perpetual bondage." However, she continued, over the course of history, many other groups had been enslaved and had worked to overcome their circumstances, which she felt was a vital part of the process. Zina argued that a better approach would have been to provide education, grant lawful marriage, and allow enslaved people to buy their freedom after the age of twenty-five. Freedom, she argued, should be earned rather than granted, no matter how high the obstacles.[2] Exactly how she envisioned them doing that was unclear. It seems Louis Agassiz's polygenism had left an indelible mark on Zina. Her hardline stance, insisting enslaved people pull themselves out of their situation, was not unlike her approach to suffrage and is painful to read today.

Zina never held back. She spoke her mind unequivocally. In *The Democratic Party*, she called out various politicians for what she viewed as their failures, beginning with departed U.S. Representative Horace Greeley and his "bog of ridicule, disgrace, and defeat." She moved on to Speaker of the House James G. Blaine, taking issue with his comment "the fallacy of local self-government." Next, she blasted Senator Charles Sumner and laid the blame for the Civil War largely at his feet. She summed up the Republican Party as "an aristocracy of contractors and speculators, of brokers and bankers and gigantic monopolists, until now it is a Rich Man's Party in a sense that no other ever was in this country, and probably never will be again."[3]

What, then, did she see as the solution? Zina suggested numerous ideas for improvement. Reform of the civil service and electoral system was vital, for she believed the addition of uneducated foreigners and Black men to the voting pool had created an imbalance. Papers and journals supporting the Democratic viewpoint were needed. Congress should represent a greater diversity of occupations, as fully half of all congressmen were lawyers. A national university should be created, for education was too important to be left to the individual states or private organizations. She even addressed the rise in scandalous behavior such as dishonesty, unfaithfulness, and Sabbath breaking, blaming theater and the press for an assault on decency: "Murder is the fashion, even the very children occasionally being at it; and free-love and adultery almost flaunt openly their loathsome banner."[4]

As always, Zina's strongest beliefs concerned women. She expanded on the ideas floated at the 1869 women's parliament, calling for a House of Ladies to run parallel to the two men's houses of Congress. Such a body, representing delegates from every state and territory, would meet yearly in Washington and "would be no disgrace, no laughing-stock, to the American people, but the second proudest gem in the national coronet."[5] Presumably, the first "gem" would be the men in Congress. In later years, she suggested that either the

Senate or half of all elected positions be earmarked for women.[6] Expressing frustration that women had not managed to organize, she finally acquiesced that they could not insinuate themselves into this sort of institution and requested that men "point out their seat and invite them to occupy."[7]

Zina insisted that women be respected for their distinctly feminine gifts and be given the opportunity to make their communities better in the aspects in which they had particular experience and interest, such as education, sanitation, and community work. She argued for organizing at the local level, establishing committees of matrons in each city and town: "Would the streets of our villages be as dirty, their sides as weedy, their little parks as bare and neglected, their tenement-houses as repulsive, their school-routine as mechanical, if the gentle influence of woman was little more actively about?"[8] These were, in fact, areas that women would address in the approaching Progressive era.

She still had not hopped onto the suffrage train, preferring a system in which women participated in issues that pertained to them rather than those reserved for the men's sphere, particularly the issue of war. It was not a neat divide; her suggestions of women venturing into the retail sphere and other areas actually did challenge the separate spheres, but Zina seemed blind to her own contradictions.

There was clearly an audience for Zina's beliefs, for she wrote frequently for *The World*, *Boston Daily Advertiser*, and later *The Boston Post*. While in Europe, she sent in a column titled "Musical Hours in Weimar," as well as a series of travel notes. In between her articles on meaty issues such as coeducation, female suffrage, and political reform, she contributed regularly to the Home Circle section of *The Statesman* on a wide variety of lighter topics for women. These included fashion (bonnets, dresses, gloves, hose, fashionable colors), home decor and arrangement (ventilation in sleeping rooms, keeping moths out of carpets, cleaning tips, colors), spitting, Christmas presents, store offerings, issues pertaining to schools, and ironically, how to maintain a happy marriage.

In "Married Happiness," which ran on November 16, 1877, an unexpectedly romantic Zina chastised the women prioritizing "the pursuit of art or music, women's meetings," even housekeeping and their own children over their husbands' happiness. Both men and women, she believed, needed to make the happiness of their spouses their first concern.[9] Had she done this with Charley? Was the article her mea culpa, self-blindness, or an exercise written merely for public approval? Again, Zina was often contradictory.

In the article "Silent Husbands," she turned the tables and encouraged men to express some interest and passion toward their hardworking wives, offering a "loving glance, the kindly word . . . the gentle solicitude for her fatigues, anxieties and occupation." Without that type of interaction, Zina warned, a wife's affection would "starve," and she would grow "as reserved and unresponsive as he is."[10] Perhaps this article was directed at Charley?

Zina's opinions were strong and her standards exacting. She had no fear of making enemies, whether politicians such as Sumner and Blaine, the musicians or artists she reviewed, or *Middlemarch* author George Eliot (Mary Ann Evans). Her relationship with Eliot began when Zina wrote an adoring letter, to which the author replied, "I am so deeply touched by your words of tenderness and by the details you tell me about yourself, that I cannot keep total silence towards you."[11]

Zina viewed Eliot as the first woman writer to rise to the level of the finest male authors. After heartily complimenting the author, Zina expressed regret for not having completed a book herself. Eliot reassured Zina and told her not to rush: "It is a misfortune to many that they begin to write when they are young and give out all that is genuine and peculiar in them when it can be no better than trashy, unripe fruit. There is nothing more dreary than the life of a writer who has early exhausted himself."[12]

The two women kept up a regular correspondence, finding much common ground and deepening their friendship. Zina later wrote, in the passionate style then common among women, "I love to love you, you are so loveworthy. And once in a long time I love to say so to you."[13] Her letters to Charley had likely never been so effusive.

But after publication of Eliot's novel *Daniel Deronda*, Zina wrote a review in the *Boston Advertiser* that turned vicious. She began with lavish praise: "Her powerful pen alone has changed the relative intellectual position of the sexes." However, further into the review, Zina explained that her enthusiasm for the writer had diminished over the last few years, in large part because of how she portrayed her women characters. Zina's review disclosed more about her own perceptions of a woman's role and current standing: "But never was there a more conspicuous example of disloyalty to her own race and to her own class than George Eliot herself. This is the age of the awakening of womanhood to self-consciousness through education. Whether wisely in their methods or the reverse, women are struggling to find out what they are, what they want, and of what they are capable. And they are doing it on the grand scale. The ferment is universal. They are making their experiments, their mistakes, their successes, all the time, and in every civilized land."[14]

While Zina continued to marvel at Eliot's writing skill, she accused the author of painting all educated, ambitious women as failures in her novels. She concluded, "I think that no woman who is trying to do anything can draw aught but despair for herself out of George Eliot's novels. . . . Instead of wearing womanhood as a crown, she has tried to make men forget it, and for fear of being womanish she has discarded, instead of reverencing, the traditions of her sex."[15] Eliot's depictions of women in *Daniel Deronda* were at odds with Zina's belief that women had different strengths than men did and needed to take full ownership of those feminine skills. It also angered Zina that Eliot had abandoned any trace of Christian beliefs. Her review criticized the novelist for not mentioning Jesus Christ in her books. Left unwritten was Zina's certain disapproval of Eliot's unconventional relationship with philosopher George Henry Lewes, whom Eliot wedded even though he was already married to someone else. This review apparently ended the friendly correspondence between Zina and Eliot.

Even sisters were not safe from Zina's written tongue-lashings. When Laura stepped forth as president of the Women's Temperance Association of St. Albans, leading the meetings and placing notices in the local newspaper, Zina replied publicly.[16] Acknowledging her familial link to Laura, Zina went on to state that she found no greater sin in a glass of ale than in a cup of coffee and that, in fact, there was acceptance of alcohol in the Bible (this harked back to Bishop Hopkins's treatise on slavery). She believed that banishing pleasures simply drove them underground and that a little harmless fun—whether drink, dancing, billiards, cards, or theater, all things denied her as a child, she pointed out—went a long way toward a happier society.[17]

The mid-1870s served as a time of transition for Zina. Charley, in New York, pressed for a reconciliation. "My darling little girl," he wrote in one letter, "I am downright homesick for the sight of my own heart's darling, my sweet and precious little wife . . . let me know how you are doing and whether you will come here or want me to return."[18] Zina had no intention of returning to the unhappy marriage. Eking out every penny she could by writing for numerous local newspapers, she continued to espouse her ideas and beliefs, but her separation had weakened her leverage in the Cambridge community. Her future no longer clear, Zina needed a new plan.

Scherzo

Amy

Germany

1869–1871

WHILE ZINA WAS PONDERING AND pontificating on women's reform issues, Amy was exploring the musical scene in Germany. Thanks to Uncle Storey's generosity, she was able to pursue a first-rate education. In the nineteenth century, Germany was perceived as the center of the music world, producing a host of composers, conductors, and performers. Starting in the 1850s, a number of conservatories sprang up in Germany, and they offered a sort of education not yet available in the States.[1]

Amy's mentor, John Knowles Paine, had studied organ in Berlin and reported that a Polish pianist there, Karl Tausig, played "like forty thousand devils." However, in late 1869, after getting settled into a boardinghouse and renting a piano, twenty-five-year-old Amy had to shift gears when she discovered that Tausig was rarely in town because of his busy touring schedule.[2] It was four months before she even met the virtuoso.

In the meantime, she took classes with his associate, Louis Ehlert. In addition to practicing six hours each day, Amy attended both private and group lessons and took courses in skills such as ear training, sight reading, and harmony. She had to learn the language as well, taking German lessons from her landlady's daughter. Though Amy benefited from Ehlert's instruction, he left after six months because he found the temperamental Tausig too difficult.[3]

Finally able to study with Tausig directly, Amy found the experience disappointing. In the few sessions they had together, he berated her and brought her to tears. Then he abruptly announced that he was closing the conservatory. Amy described him as "a capricious genius, entirely spoiled and unregulated," saying, "the conservatory is merely a plaything to him. He amused himself with it for a while, and now he is tired of it, and doesn't like to be bound to it, and so he throws it up."[4]

The crushing disappointment of the closing of the Berlin Conservatory coincided with a personal tragedy, the loss of Amy's first great love. Starting in 1863, Amy had a serious romance with Charley's brother, Ben Peirce. Born the same year as Amy, Ben was the renegade of the Peirce family. Whereas the others were scientific, philosophical, and probing, Ben was humorous, irreverent, and buoyant. He loved theater and games, played pranks, and had to briefly attend a tutoring school in Westford when he got in trouble at Harvard. Fun-loving Amy was quickly attracted to him. It appears that she hoped for an engagement, but Ben did not fully reciprocate her emotions.[5]

In 1870, Ben became seriously ill. Working as an engineer for Champion Iron in Michigan, he weathered a difficult winter in remote conditions in Ishpeming, a town outside of Marquette, where Charles, Sophronia, Kate, Norman, Rose, and Lily had settled. Upon completion of a rail line from Marquette to Ishpeming, Kate went to visit Ben, and Norman sent the following update to the Peirce family: "His case has grown very desperate. . . . The reports are so discouraging that they and we all here thought we had better write you about it. . . . Your only certainty in seeing him alive is in coming soon."[6]

When Amy received the news from Zina, she quickly began to despair:

> I can do nothing but cry all the time, & if the news of his death actually comes I feel as if I should go crazy. I can't bear it, so it is no use for you to talk to me about religion & resignation, & all that sort of stuff. It is too great a blow, & I can't feel that God has any love or mercy for me if he condemns me to it. . . . I am very sorry for poor Mrs. Peirce, & for the whole family. It must

> be terrible for them all, but it is still worse for me, & nobody can feel it as I shall, out of whose mind Ben has never been for one moment, since I first knew him.[7]

After reading Zina's next letter, confirming Ben's death on April 22, Amy wrote, "Oh! If I could have married him and taken care of him I believe he would be alive and well this day, or at least if he had died he would have had a good nurse until his last breath, for I know by instinct how to manage sick persons."[8] Charley and his father traveled to Michigan to retrieve Ben's body. On the return trip, the elder Benjamin expressed concern that if Charley concentrated his efforts on the obscure field of logic, rather than mathematics or chemistry, his long-term success was unlikely. Charley chose to ignore his father's prescient advice.[9]

Ben was only twenty-six when he died. It is unknown whether the actual cause of his death was tuberculosis, syphilis (family legend), or the extreme conditions and excessive drink (Amy declared, "That he should have ruined himself so with drinking and dissipation is too terrible").[10] His death haunted Amy and made her doubt God's existence. She was reluctant to ever give her heart fully again.

The twin losses of the conservatory and her beloved Ben sent Amy reeling. Her biographer, Margaret William McCarthy, maintained that Amy never resolved her grief, merely pushing it aside to continue on. McCarthy believed these suppressed emotions resulted in lifelong issues with nerves that plagued Amy, particularly at times of extreme stress. In 1871, Amy wrote, "I am such a nervous creature . . . that the least thing gives me a violent headache, or robs me of sleep; even a call upsets me, if the person is animated or excited."[11]

Determined not to let her nerves ruin her promising future, Amy next found a seat in the Neue Akademie der Tonkunst, an academy run by acclaimed German pianist Theodor Kullak. At Amy's audition, he exclaimed (in German), "Madame, you are a born artist!"[12] His teaching style was to play alongside his student on a second piano. Amy jubilantly wrote home that Kullak was "not nearly so terrible a teacher as Tausig. He has the greatest patience and gentleness."[13] She found so much benefit from her classes with Kullak that she remained with him for three years. However, looking back in later years, she tempered that opinion, frustrated by his extreme attention to technique as opposed to interpretation: "Kullak is the most awfully discouraging teacher that can be imagined. When you play to him, it is like looking at your skin through a magnifying glass. All your faults seem to start out and glare at you."[14]

A young woman alone in a foreign country, Amy was making her own decisions and taking charge of her destiny. She was acutely aware that these were precious privileges not to be squandered.

Letters Home

1871–1875

WHILE ABROAD, AMY WAS A conscientious family member, writing to her parents and siblings frequently. In these many letters home, Amy described the various concerts she attended, composers and performers she met, social events to which she was invited, and personalities she encountered along the way. George Bancroft, the U.S. minister to Prussia and Germany, and his wife, Elizabeth, took Amy under their wing. Bancroft, originally from Cambridge and a Harvard alum, was a good friend of the elder Benjamin Peirce. Through the Bancrofts' connections, Amy slipped easily into Berlin society and was frequently their guest at the symphony and opera. Her outgoing, cheerful persona proved a welcome addition to gatherings, and being a young female American pianist made her a novelty. She was delighted by how convenient it was in Germany that young women could go out unescorted, something socially unacceptable in the States.

Amy's letters also serve as a firsthand account of notable world events happening in Germany, particularly the Franco-Prussian War, which broke out shortly after her arrival in Berlin. She described the streets filled with regiments, horses, cannons, and other implements of war; scenes of trains packed with soldiers and women weeping at the stations; and later, the capture of Napoleon and the Prussian invasion of Paris. She watched the celebratory parade in June 1871 from her boardinghouse window, glimpsing Kaiser Wilhelm, Chancellor

Otto von Bismarck, the royal party, and what seemed to her to be the entire Prussian Army.[1] Her letters contain a sense of freshness, honesty, and delight that make them a pleasure to read, even over a century later.

Though Amy pinched pennies, living in inexpensive boarding-houses and trying to stretch Uncle Storey's financial support to its limit, her association with the Bancrofts granted her access to high social circles. She wrote, "On Wednesday, the Bancrofts most kindly called for me to go to the opera with them. They came in their carriage, with two horses and footmen, so it was very jolly, and we bowled rapidly through Unter den Linden (the Broadway of Berlin), in rather a different manner from the pace I usually crawl along in a droschkie."[2] Her letters indicate that occasionally her father or Zina sent her money as well, though she would always protest that they needed it more than she did. Having enough appropriate apparel to wear to her many social events became an ongoing source of concern for Amy, and she wrote frequently about repurposing dresses or finding other creative ways to broaden her wardrobe.

Amy attracted numerous admirers, young gentlemen who offered to escort her to concerts and invited her to events. She wrote to Laura, "I've been having a dreadful time with Betancourt, who fell madly in love with me & was determined to force me to marry him. Such scenes as he made! He is only 22 but if you will look back upon Charles Peirce at that age you will realize that a man can be very difficult to manage and that in spite of yourself you get sort of in his power."[3] But, committed to her piano and wedded to her career ("I don't care for anything but my profession!"), Amy resisted her suitors' efforts and turned down a couple of marriage proposals.[4]

Germany was rife with musical opportunities, but they were simply not yet available in the United States. From leading composers to top-name soloists, from operas and full orchestras to chamber concerts and recitals, music seemed omnipresent. Student tickets were inexpensive, and orchestra rehearsals were often free for young musicians to attend. When Amy heard the Berlin Symphony, she reported back, "We have no conception of such an orchestra in America. The Philharmonic of New York approaches it, but is still a long way off. This orchestra is so perfect, and plays with such precision, that you can't realize that they are any performers at all. It is just a great wave of sound that rolls over you as smooth as glass."[5] These observations on the lack of good orchestral music in the States were accurate. New York had the only full-size resident ensemble in the country that regularly performed classical music. But that would soon change, thanks in large part to an upcoming key player in the Fay history.

Among the famous musicians Amy encountered and wrote about during her time abroad were conductor Hans von Bülow, pianist Clara Schumann, the pianist brothers Nikolai and Anton Rubinstein, violinist Joseph Joachim, and controversial composer Richard Wagner. Of him, she wrote, "The whole musical world is in a quarrel over Wagner. He is giving a new direction to music and is finding out new combinations of the chords. Half the musical world upholds him, and declares that in the future he will stand on a par with Beethoven and Mozart. The other half are bitterly opposed to him, and say that he writes nothing but dissonances, and that he is on an entirely false track. I am on the Wagner side myself. He seems to me to be a great genius.—Pity he is such a moral outlaw!"[6] While Wagner's operas and other compositions have stood the test of time, the composer lived a tumultuous and scandalous life. A highly temperamental and narcissistic individual, Wagner was accused of domestic abuse, infidelity, anti-Semitism, and revolutionary intentions. After hearing him perform, Amy wrote, "His whole appearance is of arrogance and despotism personified."[7]

Father Charles grew concerned about Amy's long stay in Germany and urged her to come home. But Amy knew she was benefiting from her studies and held firm, writing to Zina, "I am continually distracted by my desire to go home, and my equally intense one to be an artist. . . . In Music one must resign oneself to gradual growth, and it's no use trying to hurry up matters."[8] That Amy, still in her twenties, had the independence to select the teachers she felt best suited her needs and the courage to establish herself in new cities in a foreign country indicates a remarkable self-confidence.

In 1873, Amy traveled to Weimar to audition for Hungarian-born composer-conductor Franz Liszt, who ran a free salon for talented students in the summer. An 1858 essay in *Dwight's Journal of Music* had declared that if a piano student wished to become a virtuoso, "it is clearly his best course to bury himself in the little city of

Weimar and study with Liszt,—if Liszt will take him." The author of the essay, Alexander Wheelock Thayer, compared Liszt, at the apex of music instruction, to Benjamin Peirce, "in the highest region of mathematics."[9]

In his heyday thirty years earlier, Liszt, a piano virtuoso as well as a composer, had created a frenzy in Europe with his passionate playing and good looks. Writer Heinrich Heine coined the term "Lisztomania," considered by some to be a contagious physical malady that resulted in hysteria and fainting.

Amy wrote to Zina about her experience performing for the superstar, describing him as a magician and a wizard: Playing to Liszt "reminds me of trying to feed the elephant in the Zoological Garden with lumps of sugar. He disposes of whole movements as if they were nothing, and stretches out gravely for more! One of my fingers fortunately began to bleed, for I had practiced the skin off, and that gave me a good excuse for stopping."[10] The opposite of Kullak, Liszt refused to teach technique and focused solely on interpretation. Credited as being the originator of the master class, Liszt preferred to teach in groups.[11] At the beginning of the summer, Amy was one of but five students, which meant she had many opportunities to play. A few months later, the group had grown to twenty, an energetic, convivial crew (mainly male) who delighted in each other's music and Liszt's stories. Meanwhile, Amy's relationship with Liszt developed into a true friendship. She was invited to his daily games of whist, and he even granted her the honor of appearing at her boardinghouse door one day.[12]

But playing before others continued to cause anxiety for Amy. She confessed to Zina how stressful she found her lessons with Liszt, despite her fondness for him: "I cannot tell you what it has cost me every time I have ascended his stairs. I can scarcely summon up courage to go there, and generally stand on the steps awhile before I can make up my mind to open the door and go in!"[13] Whatever the root cause of her nervousness—unresolved grief, increased stakes, more discerning listeners—it was left unaddressed and continued to grow.

Also in Liszt's salon was a short, sturdy Belgian pianist named Camille Gurickx, who managed to capture Amy's fancy despite her determination not to fall in love. But Gurickx proved hard to resist. At a dinner party, he sculpted a rose out of bread and passed it down the table to Amy, who later wrote, "Every little leaf and petal was as delicately turned as if nature herself had done it. The bread was fresh, and Gurickx had worked it between his fingers to the consistency of clay, and then modeled these little flowers which he stuck on to a stem. It was so artistically done, and it was such a dainty little thing to do, that I saw at once that he was interesting and that he possessed that marvelous French taste."[14] What began as a friendship turned into a romance, as Amy set aside the reluctance she had adopted since her experiences with Ben Peirce.

Her precious time in Weimar lasted six months before Liszt closed up his summer salon and Amy returned to Berlin, though she was loath to leave both Liszt and Gurickx. This time she chose to study with Ludwig Deppe, who focused on elbow, wrist, and hand positioning. Deppe also recognized Amy's issues with anxiety and worked with her to try to overcome them, including having her perform together with other artists instead of playing solo concerts. Amy's father continued to urge her to come home, even sending a letter to Deppe himself. But she held fast and studied with Deppe for a year.[15] This round robin of instructors—all with different methods, strengths, and weaknesses—shaped Amy's playing and her own teaching in years to come.

Meanwhile, Zina had plans of her own for Amy. Recognizing the value of Amy's charming writing style, she edited a number of Amy's letters from Weimar, removing personal family news, and submitted them to *The Atlantic Monthly*, where they ran in April and October 1874 under the headline "Letters Home." The success of this endeavor not only helped position Amy in the music world but also developed name recognition. More critically, it provided the seedling of an idea that blossomed several years later.

In August 1875, when Zina passed through Germany with Charley, their marriage no longer tenable, Amy was finally ready to go home. The two sisters returned to the States together, leaving Charley behind to fend for himself. Amy had been abroad for six years. Thanks to the popularity of her "Letters Home," the press took note of Amy's arrival, and a promising future beckoned.

Cambridge Encore

1875–1878

UPON AMY'S RETURN, SHE STOPPED first in New York, where she and Zina collaborated on a unique program. Perhaps to ease Amy's transition back into performing in the States, Zina booked the Chickering piano warehouse for a joint program featuring a lecture on women's reform by Zina and several pieces by Amy. The ensuing review in the *Buffalo Courier* indicated how much the "Letters Home" articles had paved the way for Amy's return: "Miss Amy Fay, who wrote the brilliant letters from Weimar about Liszt, in the Atlantic, is now in New York. She has lately returned from Germany where for six years she has studied the piano-forte under masters of world-wide celebrity. Her letters interested the musical world as much in their author as in her subject, and no one can hear her play without predicting for her an unusually brilliant career."[1]

Returning, then, to the Boston area, Amy moved in with Rose and Lily at 101 Pinckney Street. She placed ads in the newspaper to elicit work, emphasizing technique: "Miss Amy Fay, Pianist and instructor in the best method of forming the pianist's hand. Specially important to professionals and talented children." Her time in Germany, under different piano masters, had brought to the fore the various approaches to hand and wrist positioning, which became her specialty in teaching.[2]

In addition, Amy quickly booked a number of performances, garnering good reviews in local papers, as well as brief mentions in newspapers across the country heralding her as the up-and-coming American pianist. *The Boston Globe* wrote, "Her first appearance here was . . . the subject of the most vivid interest, and it is scarcely too much to add that the expectations of music lovers have been quite fulfilled with regard to her talents. . . . Her touch is vigorous and masculine, yet elastic and assured in style, and her reception yesterday was most gratifying."[3] For Amy, it felt good to be back among friends and family. Henry Wadsworth Longfellow and John Knowles Paine were among the audience members.[4]

Capitalizing on the attention generated by her articles and her return to town, she performed recitals and orchestral concerts throughout the greater Boston area. Uncle Charles Jerome Hopkins, by now an established composer and performer, helped his musical niece by adding her to his April 1876 program at the Academy of Music in New York City. In between, she juggled invitations for social engagements, such as with Longfellow, who frequently invited her for dinner, including such intimate gatherings as those on his birthday and Christmas Day.[5]

For Amy, this time was a whirlwind. Following the performance at the Academy of Music, Amy and Zina traveled together to Europe again. Zina, having abandoned Charley in Paris the previous summer, returned, perhaps on his father's request, presumably to escort him safely back to the United States. But first the two sisters stopped in Weimar to spend some time with Liszt, who was once again holding his summer salon. Zina, now needing to be financially self-sufficient, had been commissioned by the *Boston Daily Advertiser* to write a column based on her travels, under the pseudonym Zero. Of Liszt, she wrote, "His figure is a little bent, and he begins to show his sixty-five or more years, but there was never a more wonderful head, or a more singular, tragic and changing face, or rather mask, than his."[6] Amy's relationship with the charismatic, dynamic Liszt was one of the most meaningful in her life.

Also in Weimar for the summer was Camille Gurickx. Amy eagerly introduced Zina to her beau and was pleased when her older sister approved. Amy was reconsidering her opposition to the institution of marriage. A few years earlier, she had written to Zina, "I wouldn't marry for anything and it is the worst thing you can wish on me."[7] She had harsh words for housekeeping as well: "As to housework, never will I do it, & if I go home I shall make Mother [Sophronia] understand that immediately. If I were earning money, I should take an entirely independent stand & do as I liked."[8] But Gurickx had turned her head, and in time, he proposed. A decision would have to wait: Proper decorum dictated that Amy needed approval from a male member of her family before accepting.

Next, the sisters stopped in London, where Zina visited the National Training School for Cookery, met with more leaders in the British cooperative movement at their annual meeting, and enjoyed the theater and museums. Zina, Charley, and Amy returned to the States in August. Charley had work to do in New York City, and Zina opted to return to Cambridge with Amy, making the separation official.

Amy felt she had reached the very pinnacle of success when, in February 1877, prominent conductor Theodore Thomas invited her to play a Chopin concerto with his traveling orchestra at the Sanders Theatre in Cambridge. The Theodore Thomas Orchestra was known as one of the nation's finest ensembles, and its annual appearance in Cambridge was a local highlight. Patrons packed the theater, filling every seat. Several of Amy's sisters helped her pass the anxious moments of waiting in the green room. Amy knew the stakes were high: A success with Thomas was a ticket to a sterling career. But once on stage, she battled stage fright, which caused her to forget brief sections of the concerto. She fared better on a short concert dance composed by Liszt and was even called back for an encore. In the end, the reviews were mixed. Influential critic John Sullivan Dwight referred to "the certain nervousness" that marred her performance.[9]

For the remainder of 1877 and all the following year, Amy filled her calendar with performances on the East Coast, including a return to St. Albans, Vermont, and a concert in nearby Burlington, where so many Hopkins relatives lived. At the Worcester Festival in Massachusetts, the oldest classical music convention in the country, she performed an entire concerto, Beethoven's B-flat Major, becoming the first artist to do so at the festival.[10] She presented a series of three recitals in Boston, the reviews for which were mostly complimentary. Her strengths were becoming clear: She excelled when performing pieces by Chopin, Liszt, and old friends John Knowles Paine and Charles Jerome Hopkins. Her weakness, however, was her apparent nervousness. Amy had the talent and the technique, but her emotional fragility threatened to keep her from achieving her musical ambitions.

Chicago

1878–1881

IN 1878, FIVE OF THE Fay siblings made a dramatic change, moving to Chicago. It happened because of the telephone. During the nation's centennial in 1876, Alexander Graham Bell had demonstrated the first phone and ignited a new industry. It was the age of opportunity, and brother Norman was always keen on the latest invention. When the Chicago Telephonic Exchange was established, Norman hopped on board. The company began with seventy-five telephones in the city; a mere two years later, there were three thousand. After the first long-distance call to New York rang through in 1892, the breakneck growth continued, until over 1.2 million people had telephones in 1930.

Norman, in the right place at the right time, worked his way up the managerial ladder to the vice presidency. His paychecks increased alongside his responsibilities, and soon he summoned his single sisters to join him in Chicago. One by one they did: Amy first, then Zina (separated though not yet divorced from Charley), Rose, and finally Lily. In the Fay family, home was where your siblings were. Until you married, that is. Laura and Kate stayed behind in New England with their husbands and families.

Chicago experienced a tremendous rebirth after the 1871 fire, which had destroyed over seventeen thousand buildings and seventy-three miles of street, leaving nearly one hundred thousand people homeless. In *City of the Century*, author Donald Miller wrote, "No city in the world grew faster in the 1880s or was more chaotically alive than Chicago, a place people went to see the shape of the future."[1] Because of its location at the nexus of Lake Michigan and the Chicago River, linking it to the Mississippi River, Chicago emerged as an important hub in industry and agriculture. With the addition of several railroad lines, it became a prime location for large businesses such as meatpacking, lumber, agricultural implements, iron and steel, and textiles. New manufacturing processes made steel affordable for building, and Chicago's new postfire skyline shot skyward.

Amy soon found that the music scene in Chicago was blossoming as well. In 1865, Florenz Ziegfeld had established the Chicago Conservatory of Music, which evolved over time into the Chicago Musical College. Sara Hershey founded the Hershey School of Musical Art in 1875, bringing more musicians to town in the form of both students and teachers. A series of philharmonic societies attempted, unsuccessfully, to establish long-term orchestras, each lasting a few seasons.[2] Traveling opera companies and orchestras such as Theodore Thomas's made Chicago an annual stop. The Summer Garden Concerts were wildly popular, taking place in the barnlike Exposition Building, which was two blocks long and able to seat tens of thousands of people, on the site of today's Art Institute. That the train yard was adjacent to the Expo Building was a nuisance but did not seem to deter the crowds, who enjoyed their music with foaming glasses from the beer garden. Music was everywhere, with concert series hosted by churches, multiple local piano manufacturers, and amateur musical clubs. In the mid-1880s, no less than four musical publications operated out of Chicago.[3] The city directory boasted advertisements for piano sales, musical instruments and instruction, and sheet music on virtually every page.

In 1880, Zina, Amy, Norman, Rose, and Lily stayed at the Walton Hotel, on Clark Street where it intersected with Locust Place at the time, near Washington Square Park.[4] Next, they resided in a boardinghouse on East Indiana Street, just a few blocks north of the Chicago River, while Norman searched for a suitable house. Whereas the south side of the city had long been considered the fashionable part of town, dry goods merchant and real estate mogul Potter Palmer was in the process of developing the north side. He filled in the marshy areas north of the Water Tower with sand and started building homes on speculation.[5] Charles Palmer (no relation) served as architect. Norman purchased 43 Bellevue Place, a Romanesque Revival graystone just a block from Lake Michigan and within reasonable distance of his office. He got in just in time. Land values for that area quadrupled in the next ten years, and the former swamp became known as the Gold Coast.[6]

Norman proudly provided a home for his sisters, and in return, they helped create a household for the up-and-coming bachelor. They contributed financially as well, as their mother, Emily, had attempted to do. Zina ran a boardinghouse and freelanced for local newspapers; Amy performed and taught piano; Rose, talented with the paintbrush, accepted commissions for interior design work; and Lily took in sewing, though she had just finished a course of study in teaching at St. Mary's Hall, an Episcopal school for girls in New Jersey.

The Fays found a city ready for a bright new music scene. The *Chicago Tribune* expressed excitement about Amy's arrival: "It will be good news to our musical circles that Miss Fay contemplates coming to this city to reside. Both as a musician and a lady of exceptional culture, she will be warmly welcomed."[7]

Chicago suited the family, despite a difficult start. Amy wrote to Henry Wadsworth Longfellow: "I have never had such desperate and protracted fits of homesickness as I have had here, notwithstanding my sister, Mrs. Peirce, and my brother are both with me."[8] But by the next letter, more sisters had joined her, and Amy had softened: "There is no denying that Chicago is a fascinating sort of place to live in, after one gets accustomed to its ways. Rose says she is less bored here than in any place she ever was in. The busy, wide-awake atmosphere gives life a hopeful aspect. Life is not less of a struggle here, but one has more heart to contend, and the very rapidity with which the city has rebuilt itself, is a constant reminder of how much can be done where there is a will."[9]

Furthermore, they felt welcomed socially. Thirty-one-year-old Norman, a well-connected businessman and glib conversationalist, standing five feet, ten inches tall and with the Fay blue eyes, provided his sisters with easy access to gatherings and clubs. The *Chicago Tribune* wrote, "Coming to Chicago with the prestige of social position in the East, to which were added marked talents and accomplishments, the members of this family enjoyed from the first an enviable social rank. They have been familiar figures in gay life, and, while not conspicuous for the extensiveness of their entertainments, have had the taste and tact to draw charming circles around them."[10] The Fays had come a long way since their struggles in remote parishes and the hills of Vermont.

Coming from historic, academic Cambridge, the sisters must have found the burgeoning city both vibrant and gritty. Zina penned the most colorful description, comparing the city to "an enormous cabbage which might at any time turn into an equally enormous rose."[11]

Norman provided a more analytical view of the city, though not until 1909, when he wrote a series on business for *Outlook* magazine:

> Chicago is a sort of social forge, where things moral, economical, and political get "all het up," as they say in Vermont, fuse together, are hammered out, and cool off in new and generally in better form. There is always something doing in Chicago. Parties and politicians come and go, 'isms and 'ocracies wax and wane: . . . sinister figures of bomb-thrower, demagogue, slugger, grafter, frenzied financier, one after the other stalk, menace, fight the town, lose, and fade away; while it grows always greater and more free. Soon even its smoke and dirt must give up the unequal combat, and along the gleaming border of the lake must rise Dan Burnham's magnificent conception, the City Beautiful.[12]

The move provided an opportunity for Amy to leave behind her reputation as a nervous performer and start afresh. However, after she performed a series of three piano recitals in Hershey Hall in the spring of 1879, her hopes were dashed. George P. Upton, the influential *Chicago Tribune* music critic, noted that while Amy played with deep feeling and impressive technique, her physical nervousness would keep her from a career on the stage. Despite real talent, he concluded, she was better suited to teaching.[13]

Once again, big sister Zina stepped up to assist. Pleased with the results of the "Letters Home," which had run in *The Atlantic Monthly*, Zina edited dozens more of Amy's letters and sent the manuscript off to book publishers. She met with rejection after rejection until Henry Wadsworth Longfellow provided a letter of recommendation to accompany the manuscript, "If I know anything about books, that is a good book. It is as good as my favorite novel, *Charles Auchester*.

And I hope it will impart to youthful aspirants the indispensable conception that mastery in any Art means long years of study and effort and self-discipline."[14] (*Charles Auchester*, an 1853 novel by Elizabeth Sara Sheppard, was a fictionalized account of the composer Felix Mendelssohn set in Germany and therefore an apt comparison of a woman writing about music.) Amy acknowledged Longfellow's support: "They took a great deal more interest in it after you had seen and talked with General McClurg about it. I was so much obliged to you for what you said to him."[15]

Published in 1881 by Jansen, McClurg and Company, *Music-Study in Germany* became tremendously successful. Though writing was still considered primarily a male undertaking, Amy's book was deemed acceptable because it consisted of her familial letters rather than being an effort to establish herself as an expert on a topic. Reviews and sales were both positive. Upon Liszt's suggestion, it was translated into German in 1882. A French translation followed. All told, *Music-Study in Germany* went through twenty-five printings and made Amy a bit of a celebrity. Virtually overnight, she became sought after not only as a performer but also as a lecturer, writer, critic, and teacher.

To overcome her biggest obstacle, her nervousness, Amy evolved a new type of recital that allayed her anxiety. Billed as "Piano Conversations," they consisted of Amy talking to the audience for several minutes about the piece she was to play. Amy may have been influenced by her uncle Charles Jerome Hopkins, as he had been giving "concert lectures" in New York as early as 1867.

With her reputation growing and her Piano Conversations easing her nerves, Amy enjoyed a moderately successful concert career. Though she never again achieved the heights of performing with the Theodore Thomas Orchestra, she played frequently throughout Chicago and neighboring cities in the 1880s, as well as touring with the Thursby Concert Company to cities such as Des Moines, Detroit, Louisville, Rochester, and Washington, DC.[16]

Amy honored one of her teachers, Ludwig Deppe, by publishing a book of finger exercises based on his methods. Conversely, one of her students, composer John Alden Carpenter, became a mainstay in the Chicago musical scene. Carpenter later dedicated a song, "A Norse Lullaby," to Amy.[17]

Norman and Amy combined their interests in 1880, when she played piano accompaniment to four vocalists, all singing into telephones at different locations. The novelty made the papers: "Four singers in Chicago and its suburbs, no one of whom was within two miles of any other, sang a quartette, the accompaniment to which was played by Miss Amy Fay, who was also some miles from the singers."[18]

Charles moved to Chicago in 1881, both to be nearer to his children and to bring Sophronia closer to her sister and mother, who lived in downstate Illinois, though they still summered on the farm in Grand Isle. He served for a short period as interim priest at St. James Episcopal Church. In 1881, in one of his frequent letters to Kate, he reported, with fatherly pride, "Amy seems to have struck her roots into the soil at last and blossoms of fruit are showing promise. Her book has made for her quite a reputation and as she is a first rate teacher, her pupils are increasing."[19]

Female performers faced an uphill battle in terms of booking engagements and garnering good reviews in a field that had historically been dominated by men. Orchestras were still entirely male, with the exception of an occasional harpist. While female singers enjoyed successful careers, most instrumental soloists were men, in large part because the training channels for aspiring women musicians were not yet in place. Newspaper critics were wary of admitting women to the field, often suggesting women didn't have the constitution necessary for public performance. An 1895 article in *Scientific American* suggested that even if a woman had the talent, her stamina was roughly one-third of a man's.[20] To challenge this network took not only talent but also thick skin, determination, and extraordinary confidence.[21]

Though Amy was not immune to this gender discrimination, she carved a unique niche for herself through her accessible writing, expressive performing, and delightful personality. Her experiences in Germany, documented in such an engaging fashion, encouraged aspiring woman musicians to study abroad. While it is difficult to quantify her influence, attendance by American female musicians in European conservatories spiked in the late nineteenth century.[22] Liszt biographer Alan Walker, writing in 1997, held that her book "acted like forked lightning" on young pianists in America, "firing them with the ambition to go to Liszt and Weimar, regardless of the effort."[23]

Clubs

1881–1884

IN CHICAGO, THE FAY SIBLINGS did what so many others were doing in the late nineteenth century: They joined clubs. Norman, in one of his annual reports to the Harvard alumni group, joked, "Chicago is clubbed to death." He was certainly an avid participant, as a member of the Union League Club, Union Club, Chicago Club, University Club, and Washington Park Club, among others. Amy joined the French Literary Club, and Zina, while not a member of the prestigious Fortnightly of Chicago, gave several lectures there.[1]

In the 1880s, clubs provided a way forward for women. At a time when only 2 percent of women attended college, clubs offered educational, cultural, and social opportunities that stretched beyond the confines of home life.[2] Starting with Sorosis and the New England Women's Club, the club movement grew exponentially. It is estimated that between 1880 and 1920, over two million women joined clubs.[3] Many of these ladies were not radical enough to join reform movements, but clubs got them out of the house.[4] What started as a trickle soon became a flood, as women ventured into the public in greater and greater numbers.

Amy and Rose (also talented on the piano, though not at Amy's level) both became deeply involved in the Amateur Musical Club. The club was begun in 1873 on a small scale by four women who met weekly to play piano quartets together. By the time Amy and Rose joined in the late 1870s, the club was growing rapidly by adding more pianists and singers. Though Amy was a professional, she and other female teachers and performers were allowed to join, since the male musical organizations were not open to them. As with many of today's book clubs, the group's gathering had social undertones as well. After becoming too large to fit comfortably in most of the women's homes, the club began meeting in local piano warehouses. With the additional space, membership grew even faster, as other women would stop by just to listen. The club started charging the listeners a modest fee to help cover expenses.

Amy, writing about the Amateur Musical Club in 1887, stressed, "I must state that women only constitute this club. No ungodly males are admitted, except to its public concerts, by invitation."[5] To avoid challenging gender norms and more clearly delineate themselves from professional concerts in public spaces, the members created domestic settings for their events, decorating the performing spaces with flowers, rugs, sculptures, pictures, and curtains from their own homes.

No longer just a casual gathering by the early 1880s, the Amateur Musical Club began offering regular concerts once a fortnight, with printed programs and increasingly higher musical standards. Having now outgrown the piano warehouses, organizers hired more expensive rooms and started inviting traveling musicians who were in town for other performances. The social-gathering element diminished as the musical focus intensified.

The Amateur Musical Club became very popular and soon had a membership of four hundred, necessitating further changes.[6] The club made a distinction between active members, who were the performers, and associate members, the listeners. A board coordinated the concerts and helped with logistics. Rose recognized this as a place where she could help and stepped up to serve as both secretary and librarian.

Overwhelmed by the work required to present concerts every other week, as well as the rental costs of the performance spaces—which ran to over $3,000 annually—the board opted to cut back to once a month in the rented Apollo Hall. To compensate for fewer programs, they raised the performance level to offer consistently high-quality concerts.

Amy also helped launch a second musical club in Chicago. The Artists' Concert Club had a highly selective membership of skilled performers, including men. The club aimed to "further art" and to work collectively to advance its musical goals. Amy wrote that "congenial and trusted members were to be relied upon to write press criticism."[7] She performed three pieces during the opening concert in December 1884, again playing to her strengths, with one by Liszt and one by Charles Jerome Hopkins. One of Chicago's chief music critics, W. S. B. Mathews, later wrote that the Artists' Concert Club had "exerted an important influence on the music of Chicago since its inception. It would be well if such a one existed in all cities."[8]

While musical clubs seemed like innocuous entertainment, they served as petri dishes for organization among women, allowing leaders to practice management skills, budget money, and build solidarity among their members. These techniques proved useful as women gained slow momentum toward obtaining the vote and broadening their sphere.

Zina had burst forth as an early voice in the women's reform movement; now two other sisters joined her as organizers and leaders in the club society. Amy served as a driving force behind both the Amateur Musical Club and the Artists' Concert Club, and within a few years, Rose became the second president of the former. The Fay women were on the rise.

Rose Fay and Theodore Thomas, as they appeared in 1903. Felsengarten Collection, Rosenthal Archives of the Chicago Symphony Orchestra Association.

Felsengarten, in the White Mountains of New Hampshire. Rose and Theodore treasured their summers here. Reprinted from Rose Fay Thomas, *Memoirs of Theodore Thomas* (New York: Moffat, Yard, 1911). Felsengarten Collection, Rosenthal Archives of the Chicago Symphony Orchestra Association.

Theodore Thomas with the Chicago Orchestra, taken in the Auditorium Theatre in 1897. Lawrence & Dinius photo, Rosenthal Archives of the Chicago Symphony Orchestra Association.

Theodore working at his desk at the Bellevue home in 1896. Theodore Thomas Collection, Rosenthal Archives of the Chicago Symphony Orchestra Association.

Orchestra Hall under construction in 1904, advertising offices for rent. Rosenthal Archives of the Chicago Symphony Orchestra Association.

Horses drinking from one of the numerous troughs and fountains installed around Chicago by the Anti-Cruelty Society. Courtesy Anti-Cruelty.

The Anti-Cruelty Society's building as it appeared in 1910. Courtesy Anti-Cruelty.

John and Frances Glessner's son George captured this photo of Rose and her dog, Dickey. Courtesy Glessner House.

Katherine Maria Fay Stone later in life. Kate was always elegant and stately, as seen here in her Cambridge home. Courtesy Christopher King.

Portrait of Norman by his wife, Lillian Hale Fay. A talented painter, she created this likeness of him in 1931. Courtesy David Fay Smith.

Amy and Zina's conjoined tombstone. The epitaph reads, "They were lovely and pleasant in their lives, / And in their death they were not divided." Photo by author.

Concerto Grosso

Rose

Chameleon

1878–1883

WHILE ZINA WROTE ARTICLES AND speeches about women taking control of their sphere, and Amy tried to make headway in the male-dominated music world, Rose had a quieter presence. Whether slipping quietly into the Selden family at a young age to bring cheer to a grieving household or joining the Longfellow girls in their studies, Rose had a chameleonlike ability to adapt to her surroundings.

In 1878, when she moved to Chicago with Norman, Amy, Zina, and Lily, Rose was twenty-six years old. She took out a listing in the city directory as a decorative artist and found occasional work painting floral designs on interior walls. The 1880 census lists her occupation as artist.[1] The only record of a romantic attachment had been four years earlier, when a love interest, Sam Lynde, the son of stepmother Sophronia's sister, had broken her heart, though exactly how is unclear.[2]

Perhaps Rose was content staying in the background. She had scant desire for attention, preferring to shine the light on others. Her role on the board of the Amateur Musical Club as a diligent behind-the-scenes worker suited her perfectly. Though her piano playing paled in comparison to Amy's (or sister Kate's, for that matter), her appreciation and understanding of music was considerable. Zina, as a music and theater critic for the *Chicago Evening Journal*, received two complimentary tickets to many concerts, and Rose was her usual guest.[3] Occasionally, Rose wrote critiques as well.

Rose had a talent for friendship. Whether it was the students in the Longfellow school, other girls in the Cambridge Bee, or fellow music lovers in the Amateur Musical Club, people liked Rose and her gentle manner. She excelled at lifting up those around her. She even inspired Henry Wadsworth Longfellow to write a snippet of poetry for her one Christmas:

> To the Rose of Roses
> And Fay of Fays,
> Health and happiness,
> Length of days,
> And all good wishes
> In all good ways![4]

Thanks largely to Norman, the 1880s were a time of relative affluence for the Fay family. A self-made man, Norman used his acumen and social connections to work his way up in the business world. While serving as vice president and general manager of the Chicago Telephone Company, Norman was also elected president of the National Telephone Exchange Association, a consortium of telephone companies nationwide. In his capacity with the telephone company, Norman had occasion to write to Thomas Edison in 1882, asking for information on his invention of a chemical printing register.[5] From the Chicago Telephone Company, Norman moved on to the presidency of the Chicago Gas Trust Company, then to the Chicago Arc Light and Power Company, capitalizing on the new industries forged by the discovery of electricity.

Most of the Fay siblings had found their life paths. By this time, Laura, in Vermont with her husband, Frank, had borne six children, four of whom survived to adulthood. Kate and her husband, Will, in Cambridge had two children, with more on the way. Both had chosen traditional roles for women.

Rose, largely free of commitments and quietly capable, was the extra pair of hands wherever needed. Norman gave her credit for keeping 43 Bellevue Place running smoothly.[6] She sometimes served as a mother's helper, traveling to the East Coast for weeks at a time.

In 1871, after another difficult delivery and birth for Laura, Rose went to Vermont to assist her older sibling for a few months. After she left, Amy wrote to Laura, "You must miss Rosie a good deal I think. I was quite desolate when I bid her good bye. She had made herself almost indispensable to me & I hardly knew which way to turn without her for a long while."[7]

In the early 1880s, of all the sisters, it was surprisingly her eldest sibling who needed Rose's help the most. Zina had been separated from Charley since 1876 and struggled to be financially independent. It was no easy path, but life with her husband had been far worse. In 1881, Charles wrote about his daughter's trauma: "Zina was very sick and I thought at one time that she would die. But she struggled back to life . . . but she is so broken in constitution from years past, that I fear she will live to suffer more than to enjoy. Then again, her husband's brutal treatment has been, and is, a source of mortification, which I have no doubt wears upon her."[8]

In 1882, Charley finally filed for divorce, something Zina never pushed for because of the social stigma (the divorce rate in 1880 was estimated at 2.4 out of every 1,000 marriages).[9] When the divorce was final in 1883, Charley immediately married Juliette Pourtalai, a woman of mysterious background. The couple obfuscated her life story so successfully that her true identity is still in question. According to her death certificate, Pourtalai was born in 1865, which would have made her eighteen to Charley's forty-four at the time of their wedding.[10] However, her date of birth ranges from 1851 to 1865 on other official documents; her immigration date similarly varies.

Rumors swirled that she had connections to the Austrian Habsburg family. According to neighbors, she had a hidden closet filled with evening dresses and fur coats, and they reported seeing Pourtalai dressed in a royal purple velvet robe emblazoned with the czar's crest. Novelist Henry James, who helped Pourtalai with legal issues, believed her to be connected with the royal court of Austria. Neighbors and friends speculated that she was an illegitimate child of the royal family, "born on the wrong side of the blanket."[11]

When it became clear that the couple had been living and traveling together while Charley was still married to Zina, Johns Hopkins University dismissed him. In fact, the situation so badly damaged Charley's reputation that he was never again able to land an academic position.[12] The Coast Survey job ended as well. Though Charley continued to write and made a profound mark on the field of logic, and while the couple seemed truly in love, they faced economic, social, and physical hardships for the rest of their lives.

Zina was probably happier single, having written about the phenomenon of "husband-power, which is very apt to shut down like an invisible bell-glass over every woman as soon as she is married, and affectionately say to her, 'My dear, thus far shalt thou go and no farther.'"[13] She expressed her doubts about the institution of marriage in a letter to Kate: "One of the interesting things to find out when we get to the next world is—*where are* marriages made—in Heaven, as the proverb has it—or in the other place?"[14]

But running a boardinghouse single-handedly was not easy, and other family members pitched in where they could, Rose chief among them. Zina ran a tight ship. Charley's aunt Lizzy wrote about a friend's experience in Zina's boardinghouse: "In some ways the boarding house was the best in Chicago. Everything was very neat and dainty—glass, china, linen, etcetera, but the eatables were nothing extra—only the way in which they were served—but sometimes the boarders would leave—having got offended—or not wishing to conform to Mrs. P's rule of etiquette—but their places would soon be filled up."[15] Despite her eldest sister's determination and fortitude, Rose, younger and more energetic, served a critical role in keeping the boardinghouse running and mending Zina's broken spirit.

Between her club work, interior painting, running the household, and helping her sisters, Rose kept herself busy. She abhorred idle hands. Thanks to Rose's ability to form strong friendships, those hands were soon juggling even more projects.

Famous Friend

1880–1883

ROSE FIRST MET THEODORE THOMAS backstage at the Sanders Theatre in Boston, when Amy performed with his orchestra in 1877. Thus began a steady friendship, strengthening gradually over the years whenever Theodore passed through Chicago with his traveling ensemble. Biographies of the conductor indicate he had just a handful of close friends, but somehow the Fay family, most of all Rose and Norman, managed to forge true connections with him.[1]

Though Amy's chance with the orchestra had come and gone, the contact initiated in the Sanders Theatre turned into meaningful companionship. Rose wrote, "The acquaintance thus professionally begun had been continued from time to time, as he visited Chicago, and gradually included other members of the family, for we were all ardently devoted to music, and more or less connected with the musical interests of the city."[2] Theodore's biographer Charles Edward Russell said likewise, "From the beginning, all the Fays seem to have had an odd intuitive understanding of Thomas. If there is any such thing as spiritual kinship, it must have existed here."[3]

Originally from Germany, ten-year-old musical prodigy Theodore Thomas immigrated to the States with his family in 1845. They arrived in New York City, which he later described as "a provincial town of two-story houses" where "the pigs ran through Broadway and ate the refuse."[4] In the struggle to help feed the family, Theodore eschewed school, instead performing on his violin at every opportunity, playing in theater orchestras, barrooms, and a brief stint in a navy band. At the age of fourteen, he traveled solo south on horseback, with just his fiddle, some clothes, cigars, a pistol, and posters advertising music by "Master T. T."[5]

Returning to New York, Theodore played everywhere he could, in pickup orchestras, operas, and small ensembles. In 1864, as casualties continued to rise in Civil War battles, Theodore assembled his own orchestra, certain that "what this country needed most of all to make it musical was a good orchestra, and plenty of concerts within reach of people."[6] At the time, the only full-scale organized orchestra in the country was the Philharmonic Society in New York, and it performed just five or six concerts per season.[7]

Theodore set up his own ensemble of sixty musicians—most of them German, all of them male—and he did it all: programming, hiring, marketing, rehearsing, ticket sales, conducting. After starting in New York with a summer concert series, then playing in Boston, he soon figured out that ticket sales boomed when he played in other cities, so beginning in 1869, in the off-season, he took the show on the road. His orchestra traveled by train, going farther each year and adding more cities. Over the years, his annual trips to Chicago, St. Louis, Philadelphia, Cincinnati, and dozens of smaller cities became a regular parade of stops the press dubbed the "Thomas Highway." One particularly long tour involved seventy-four concerts over a three-month period, covering fourteen thousand miles of railroad track.[8] Immigrant Theodore saw far more of the country than the vast majority of native-born Americans.

On October 9, 1871, the Theodore Thomas Orchestra chugged into Chicago, scheduled to dedicate the newly renovated Crosby Opera House. Reaching the Twenty-Second Street Station, they pulled into a city in flames. The opera house and everything around it for blocks, including the streets themselves, were ablaze, the fire completely out of control. There was nothing to do but to find the first train out of the burning city. They stayed in Joliet for twelve days before the next scheduled performances in St. Louis.[9] It was a tough pill for Theodore, who had all his expenses but none of the ticket revenues. It took many years for him to recover financially from this loss.[10]

The orchestra's reputation spread rapidly. Through patience, skill, and determination, Theodore shaped his musicians into an ensemble unlike any heard in the States at that time. There were plenty of opportunities to hear live music—in church, theaters, traveling operas, summer concerts, dances—but Theodore's orchestra was superior because his men rehearsed together year after year, developing their skills and ensemble playing into a cohesive sound beyond what temporary groups could do. They spent the 1870s and 1880s touring the country, introducing new audiences to classical music. Before the invention of radio or recordings, the only possible exposure to music was live performances. Theodore crafted his programs with care, interspersing heavier or modern pieces with lighter pieces to educate his audiences without losing them. Music historians believe his skill in creating compelling programs equaled in importance his ability to shape an orchestra.[11]

It is impossible to overstate Theodore Thomas's influence on American music education. In addition to leading his own traveling orchestra, he helmed the Brooklyn Philharmonic Society from 1866 to 1891 and the New York Philharmonic Society from 1877 to 1891. In his lifetime, it is estimated he conducted the U.S. premiere of over three hundred pieces. Because of Theodore's commitment to championing new music, Richard Strauss's *Till Eulenspiegel* was performed in Chicago eight years before it was heard in Vienna; similar statistics are available for works by Franz Liszt, Pyotr Ilyich Tchaikovsky, César Franck, Anton Bruckner, and Jean Sibelius. Biographer Ezra Schabas referred to Theodore as the "Johnny Appleseed of Music."[12]

In 1883, when the orchestra came to town again for the summer garden concerts, Theodore wrote to Rose, looking for lodging. He hated the Chicago hotels and wondered if Zina might have space for him in her boardinghouse:

> I will tell you what I need. Two rooms, connecting, one as a sitting-room, the other to sleep in. I would like a bathroom, but would be satisfied with a "Sitzbad" in my bedroom. I must have strong coffee (poison) for my breakfast and plenty of meat for my dinner. Also a little cold luncheon, consisting of bread and meat,

> aft the concert, if possible in my room. My wine I, of course, provide for myself. I receive no calls. . . . In return for giving you all this trouble I will help you with the winter programs of your Amateur Musical Club, or with anything else in which I can be of service. Our stay in Chicago will be five weeks.[13]

Zina replied that she had but one room to offer, and Theodore quickly accepted.[14] Rose enjoyed having Theodore nearby, and she later wrote of his stay, "All formality between Thomas and the Fay Family naturally vanished, and, as the years went on, the tie then formed drew ever closer and closer until, at last, it became the dominating influence of the closing period of his life."[15] On the flip side, having access to such a well-known and highly regarded musician increased Rose's standing in the Amateur Musical Club as well as her reputation in society.

Like Rose, Zina was a fan of Theodore's. In her role as music critic, she urged the public to embrace him, reminding them that he owed Chicago nothing: "It seems all the time but a chance, a rare piece of fortune, a something 'too good to believe,' that we have him at all."[16] It was a repeated chorus for Zina, referring to him as "too precious an element in our national life to spare him yet for many a long year."[17]

Though Theodore was happily married to Minna Rhodes and had five children back east, when in Chicago, he had a home away from home, a place among people who were musically astute and welcomed him. There was no impropriety. Theodore was a deeply moral man, believing "a musician must keep his heart pure and his mind clean, if he wishes to elevate instead of debasing his art."[18] Furthermore, he believed music to be an ethical force, pure, uplifting, therapeutic, inspiring. Good music would create good men. Theodore's goal was to perform the greatest music perfectly, for the betterment of all listeners. He wrote, "Music has the strongest influence of any art if properly controlled, because of its powerful appeal to the emotions."[19]

His comments on Beethoven's music stand as an example of his belief in the power of great music: "I care not from what station in life come the thousands who sit back of me. Beethoven will touch each according to his needs, and the very same cadence that may waft the thoughts of one to drowsy delight or oblivion may stir the heart of another to higher aspirations—may give another hope in his repair, may bring to yet another a message of love."[20]

For the Fays, a family raised on equal parts religion and music, Theodore, a deeply gifted musician on a lifelong quest for musical perfection, must have seemed almost holy.

Family Dynamics

1884–1889

FOR A LONG TIME, ROSE stood in the shadow of her more outgoing and public-facing older sisters, Zina and Amy. Splitting her time between her Chicago projects and trips back east to assist Laura and Kate with their growing families, it must have felt as if her own path might never materialize.

Meanwhile, family dynamics were changing once again. In 1884, fifteen years after the publication of her first *Atlantic Monthly* articles, Zina succeeded in getting *Co-operative Housekeeping: How Not to Do It and How to Do It; A Study in Sociology* published in Boston by J. R. Osgood and Company. In this updated version, Zina outlined the mistakes made by the Cambridge Co-operative and provided ideas for future success. She continued to argue against suffrage and for a separate House for Women, believing that this third House would eventually replace the Senate, once men realized that women had stepped forward to assume their full responsibilities.[1]

Overall, reviews for the book were good but mentioned that her innovative ideas were probably too idealistic for "earthly realization," an observation similarly noted in the introduction to the 1870 Edinburgh edition.[2] Suffragists felt she was missing the boat, as printed in the *Woman's Journal*: "Try again, Mrs. Peirce, when we have placed in your hand and in those of your fellow-workers that wonderful little lever entitled the ballot. Depend upon it, you will then be better treated!" The *New-York Daily Tribune* suggested that some enterprising women should give cooperative housekeeping a "fair, persevering trial."[3]

Some newspaper reviewers took issue with Zina's attitude toward men. She had been through so much since her original *Atlantic Monthly* articles in 1868–69, and her words had become increasingly pointed. She took aim at men's despotic power over women: "It covers not only the political area. It owns not only the bodies of its subjects. Its hand lies heavily on their innermost personality, and its power is so tremendous that whatever they are, it is because these absolute lords have willed it." *The New York Times* took umbrage, saying, "This peppery element does her cause no good," and suggested she contain her reform ideas to women.[4]

Rose helped Zina pack up her belongings and close her Chicago boardinghouse, and Zina moved to New York City shortly before the Statue of Liberty's June 1885 arrival. She took on three boardinghouses in a single block, charging $3 a day. The brilliant woman who had for years reenvisioned communal cooking and cleaning had become an expert at both and wound up spending years fulfilling these mundane roles for strangers. Socially speaking, she had fallen significantly since her days as part of the Cambridge intellectual scene. But true to form, she got right to work on social issues, helping organize the Street Cleaning Committee of the Ladies' Health Protective Association.

As for Amy, she took advantage of Norman's affluence to return to Europe in the summer of 1885 to attend a grand birthday celebration for Franz Liszt. She stopped in Brussels for a reunion with her former beau, Camille Gurickx. Both Amy and Camille were still quite fond of each other. However, for some unknown reason, Norman had opposed the marriage, and that spelled the end of the romance.[5] For the remainder of her life, Amy wore a heart-shaped locket around her neck with a photograph of her "Gu-Gu." Her correspondence shows no indication that she bore Norman any ill will for his interference; given her misgivings about marriage and housekeeping, perhaps her brother's edict had been a relief.

After Brussels, Amy continued on to London, where she met with Sir George Grove, head of the Royal Academy of Music. She presented Grove with a copy of her book *Music-Study in Germany*, which continued to sell well. Based on his recommendation, Macmillan published a new edition that included a preface from Sir George: "The freshness and truth of the letters is not to be denied. We may laugh at the writer's enthusiasm . . . but no one can laugh at her indomitable determination, the artistic earnestness with which she makes the most of each of her opportunities, or the brightness and ease with which each successive person is placed before us in his habit as he lives. Such a gift is indeed a rare and precious one."[6]

Next, Amy caught up with Franz Liszt in both Antwerp and Weimar. There were many opportunities for shared music, enjoyable games of whist, and spirited conversation. She relished her time in Liszt's salon with about twenty other Liszt disciples, who gathered around his piano, taking turns playing and singing. These were playful days of "endless fun."[7]

Back in Chicago, Amy and Rose kept busy with their club activities and other concerts. In June 1887, they both accompanied Theodore to St. Louis, where he was conducting the American Opera Company in Anton Rubinstein's *Nero*. Technically, they went as music critics for Chicago papers, but by now all objectivity had been lost. In a letter to Laura, Amy wrote:

> We were Thomas' guests at the Hotel, and he treated us in his usual royal style, and we had a charming visit. . . . There is a very nice Opera House in the Exposition Building in St. Louis. We went with Thomas in his carriage, of course, and came in through the stage entrance. He had a private room facing upon the street in front of the Opera House, and it was quite a novel sensation to sit in it with the great conductor before the beginning of the performance and watch the people alight from their carriages and walk up the steps.[8]

Theodore, trying to establish an auxiliary of the American Opera Company in Chicago, recruited Norman to serve as secretary of the committee.[9] (The failure of this company eventually set Theodore back $18,000.)

The biggest change to the family dynamic was the loss of its patriarch. In November 1888, diagnosed with heart issues during a doctor's visit in Burlington, Charles summoned Norman, who escorted him to New York City for consultation with top physicians. Charles died a few days later at Zina's home. In Norman's opinion, "He was a man who, as far as I know, never had an enemy. His death was the peaceful ending of a noble and gentle life, of unselfish devotion to others."[10] Laura wrote that he was saintlier than anyone she ever knew.[11] Charles's funeral took place at Christ Church, Cambridge, where he had been christened eighty years earlier. He was buried in the lot belonging to his father, Judge Fay, at Mount Auburn Cemetery. In his honor, his widow, Sophronia, gave his former parish in St. Albans a new marble pulpit. Four years later, she died as well.

After a six-month mourning period, on June 12, 1889, thirty-three-year-old Lily married Charles Henry (Harry) Wilmerding, an engineer who worked with Norman as the general manager of the Chicago Arc Light and Power Company. Like Theodore, Harry had also been one of Zina's boarders. Norman hosted the wedding reception at 43 Bellevue, with Amy and Rose receiving the guests.[12] The newlyweds set up house just a few blocks north of Bellevue on Division Street.

Watching her younger sister wed, Rose, now thirty-seven, may well have wondered whether she would ever find her own mate. She had no idea that her great love was just around the corner and that the relationship would entail major roles in society.

Wedding

1889–1890

IN APRIL 1889, A WIFE and mother in New York named Minna Rhodes Thomas died after several years' illness. This meant that after twenty-five years of marriage, fifty-four-year-old music icon Theodore Thomas was widowed, alone, and heartbroken.

It had been a happy marriage, though certainly Minna would have been almost entirely responsible for managing their household and raising their five children, as Theodore toured for months at a time. The day Minna died, Theodore was conducting in Philadelphia and honored his commitment to the concert the following night. As he led the orchestra in Chopin's *Marche funèbre*, tears ran down his cheeks.[1]

Theodore, "nearly prostrated by the blow" of Minna's death, wrote to Rose of his efforts to keep his grief at bay and not neglect his responsibilities: "I have had no sense for music or anything else, since my loss, except to be with my children. These lines are the first I have written, or, in fact, the only thing I could bring myself to do, except the few concerts I had to conduct, and in which I took no interest."[2]

Through their correspondence (of which, sadly, only his letters survive) and the occasional time they spent together, their relationship deepened, and Theodore turned to Rose for comfort. With her gentle, unobtrusive manner, her knowledge and passion for music, and above all, her compassion for others, Rose made a perfect complement to Theodore. In an interview, he maintained, "I do not care for so-called 'pretty women.' What I admire is character and intelligence. If a woman has these, she does not need beauty, but I will confess that if a woman of character and intellect has beauty in addition, it is like a lamp shining through an alabaster vase. But this is a rare combination."[3]

As for Rose, a newspaper described her as follows: "Her personal appearance is pleasing. Tall, slender, and well-formed, she has a graceful carriage, but is so retiring as to seem distant in her manner. Her features are regular. Fair brown hair and blue eyes, a straight nose and oval contour mark a face that, if not beautiful, is decidedly good-looking."[4]

At thirty-seven years old, Rose had suffered a few broken relationships, had watched nearly all her sisters—including the younger Lily—wed, and had lived quietly in the shadow of her more outgoing sisters. Now she burst suddenly into the Chicago spotlight, in a role for which she was perfectly suited. The little girl from Vermont, shunted around from caregiver to caregiver for so many years, had finally found her place.

Theodore had five children with Minna: Franz (1865), Hector (1866), Minna (1869), Hermann (1873), and Marian (1877). Most were young adults at the time of mother Minna's death, but Marian was only twelve and still needed nurturing. Norman recalled that there was considerable hesitation on both sides, but Rose gradually won the children's affection.[5]

Theodore's biographer, Charles Edward Russell, wrote that Rose "was kind, gentle, sweet, wise, had long understood and shared Thomas's ideals, and was now the influence he most needed in his life."[6] A man of sturdy build—to match a sturdy personality—Theodore carried himself firmly, without pretense or flash. He dressed impeccably but modestly and was largely undemonstrative, unless circumstance demanded otherwise. Though generally understated on the podium, he could erupt in anger on occasion.

Rose wrote an unflinching portrayal of him in her *Memoirs of Theodore Thomas*: "In his professional life he was stern, serious, intensely in earnest, and absolutely uncompromising. His personality was so commanding that he was instantly and unquestioningly obeyed by everyone who came near him, and I have never known anyone who did not fear him. . . . He made the impression of holding, pent up within himself, some kind of tremendous force which would annihilate everything in sight if it broke loose." She went on to say that "[when] it did break loose, . . . he was "terrible and no one could stand against him." Despite the conductor's dominating personality, Rose believed that the intensity stemmed from a deep sense of truth and justice and that while he was feared, he was loved to a greater degree. At home, he was warm, tender, dependent, and docile.[7]

Their wedding constituted a major social event covered by newspapers across the country, the *Chicago Tribune* devoting a considerable portion of its front page to the occasion. Invitations had been sent to 150 guests after the formal engagement in February, but on Wednesday evening, May 7, 1890, at the Chapel of the Church of the Ascension at the corner of Elm Street and LaSalle Avenue, a crowd of several hundred gathered for a glimpse of the wedding party.

The *InterOcean* reported, "The favored of society were there to witness the pledging of the vows. Riches and fashion and beauty smiled upon the happy couple; flowers beamed brightly upon them, the gladdening strains of noble airs wafted in from the church organ adjoining, while from without came the boisterous echoes that told of the presence of the multitude, the curiosity of the larger, plebeian, uninvited throng."[8]

Under the watchful eye of the Reverend E. A. Larrabee, Rose, in a white, square-necked satin dress brocaded with roses and with a long train, made her way down the aisle, with Norman and Amy (in yellow brocade with train) right behind. Rose had orange blossoms in her hair, offsetting a tulle veil. In Theodore's buttonhole and in the bridal bouquet were white roses.[9]

The right music was crucial for the event, and Theodore had chosen carefully. His friend and noted musician Clarence Eddy was the organist, performing airs from Wagner's *Die Meistersinger* and *Die Walküre* during the processional. Theodore met Rose at the altar, with Norman and Amy taking spots on either side of the couple. All of Theodore's children were present but not at the altar. A large floral lyre stood to the right of the altar, and bright LaFrance roses, Calla lilies, and maidenhair ferns filled the chapel.

The ceremony was short and simple, including the march from Weber's *Konzertstück*. After the declaration of vows, the bridal party exited to the finale of Beethoven's Fifth Symphony. The reception, in keeping with the private and reserved nature of the bride and groom, took place at 43 Bellevue, with Amy and one of Theodore's daughters (it is unclear which one) helping receive. All the Fay siblings, with the likely exception of Laura, attended; Zina came in from New York and Kate and Will from Cambridge.[10]

The wedding gifts included a grand piano from Steinway and Sons, a solid silver salad bowl inscribed with their names from the Amateur Musical Club, an ornamental clock with two candelabras from the New York Philharmonic,[11] and a gold-bangled necklace and four Venetian glass vases from Zina. Norman, at the apex of his success, gave the pair the Bellevue house and a staggering $25,000 (over $860,000 in 2025 dollars).

The newlyweds spent their honeymoon night at the new Auditorium Building, then traveled to Cincinnati, where Theodore was conducting at the May Festival. With Theodore's national prominence as orchestral leader and Rose at the helm of Chicago's Amateur Musical Club, the couple resolved to reshape Chicago's musical landscape.

Orchestra

1891–1892

ROSE'S MARRIAGE TO THEODORE CATAPULTED the Fay family into a new level of society. Furthermore, it was a good match, the type of marriage Emily, Zina, and Amy had concluded impossible. Years later, Rose described it as "one of those rare and exquisite unions such as seldom occur in this imperfect world." She continued, "As long as I had my husband with me I was absolutely happy. We never had a quarrel or an unkind word or inconsiderate act pass between us, and we were always each other's most cherished companions and were never separated a moment longer than we were obliged."[1]

Norman was delighted. He moved out of the Bellevue house, as did Amy, who relocated to a boardinghouse in New York to be near Zina and try the musical scene there, leaving the graystone to the newlyweds and teenage Marian. Norman took up residence in the Chicago Club, a perfect home base for his social activities. He relished his position in Chicago's social scene and happily participated in hospital fundraisers, art shows, horse shows, and benefits.

In 1877, when Amy performed with the Theodore Thomas Orchestra in Boston, Norman had been in the Midwest and unable to attend. But a few months later, he happened upon the ensemble in Chicago. He recalled, "That evening, wandering out for a breath of air, I came upon the old Exposition Building down on the Lake Front, and from its open doors and windows floated . . . the divinest music. Theodore

Thomas was giving there his first Chicago season of Summer Garden Concerts, and for the first time I heard a great orchestra."[2]

From that point on, Norman had advocated for Theodore to make a commitment to Chicago. He first wrote to Theodore in September 1879, proposing a new Philharmonic Society with local musicians who would perform twelve concerts a year.[3] However, at the time, Theodore was based in New York, still raising his family, and had his own orchestra. He was scarcely inclined to take on training a new ensemble. In a letter to Rose during those busy years, Theodore wrote, "I long for rest, and the opportunity to devote myself to my specialty. I ought not to be expected to travel about and do pioneer work any more, and I have not the physical endurance for it now, either; it will be my ruin if I have to keep it up much longer."[4]

After the Theodore Thomas Orchestra disbanded and Rose and Theodore became engaged, Norman tried again. While in New York on business, he had dinner with Theodore at Delmonico's restaurant. Norman later recalled, "My thoughts went back to those ten years of Summer Garden Concerts, and to some powerful and devoted friends of Mr. Thomas and his music at home, and I asked, 'Would you come to Chicago if we could give you a permanent orchestra?' The answer, grim and sincere, and entirely destitute of intentional humor, came back like a flash: 'I would go to hell if they gave me a permanent Orchestra.' . . . And then and there we roughed out in talk the general principles of an agreement."[5] Much more substantial than merely twelve concerts a year with local musicians, this endeavor was to be a large, permanent symphony orchestra of the highest quality that would give two performances a week for twenty weeks. Norman's plan afforded Theodore all the musical decision-making while releasing him of the logistical details.

In this, they were expanding on the model that businessman Henry Lee Higginson had established in Boston in 1881. In founding the Boston Symphony Orchestra, Higginson inaugurated a new type of orchestral structure. Up until this point, most orchestras had operated either as cooperatives, with the musicians starting the ensemble and sharing the financial and organizational burdens, or, as with the Theodore Thomas Orchestra, the leader solely taking on these obligations. The Boston Symphony Orchestra was the first major ensemble to run on the benefactor model, freeing the conductor and the musicians of the financial side and guaranteeing a certain annual income.[6] This enhanced rehearsal-and-concert schedule (twenty concerts per season) allowed for steady improvement in ensemble playing and alleviated the need for the musicians to work outside gigs; in fact, Higginson forbade them to play in other orchestras.[7] Norman's plan took Higginson's idea one step further, creating a corporate model for orchestral management in which a civic-minded group of directors and a professional staff handled all the logistics.[8] And unlike the Boston Symphony Orchestra, which relied heavily on Higginson's pocket, the Chicago plan called for a larger group of investors. The Fays were familiar with the Higginsons—Henry's wife, Ida Agassiz, had helped her parents run the school that Zina had attended years earlier in Cambridge.

The Chicago model of orchestra administration caught on quickly, and just in time, as other cities assembled their own ensembles based on this model. The St. Louis Symphony was founded in 1893, Cincinnati's the following year, and Pittsburgh's in 1895. Philadelphia, Minnesota, San Francisco, and Detroit launched orchestras of their own in the early 1900s.[9] Theodore's cross-country pioneering work had helped create audiences large enough to support permanent resident ensembles.

Thus because of his relationship with Rose, fifty-four-year-old Theodore Thomas had a completely fresh start. Within a couple of years, he had found a new wife, a new city, and a permanent orchestra.

Most biographies of Theodore Thomas and histories of the Chicago Symphony Orchestra give Norman credit for establishing the organization, and not unjustly. Norman made the approach, secured Theodore's participation, formulated the organizing principles, and rallied the support necessary.[10] However, the lack of mention of Rose's role is striking. Without the second marriage, the warm Fay family embrace, or the new place to call home, one wonders whether Theodore would have been able to muster up the energy and enthusiasm for this endeavor.

Norman's memberships in numerous business and literary clubs now paid off in full. He moved quickly. Having gotten support from Marshall Field, Charles Hamill, N. K. Fairbank, and George Pullman, Norman pulled together a subscription paper for distribution. The Commercial Club was hosting an excursion north on the train to see the new army base, Fort Sheridan, and Norman set to work, going up and down the aisle to get signatures. By the end of that day, he had nineteen subscribers, with only two men abstaining from involvement.[11] In October 1890, he proudly informed Theodore that they had nearly secured $1,000 apiece, annually, from fifty men, establishing a guarantee fund for the first three years. The list of fifty included most of Chicago's business leaders, such as Cyrus McCormick, Henry Field, Charles Wacker, John Glessner, Charles Hutchinson, Martin Ryerson, and three members of the meatpacking Armour family.

Theodore signed the orchestra contract in December 1890, seven months after the wedding. Rose reported, "The prospect of a return to his old artistic standards of work banished all the gloom and depression of the past, and once more Thomas was himself again—bright, hopeful, boundlessly energetic as of yore, and intensely interested in making the new Western orchestra the best he had ever conducted."[12] He brought sixty of his former symphony members from New York to form the core of the new orchestra, then hired twenty-six local players to complete the ensemble. All were male. With the exception of an occasional female harpist (the harp was perceived as a women's instrument), it was not until 1940 that a woman, horn player Helen Kotas, was awarded a position as a permanent member of the group.[13]

Another Chicago carrot for Theodore was that in April 1890, just weeks before the wedding, President Benjamin Harrison had announced the city as the winner for the World's Columbian Exposition, scheduled to be held in 1892, celebrating four hundred years since Columbus's arrival. World's fairs were popular international expositions at which the latest and greatest inventions and artworks were displayed. Paris had held the most recent one, in 1889, at which the Eiffel Tower had been unveiled to great acclaim.

In addition to establishing his own Chicago orchestra, Theodore secured the appointment as musical director for the World's Fair, providing him with the opportunity to showcase classical music for a much broader audience. Rose, as head of the Amateur Musical Club of Chicago, had her own plans for the fair. The couple's grand ideas to shake up the musical offerings in Chicago expanded to include the entire country.

World's Fair

1892–1893

FOR ROSE, THE WORLD'S FAIR was a launchpad. For Theodore, it turned out to be a debacle.

The World's Columbian Exposition got off to a rocky start. The designers and builders quickly fell behind schedule, leading to the decision to host an opening ceremony in October 1892 but to hold off on the remaining events until the following year, 401 years after Columbus's arrival.

On October 21, 1892, Rose, with an estimated 125,000 other people, sat in the as yet unfinished Manufactures and Liberal Arts Building for the dedication ceremony. It was thought to be the largest gathering ever assembled under one roof at the time. The building was four times the size of the Roman Colosseum. The crowd included U.S. Vice President Levi Morton (standing in for President Benjamin Harrison, who had been called to his wife's bedside; she died four days later), justices of the Supreme Court, members of the House and Senate, governors, mayors, and foreign dignitaries.[1] Theodore commanded an orchestra of two hundred in addition to two large military bands, two drum corps, and a fifty-five-hundred-voice choir. Instead of using a baton, he conducted with a white handkerchief for better visibility.[2] Because there was no amplification yet, he (and much of the audience) could not hear the speakers, and Theodore had to use a telephone to communicate with organizers across the hall. (One suspects Norman's hand in this arrangement.)

Handel's "Hallelujah Chorus" was a success, at least for those who could hear it. That it coincided with the pealing of bells and chimes from nearby buildings, the firing of ceremonial artillery on the lake, the turning on of fountains, the unfurling of one thousand flags from nations around the world, and the unveiling of models of Columbus's two ships surely added to the grandeur.

Rose would have taken special note of the speech given by Bertha Honore Palmer, president of the Board of Lady Managers. This was the first world's fair to include women officially in the planning, including a separate board of women who made their own decisions on the design and contents of the Women's Building, which had been designed by a female architect and featured a sixty-foot-long mural by painter Mary Cassatt. Palmer noted that no comparable organization of women had ever before existed, applauded increased educational opportunities for women, and spoke of the new liberties women enjoyed because of time-saving inventions such as the sewing machine and the removal of garment-making to factories. Josephine Cochran's new invention, the dishwasher, displayed at the fair to great interest, was next in the line of improvements. Palmer declared, "Even more important than the discovery of Columbus, which we are gathered together to celebrate, is the fact that the general government has just discovered women."[3] It had been twenty-five years since Zina's first articles for *The Atlantic Monthly*, in which she had outlined her reform ideas for women, were published. Progress had been made.

The inaugural ceremony behind him, Theodore began planning in earnest for the music for the fair itself. Most days for the better part of a year, when he was not working with his orchestra, he worked from 8 a.m. until the early hours of the morning on programming and scheduling. The plans included free daily orchestral concerts by the Exposition Orchestra (his Chicago Orchestra, somewhat augmented), symphony concerts by visiting orchestras, outdoor band concerts, military band concerts, choral performances, children's concerts, chamber groups, artists' recitals, and concerts by famous European musicians. They also specifically called for concerts by women and performances by amateur musical clubs from around the country. American composers were invited to submit their scores for consideration for performance, and it is noteworthy that several women were among the winners.[4] John Philip Sousa's new band was booked for the fair, as was pianist Scott Joplin, who performed his upbeat, syncopated rags among the carnival rides and games on the Midway Plaisance.

Of the almost two hundred concerts given during the six months of the fair, Theodore conducted 125, a magnificent but grueling undertaking.[5] Meanwhile, he was under attack in the press.

The fair got off to a slow start, with bad weather and a poor national economic situation leading to lower-than-expected attendance. As a result, Theodore's concerts were poorly attended, bringing in far less income than anticipated. Some surmised that "too much Wagner did it," insisting the highbrow programs failed to draw crowds. This was a common struggle for Theodore, whose life mission was to educate the American public on art music. To critics who complained that people didn't like Wagner's new pieces, he coolly replied, "Then they must hear them till they do."[6]

Theodore explained to Norman, "Play some light programs? Yes. To those who cannot enjoy the great music, poor fellows, I do not grudge that they can enjoy. Music is music, and I too know how to be gay. I will play for them now and then, but it is not for Tell Overture and Händel Largo that Chicago supports my orchestra. One does not buy a Krupp cannon to shoot sparrows."[7]

A more serious accusation of bribery accompanied the difficult financial situation. The commercial piano business was a highly competitive field, with over one hundred manufacturers in the game.[8] Steinway and Sons had decided not to exhibit at the fair because they did not wish to subject their instruments to a panel of politically appointed judges. The organizing committee therefore declared that Steinways could not be used in concerts, specifying that if they were brought in, "the Director-General is authorized to send teams and dump pianos outside the gates." But star international pianist Ignacy Jan Paderewski insisted on his Steinway. His piano was brought in under the cover of night, and the concert proceeded nonetheless.[9]

Theodore made a statement that he did not dictate what types of instruments his musicians would play: "It is a question of art, pure and simple." However, this coupled with a public statement from one of his harpists that Theodore had forbidden her to play a Lyon and Healy harp led to accusations that Theodore had been bribed by instrument manufacturers.[10] The harpist later changed her story.[11]

Ironically, Zina may have seen it all coming. Back in 1875, in a letter to *The Sun* written before she had ever met Theodore, she praised his musical brilliance and his work in educating the public but bluntly took him to task for insisting his artists perform exclusively on Steinways, "It is a strange thing to see one of the greatest orchestra leaders in the world thus tied to a single firm, and one cannot but doubt whether so stupendous an advertisement of the famous piano can be altogether a simple act of friendship or even of race feeling."[12] (By "race feeling," Zina was referring to ethnicity and the fact that both Theodore and the Steinway founder were German immigrants.)

Newspapers fanned the flames, accusing Theodore of having been bought by instrument companies. The scandal continued to grow over the next two months, with papers across the country running stories questioning Theodore's integrity. Despite unanimous support for Theodore from the fair's board of directors, an ad hoc committee was appointed to investigate any possible abuses. Summoned to testify, Theodore denied any wrongdoing, but the committee recommended his immediate removal. Theodore, bullheaded as usual, was unwilling to recognize the committee's authority and resolute in his loyalty to his orchestra; he ignored their conclusion and continued to conduct.

Rose grew quite concerned about her husband. The scandal combined with the manic schedule of the rehearsals and concerts was taking a toll. She wrote to fair organizer Daniel Burnham, who had become a close friend of the couple's, "Mr. Thomas is sick in bed with a high fever and a pair of congested lungs, and asks me to write a line for him and thank you for your kind interest and friendly suggestions. He will try to follow your advice, and I suppose matters will now soon be decided. I fear more for his health than for his official position, and would not be at all sorry if he should resign the latter and take care of the former, for he is badly in need of rest."[13]

Theodore resigned as the fair's music director in early August. When attendance swelled in the very late summer, the board begged him to reconsider. He refused, having been wounded by the accusations on his character and deeply weary of the entire undertaking.

Rose ranted to a friend, "This incessant hounding & persecution, this constant misrepresentation and opposition in the public press are getting to be too much even for him to stand, & when he has so many opportunities all the time to go else where, there seems to be no particular reason why he should stay where he is all the time subjected to such insults."[14]

Rose had her own role to play at the World's Fair, and perhaps this is one reason Theodore had held off on his resignation for so long. As president of the Amateur Musical Club of Chicago, Rose had invited all the musical clubs in the country to attend the fair. Thirty-five groups responded to her invitation, eager to forge connections. From June 21 through 24, during the World's Fair Congress of Musicians, representatives met to share ideas and build a community.

In her opening welcome before an audience of eight hundred people, Rose explained her thinking:

> The branch of woman's work, which many of you have come such great distances to exhibit this week, is one which has an important bearing on the intellectual culture of America. . . . Of course it would be too much to say that these amateur clubs are the absolute foundation of the music of America, but it is not too much to say that in them, musical art has its most powerful ally, and its most beneficent friend. The fundamental value of amateur music does not lie in the facility with which the fingers can manipulate the keys or the voice can trill a song, but in the deeper and broader culture it gives to the mind and heart—the power to think and feel with the mighty creator and their noble interpreters, and to follow them into those supernal realms of art whose portals only fully open to those who hold the mystic keys.[15]

The stated objectives of the assemblage were trifold: to show the standard, the character, and the quality of the educational work being done by women's amateur musical clubs across the country; to stimulate the formation of clubs in places where they did not yet exist; and to give national recognition to this department of women's education work.[16]

During the four-day symposium, each club was allocated one hour in the auditorium of the Music Hall to present their group's undertakings and events, followed by a musical performance. Most, if not all, of these clubs had experienced a common evolution. They had been formed by small groups of women who merely desired a place to share music together, an outlet for performing and for hearing new works. Gradually, the groups grew to the point where they aimed to bring fine music to their communities, to raise the cultural offerings in their regions. In the smaller towns, they prided themselves on being able to bring in touring artists. In Chicago and other large cities, they began efforts to lift up female artists and composers, with some offering scholarships to promising young women. For instance, Chicago's Amateur Musical Club had an annual charity event that raised $1,000 to $1,500.

In *A Musical Legacy of 100 Years*, Lucile Parrish Ward wrote:

> To Rose Fay Thomas all the honor is due for originating the idea of this Woman's Musical Congress. The musical women throughout the United States hailed this convention as an event which marked an era in music in this country, and one which gave a strong impulse to the organization of clubs. Mrs. Thomas, already famous in the musical world gained an added renown for this valuable work. . . . Mr. Thomas felt so strongly the great influence these clubs would have on the musical culture of the country, that he gave great help to the movement which his wife, Rose Fay Thomas, carried out.[17]

Working together, this combination of Rose, a quiet, determined organizer, and Theodore, the nation's foremost conductor and music educator, helped raise musical awareness and standards in communities small and large.

At the conclusion of the four days, the participants voted to form a national organization of amateur musical clubs. They appointed committees and made plans to meet again the following year. Lucile Parrish Ward wrote, "Mr and Mrs Thomas expressed their gratification at the cordial sympathy with which all the clubs had worked with them in promoting the success of the convention, and their 'sincere hope that a permanent organization may grow out of this vigorous and healthy beginning, which shall be the best friend of the musical art throughout America.'"[18]

So alongside Theodore's public humiliation, the Thomases had a joint success. Amy participated as well, presenting a paper on piano performance as part of larger discussions on careers for women in the arts.[19] She then traveled to Europe to attend the Mozart Festival in Salzburg and concerts in Paris and Bayreuth before settling back in New York.

Following Theodore's reluctant resignation, the couple left for Fairhaven, Massachusetts, where he had a summer home in the seaside town, purchased in 1887 with his first wife, Minna. In later years, Rose wrote that Theodore "was never afterwards the man he had been before. His courage was gone, and for the rest of his life he would drop into despondency and be ready to give up at any little untoward happening."[20]

The winter of 1893–94 was a desperate one for Chicago as well as the country at large. Though the fair was ultimately considered a great success for the city, with attendance topping twenty-seven million, and it was forever remembered for Burnham's visually spectacular White City and the first Ferris wheel, it ended on a grim note. Chicago Mayor Carter Harrison was assassinated two days before the conclusion. Memorial services replaced the closing ceremonies. A large fire three months later destroyed the majority of the buildings.

Showmen, speculators, and curiosity seekers drawn to Chicago for the fair stayed behind when the show closed down. Public buildings such as city hall and the police stations became de facto homeless shelters on cold winter nights for fair workers, who were now jobless.[21]

But it was more than just Chicago: The great panic of 1893, caused by a number of railroad failures and the ensuing stock market crash, led to soaring unemployment and riots. Twenty percent of the city's workers lost their jobs; countrywide, sixteen thousand businesses failed, and 150 railroads collapsed.[22] Despite Rose's desire for a national organization for musical clubs, it would have to wait.

Struggling

1893–1894

AMONG THOSE SUFFERING AFTER THE 1893 crash was Norman. He later reported that he had lost $200,000, a prodigious sum, if true.[1] Family legend has it that Norman was on vacation in Florida and could not be reached during the financial crisis, or his losses might not have been as severe.[2] He never fully recovered financially. This would have implications for the rest of the family.

Up until then, Norman had done remarkably well for himself. In the early 1890s, he summered with East Coast elites in the resort town of Newport, Rhode Island, where he could be seen driving a four-in-hand down the island streets. Amy often joined him in Newport, providing the allure of sterling musical evenings for their neighbors and guests. Over the years, Norman had been generous to his sisters, inviting Zina, Amy, Rose, and Lily to live with him in Chicago; giving Rose and Theodore the Bellevue house; and providing a $50 monthly allowance to his unmarried sisters (equivalent to about $1,700 in 2025 dollars).

While Norman did not provide financial assistance to Laura or Kate, their experiences as mothers illustrate the struggles and heartbreaks inherent in those paths. Laura, a busy mother and clergyman's wife, was diagnosed with periodontitis and had all her teeth extracted. Gum disease and other major dental problems were not uncommon at the time and could be very problematic, even leading to death in extreme cases. Laura's daughter later wrote that the shock of the tooth pulling proved to be too much: "For twenty-three years after that, she was drowned in melancholia."[3] Frank hired a housekeeper to manage daily duties and did his best to help his wife recover, but she found herself unable to rally, becoming nearly incapacitated.

Kate and Will experienced a tragedy when their only son, Reginald, died at age fourteen of an embolism. Their three daughters were seventeen, five, and three at the time. Kate's life revolved around her children, and she tried to provide them with the sort of mothering and childhood she had lacked. Thanks to Will's excellent job and salary, they were the most financially comfortable of all the siblings, but Reginald's death was a bitter blow.

The nationwide Depression and grim outlook in Chicago after the fair affected the Chicago Orchestra as well. Despite great enthusiasm and hope, the first season, in 1891–92, had resulted in a $53,000 deficit, and the second season wasn't much better. The third season didn't bode well. The new Auditorium, dedicated in 1889, had nearly five thousand seats and was difficult to fill in the best of times. The orchestra had not yet cultivated a large audience, and with seats always available at the last minute, the public had little incentive to purchase tickets in advance. Theodore had come to believe that the third season would surely be the last.[4]

Orchestra boosters such as Bryan Lathrop and Daniel Burnham stepped into the breach, collecting extra subscriptions from their many friends and acquaintances, thereby pulling the orchestra into another season. But it was a tenuous situation. Norman was aware that deaths among their supporters, a health crisis for Theodore, or a change in the administration of the Auditorium could wipe out the organization in a heartbeat. He wrote, "Alas, it does not need a sledge-hammer to shatter a Stradivarius!"[5] With empty chairs and an uncertain future, supporters were losing heart.

Business leaders in New York and Boston approached Theodore about settling there instead, and it must have been tempting, especially considering the public humiliation he had suffered during the fair. But Theodore honored his commitment to Chicago and to the band of businessmen who had made a permanent orchestra possible. Furthermore, Chicago had become home. Marian lived with Rose and Theodore, Theodore's older children came to visit when possible, and Norman and Lily resided nearby.

In addition, Rose and Theodore had made meaningful friendships in Chicago. Rose cultivated strong relationships with many in the Amateur Musical Club. Now, as the wife of such a prominent man, she found herself frequently thrust into new situations and forced to adapt. Luckily, her background—having lived with so many different families, in various circumstances and communities—had prepared her well.

One couple in particular, Frances and John Glessner, became a perfect pair of friends for Rose and Theodore. An agricultural implement executive, John Glessner had been one of the first of the orchestra's fifty guarantors and remained a strong supporter throughout his life. And in John's wife, Frances, Rose had a fast friend. Musically astute, civically active, and in the inner circle of Chicago society, Frances Glessner elegantly provided Rose entrée to the more elite women's groups and clubs.

Norman and John were also well acquainted, with many overlapping club memberships (Commercial Club, Chicago Club, Chicago Literary Club), and Norman enjoyed frequent dinners at the Glessner house.[6] In fact, Norman's life was so interwoven with Rose and Theodore's that he became a virtual third wheel in their marriage, albeit a welcome one. Norman's love life served as a source of consternation for his sisters, as they saw numerous opportunities for what they considered good matches slip away. But he seemed unbothered, cheerily reporting year after year to his alumni group that he had "written no books and married no wives" and had "made no offers of heart and hand recently."[7]

In January of that first orchestra season, the Glessners hosted a dinner party with Rose and Theodore as their guests of honor—the first of many. From that point on, the couples frequently shared a box together at the opera or the Apollo Club. Theodore sent Frances a standing invitation to all the rehearsals. And there, in the cavernous Auditorium, Rose and Frances could often be seen seated side by side, poring over the musical score as Theodore took the orchestra through its paces.

The couples became tremendously close, with the Glessners invited to the Thomases' home for intimate musical evenings with select members of the orchestra or late-night dinners after the concerts, where the foursome would often talk deep into the night.

One such event included Paderewski, the source of the Steinway debacle at the fair, who was widely considered the world's finest pianist (and later served as prime minister of Poland). Norman attended as well. Frances's diary shows her delight at the intimacy of the evening: "T[homas] likes Paderewski exceedingly. They joked, laughed, sat so close together that their noses touched almost—would shake hands every little while. Thomas gave P[aderewski] a big cigar wrapped with gold leaf—and said 'the great Polish prince, the world's pianist, shall smoke that.' P[aderewski] said, 'I shall leave it for King Thomas.'"[8]

Rose delighted in meeting world-class composers, conductors, and soloists. She had all notable guests to their home sign a shiny red guest book, which she treasured. Rose asked the musicians to include a photo of themselves or a hand-drawn line from their favorite music. Edward Elgar included a line from his newest work, the "Enigma Variations." Alongside her treasured autographs, she included notes Theodore received over the years, such as from composers Camille Saint-Saens, Richard Strauss, Ferruccio Busoni, Johannes Brahms, Antonin Dvorak, and Franz Liszt. The list is impressive, though it is unclear which individuals actually visited the Bellevue house.

As a pianist, sister Amy also had a page in Rose's book. Correspondence that Amy had with fellow musicians is now included; likely these were added in later years. The names include John Knowles Paine, Ludwig Deppe, violinist Maud Powell, pianist Fannie Bloomfield Zeisler, and composer Vincent d'Indy. Rose maintained contact with several of these musicians for the rest of her life.

The Glessners' inner circle also included Dr. William Rainey Harper, president of the new University of Chicago, and many of the college's distinguished professors. Rose later wrote that Theodore had been "intellectually a very lonely man," but in this milieu, he at last found himself surrounded by other inquisitive minds.[9] For years, Harper and Theodore had discussed establishing a music department for the university, with Theodore at its head, but ultimately found that they were incompatible regarding the details.[10] Theodore wrote to Harper, "Either you do not understand my views on the subject, or, I rather think, you do not want to understand me and wish to persuade me to take your view of the case—which is impossible."[11]

Theodore stood immovable when faced with a viewpoint different from his own.

An 1892 letter from Rose to Frances defined how vital her friendship and support had become. This remarkable correspondence also underscored Theodore's musical goals. Writing of complaints about Theodore's challenging programming, Rose confided:

> One ought not to mind the criticisms of these stupid persons, but such little pin-pickings are just enough to take the life and spirit out of his work, to him, except for the generous sympathy and support of those far seeing, & noble minded men and women, like yourself and Mr. Glessner, who can grasp the situation, & understand that Mr. Thomas is there to establish a great Art Work & to make Chicago one of the first musical centers of the world—& not to provide a series of cheap musical entertainments for the riff-raff of the public.[12]

Rose continued, with lovely metaphorical references to nature but also more than a hint of classism:

> The highest forms of art whether it be in painting, sculpture, architecture, literature, music or any other branch are not within the comprehension of the masses, they are the delicate blossoms which make the crown & glory of the shrub called humanity, but which roots and branches and stems can only catch vague glimpses of through parted leaves, & never wholly see. So it is a useless task to attempt to produce the highest form in any art, in such a way that it can be appreciated by the ignorant. All that can be done is to produce it and let it stand till the ignorant acquire a little education and begin to understand it.[13]

In 1893, as the Chicago Orchestra grappled with a losing balance sheet, the Glessners stepped in to bolster Theodore's spirits. They hosted a party in his honor, gathering together twenty-two of the guarantors, and presented him with a loving cup, a Norwegian tankard inscribed with the date and, on the bottom, all the men's names, a symbol of their belief in Theodore. The tankard was passed around the table, with each man giving a brief toast. Daniel Burnham, a man of no small accomplishments, said he drank to the man who set for himself high ideals and had the courage to live up to them.[14]

Rose understood the Glessners' role in the success of the orchestra: "If it does become a permanent institution, it will be very largely due to the interest of the J. J. Glessner family, we think!"[15]

While biographies of Theodore Thomas and histories of the orchestra have recorded the vital role the male guarantors played in the success of the orchestra, women supporters were crucial at this juncture as well.[16] Frances Glessner, for example, in late 1893, hosted twenty-five women for lunch, at which Norman presented the case for why more subscribers were needed. By November, Frances had sent in twenty-four names to buttress the membership; other female friends helped spread the word as well.[17]

At the Glessners', Rose interacted with another inspirational woman, Alice Freeman Palmer, whose world overlapped with Zina's. The former president of Wellesley College (founded in 1870), Palmer, as dean of women for the University of Chicago in 1892–95, was charged with recruiting more female students and serving as their mentor. She succeeded in doubling the proportion of female students, from 24 to 48 percent, which unfortunately resulted in significant consternation among the male faculty. The university ultimately decided to segregate their undergraduate classes by gender.[18] From 1891 through 1901, Palmer served as president of the Women's Education Association in Boston, which Zina had helped found. Palmer was also a late addition to the Cambridge Banks Brigade, the "Bee," yet another point of overlap with Rose.

Theodore, typically nondemonstrative, got about as cozy as he would ever allow himself in a letter to John Glessner written on Christmas Day 1893: "Permit me to say to you that it is a source of much pleasure to both Mrs. Thomas and myself to enjoy Mrs. Glessner's and your friendship."[19]

Midnight on New Year's Eve 1893 found Rose and Theodore again at the Glessner house, along with about thirty other guests, including the Burnhams, University of Chicago literature professor Richard Moulton, and poet Harriet Monroe. Theodore brought a trio from the orchestra, who played Beethoven and Mozart by firelight. At midnight, Theodore struck the hour on their Japanese gong, ushering in a new year.[20]

Felsengarten

1894–1896

IT WAS THANKS TO FRANCES and John Glessner that Rose and Theodore found a mountain retreat where they could truly replenish their spirits and where all the Fays would spend precious summer weeks. Theodore never held any particular fondness for the vacation home he had purchased a few years earlier with his first wife, Minna, in Fairhaven, Massachusetts, and Rose felt like an interloper at Fairhaven.

The summer of 1894, while visiting the Glessners at the Rocks, their summer home in the White Mountains of New Hampshire, the Thomases found a spot of their own. Out for a carriage ride on a Monday, Rose fell in love with the views from a nearby farm. On Wednesday, she inquired at a real estate office, and by Friday, the couple had purchased fourteen acres for $800.[1]

Having acquired the new property, with the deed in Rose's name, Rose and Theodore continued on to Grand Isle, Vermont, where they were treated like conquering heroes, "As we drove through the Island the inhabitants of every farm house were watching at the windows to see us go by, & I have been really quite touched to see what warm affection these tough old farmers seem to have for our family, & for my dear fathers memory—when we go along the roads they come rushing out to greet us, & fill our pockets with apples!"[2] How the locals knew the Thomases were coming is unknown.

For Rose, as she passed through the part of the country where she grew up in tough circumstances, her family always barely scraping by, this return must have been a moving reminder of how far she had traveled—from the white boardinghouse and little schoolhouse to a life filled with great music and friendships with some of the world's finest musicians, a life she could not have foreseen. It is highly likely that the couple also stopped by Rock Point in Burlington or at the old home and St. Luke's Church in St. Albans.

Over the next few years, as their schedules allowed, Rose and Theodore tamed their new land, which they named Felsengarten, German for "garden of rocks." They spent the summer of 1895 in Europe, the only pleasure trip of their lives together. Rose later wrote that this four-month jaunt consisted of "pleasant little excursions to historic places; of dreamy wanderings in wonderful art galleries; of lovely drives and walks; of cozy little tete-a-tete meals in quaint restaurants, of operas, concerts, and delightful junketings with foreign friends."[3] Among these friends was German soprano Lilli Lehmann, with whom they spent time in Austria.[4] At a time when most of the orchestra was of European background, and in fact, rehearsals were usually conducted in German, Theodore also used the trip to audition musicians for empty spots in the orchestra; in Cologne, he found the versatile Frederick Stock, who became the orchestra's violist, assistant conductor, and ultimately Theodore's successor.[5] Their new rural plot stood quiet until the summer of 1896, when they finally had some time for it.

Felsengarten, a wild, uncultivated tract "suspended halfway 'twixt heaven and earth" on the side of a mountain served as respite.[6] In later years, when asked where he got his inspiration, Theodore replied:

> Why, up in the White Mountains of New Hampshire I have a cottage hidden away from the world. A cunning little bypath runs through the woods, and without a guide you cannot find your way in. And when you are in, you do not want to find your way out. I go in the morning and at night and talk to my trees, and my mountains that I love. And I catch a little bit—just a little bit—of what they answer me. . . . What is it they say? Ah, that is it. It is nothing, and yet everything. Nature is all music, and

> whatever she whispers to us is the heart of melody and the soul of rhythm. Some of us are lucky enough to catch a few of her disjointed words, and are allowed to tell them to our brothers. That is called inspiration.[7]

Rose later wrote that for Theodore, after having spent most his life touring and moving around, "the love of home was a passion." She continued, "In Felsengarten he now had a place which was peculiarly his own, for no white man had ever before lived upon its virgin soil."[8]

Early in her marriage, Rose had been weakened by a mild, lingering case of tuberculosis. While her physician Dr. Alfred Loomis had advised her to leave Chicago for a milder climate, Rose instead adopted a homegrown alternative that she believed did the trick: For three years, she had breakfast in bed, avoided bad weather, and drank burgundy.[9] Added to this were the fresh air and outdoor exertion she experienced in Bethlehem. "My husband's overworked nerves needed to be strengthened by some out-of-door life, and illness had made the same kind of medicine imperative also for me. Therefore, in seeking a country place, we wished for one where the air was dry, the temperature even and cool, and where there was plenty of work which we could do out of doors with our own hands."[10]

"Seated on a nail keg," Rose oversaw the building of an initial five-room cottage, twenty-eight by forty feet, simple and unadorned.[11] While Rose led the building process, Theodore began shaping the landscape. In the winters, when Theodore had trouble sleeping, he turned his thoughts to Felsengarten and imagined his landscaping plans, "till, lulled by the memory of its whispering pines, and tranquillized by pictured fantasies of mountains, woods, and summer skies, 'sleep that knits up the travelled sleeve of care' would come at last, and draw its veil of sweet oblivion."[12]

Rose recorded their transformation of the property in a book, *Our Mountain Garden*, published by Macmillan in 1904. Rose thereby joined Amy and Zina as a fellow author. Gardening was considered a female occupation and therefore acceptable for a woman to write about. This book, while meant as a folksy, hands-on guide for establishing a homemade garden, provides an intimate look at Rose and Theodore as they discovered the joys of living in nature.

The house was originally intended as a bungalow of the simplest sort. They eventually added a second floor, and the property increased in both comfort and size as they purchased additional acreage. Felsengarten became a regular summer stop for Theodore's adult children, Rose's siblings, and many nieces and nephews. Amy spent several weeks at Felsengarten every year, adding her piano practice to Theodore and Rose's frequent music making.

Theodore worked on making meandering paths through the property, dragging off dead branches, and trimming back overgrown shrubs. A messy marsh was gradually shaped into a waterfall and pond, although it took three patient attempts at damming before it finally acquiesced into its new format.

Adding flowers and color to the property fell to Rose. A fairly inexperienced gardener, she learned her lessons the hard way. Many new plantings failed entirely, placed in too much or not enough sunshine or in unprepared soil. She documented it in *Our Mountain Garden*, adding, "All these ignorant mistakes on my part have caused me no grief, for my garden would have given me but half the pleasure had I known about things at the start."[13]

The couple resolutely performed the hard work themselves, enlisting help only when they physically couldn't handle something. Rose had harsh words for those who relied on gardeners: "How much I pity the people who, owning and living in magnificent country homes, adorned with trees and flowers, do not know any of the pleasure of cultivating them, and have no sense for, or knowledge of, their characters, habits, or individuality, but regard them merely as species of extended table decoration. They lose half of the pleasure and enjoyment which their country places might yield them and are like those other unfortunates who occupy an opera box night after night without any knowledge or appreciation of music."[14]

Rose's book provides an engaging look at her learning process. When her first attempts at propagating plants from cuttings went awry, she tried again, sticking them in a layer of sand covered with water in shallow pans and dishes. She endeavored to keep them in constant sunlight throughout the day, moving them from one bright window to another as the day progressed, scaffolding her chairs and stools to capture the most advantageous angle, a painstaking effort she tried to maintain all summer.[15] The theme of nurturing comes through again and again.

Her attitude toward her plantings exemplified compassion, as Rose worked together with them rather than reigning over them. She believed, "Plants are a good deal like people, and they know perfectly well what they want and where they want to be. . . . I often think, in all seriousness, that the scientists of the future will discover that plants have something which correspond to the sense of the human being, and perhaps even to his mind."[16]

They took no servants with them to Felsengarten, preferring to cook their own breakfasts and suppers and then driving to one of the hotels in the village for dinner. Once a week, they dined at the Glessners' in nearby Littleton. They spent the time between meals working outside.[17] The landscape for Theodore and the garden for Rose provided the couple with the healing projects they needed. For Theodore, "it seemed to him a veritable paradise on earth, and he never spent an unhappy moment there."[18]

From this point on, Rose gathered seeds and clippings from nearby woods or neighbors' houses. She stole seedlings from Longfellow's property, landscape architect Frederick Law Olmsted brought willow cuttings, roses were imported from acquaintances in Cambridge, and a clutch of lady's slippers originated in a friend's garden in Vermont.[19] Her garden was a gathering of friends.

Busy Lives

1895–1897

FOR ROSE, THE MID-1890S WERE heady years. Laura's daughter Madeline recalled the dynamics between her aunt and uncle: "On Saturday nights we drove down to the old Chicago Auditorium in a 'hack,' I on a little seat facing Aunt Rose and Uncle Theodore, and I shall never forget the expression on Aunt Rose's face, on the homecoming trip after the Concert—perfect happiness was reflected there as we passed under the street lights. She adored her husband and was tremendously proud of him. Her first role in life was to make things run smoothly for him."[1]

The Thomases' lives revolved around the orchestra, with Theodore studying scores, transcribing new arrangements of piano or vocal pieces, preparing parts, communicating with composers, and hosting soloists alongside his duties at rehearsals and concerts. Nothing gave Rose more pleasure than getting to know these world-class musicians. They hosted musicales at their home, inviting a handful of close friends to dinner and entertainment by members of the orchestra or visiting soloists. The couple was often found at the Glessners, either for Sunday night dinners or private concerts.

Rose zealously guarded her husband's time and energy. The physical demands of the job were taking their toll on Theodore, who turned sixty in 1895. The orchestra season in Chicago typically began in November and ended in March. The Chicago season was followed by travel to generate box office income and boost the orchestra members' wages. In the early spring of 1895, for example, the orchestra toured for a grueling two months before Theodore went to Cincinnati for its annual music festival, of which he was founder and music director.

During this difficult stretch, he wrote to Norman, explaining that he was too old for so much travel, and asking him to notify the trustees that the next season in Chicago would be his last. Norman refused to deliver the letter, stating that Theodore would have to place it before the trustees himself.[2]

It is likely that Norman, trying to ward off Theodore's resignation, rallied the trustees, for in May of that year, they threw a gala dinner at the Chicago Club honoring Theodore. The event represented so much goodwill toward Theodore's efforts that he didn't have the heart to push his resignation. Frances Glessner presented him with a large silver punch bowl on behalf of the women of Chicago.[3]

These efforts bought Chicago and the orchestra a little more time with Theodore. He wrote to Frances Glessner in appreciation:

> Of late I have been overworked and tired, consequently had frictions of all kinds, and in all directions. The future I distrusted, the elements were my enemies, and even my life-long love "Music" had turned a cold shoulder on me. After reading your letter, signed by the names of so many representative Chicago ladies, and realizing the good will this all contained, I find that I have regained full confidence in the future—I've "made up" again with the climate and my old love, and am anxious already for the fall to come to inaugurate these handsome gifts, and to show my appreciation and gratitude to you for all your kindness to me.[4]

The celebratory dinner, followed by their enjoyable European trip and the promise of a new quiet existence at Felsengarten, caused a sense of rejuvenation. Rose wrote that "life brightened for Theodore" and that they found a new sense of equilibrium.[5]

Norman remained a vital link between Theodore and the guarantors, capitalizing on his business connections whenever possible. He was also keen to capitalize on new inventions, first the telephone, then electric lights, and later the typewriter. After the financial crisis in 1893, Norman moved away from utilities work and became president of the Remington-Sholes Typewriter Company, where he oversaw 250 employees. The typewriter, invented in 1874, had quickly become a staple of the office, and with it, doors opened for women into what had been an almost exclusively male environment.[6] In fact, an early ad for the machine boasted that "no invention has opened for women so broad and easy an avenue to profitable and suitable employment."[7]

Meanwhile, in New York City, Zina ran three boardinghouses—she skirted the stigma of her divorce by identifying herself in the directory as a "widow," although her former husband, Charley, was still alive—and somehow still found the time and energy for neighborhood improvement projects. Nearly sixty, she continued to galvanize those around her. Like many other middle- and upper-class women of her time, Zina got involved in historic preservation efforts. The movement had been gaining steam as homes of the founding fathers and other historically significant buildings fell into disarray or were threatened by the wrecking ball. In 1863, efforts to save John Hancock's house near the Boston Common failed, despite public outcry. But there were success stories as well. In 1876, Boston women raised enough money to rescue the Old South Meeting House, where patriots had assembled before heading off to the harbor to protest taxes on tea.[8] Zina does not appear to have been involved in these efforts.

An ardent admirer of George Washington, Zina would certainly have been aware of Ann Pamela Cunningham's successful founding of the Mount Vernon Ladies' Association (MVLA) in the 1850s to restore George Washington's former home in rural Virginia. Now she saw her own chance to honor the nation's first president. New York had recently formed the Society for the Preservation of Scenic and Historic Places and Objects, and Zina served as president of the Women's Auxiliary. In this capacity, she headed a group of about one hundred women whose object was to "interest American women everywhere in the preservation of all historical places and objects."[9] One of their key goals was to restore Fraunces Tavern at 54 Pearl Street, the site where Washington had bade farewell to his officers after the Revolutionary War. The auxiliary petitioned the New York legislature to acquire the tavern and the entire block on which it stood. The group also championed efforts to save Edgar Allan Poe's five-room cottage in the Bronx.[10]

Despite the failure of her cooperative housekeeping venture in Cambridge, Zina's work in that realm had not been for naught. Women in other parts of the country tried similar plans. Evanston, just north of Chicago, attempted a cooperative housekeeping program in 1890. After raising $5,000 in capital, they stocked a kitchen and laundry in the downtown area. Forty-five families enrolled at the rate of $4 per person per week in the food delivery program, and deliveries began on December 8. But the experiment was short-lived and closed in January. Maids and other servants of the families went on strike when cooks and laundresses were fired; food wholesalers refused to work with the cooperative; and mismanagement resulted in food delivered late, cold, or not at all.[11] There was still interest in Zina's ideas, but the logistics needed work.

In addition to her ideas for communal kitchens and laundries, she floated the idea of simplified houses without kitchens: "Think how much more beautiful city architecture will be now! The houses, instead of being built around a square, could be set in the middle of it. . . . Every tenth block would contain the kitchen and laundry and clothing house."[12] Discussion of apartment house architecture was rampant. Before the Civil War, shared living was considered undesirable for middle- and upper-class families. But as urban land costs rose after the war and new building techniques were developed, the luxury apartment house was born. The 1870s–90s saw tremendous growth in the numbers and types of shared living spaces. Zina, considering this an outgrowth of domestic planning, jumped into the fray with her own ideas. What better place for shared laundry and kitchen facilities?

In a letter to Rose, Amy wrote of Zina's many activities: "First she is driving down to the Mayor's office about saving the Poe cottage; anon she confers with Miss Fischer uptown about the Home Hotel for aged and indigent brainworkers like myself. Between times she has interviews with Sam Franco and musical managers about summer night concerts. Then she pours tea at the receptions of the Authors' Club, in their rooms at Carnegie Hall. Like Bryant's clouds, here she stretches to the frolic chase and there she rolls on the easy gale!"[13]

Amy was no less busy. She was frequently asked to perform her Piano Conversations in the public schools, which resulted in a regular stream of private students. Her specializations in the Deppe method and in hand positioning gave her a unique niche. Full of vitality, she enthused, "I think life gets more interesting with every year and it is a pity we have to lose our good looks as we grow older! Were it not for that, we would have a better time than ever!"[14]

Yes, they were heady years. Busy, full in every aspect. The sisters didn't know at the time how fleeting those good years would be.

Federation

1897–1898

Music was always a uniting force for the Fay family—during their childhood, with their work as music critics and the advancement of the Amateur Musical Club in Chicago, and with Theodore's orchestra. In the late 1890s, three of the sisters worked together on another musical endeavor.

The idea floated four years earlier at the Chicago World's Columbian Exposition finally sprang back to life in June 1897 at the Music Teachers National Association (MTNA) in New York City. Amy and Zina both attended the organizing meeting. Amy, very involved with the MTNA, presented a paper on music study abroad. About fifty women, representing amateur women's musical clubs from around the country, gathered to revisit the idea of uniting under a national umbrella organization to promote cooperation among musical clubs and hold an annual conference.

Because of Rose's initial work with women's musical clubs during the 1893 World's Fair, she was held in high esteem, and the group voted unanimously to ask her to be chair.[1] Amy and Zina sent Rose a telegram asking her to accept. The trouble arose when Rose declined the honor, replying that she didn't have time to take it on. However, it was more complicated than that.

A temporary committee was formed to discuss how to organize the federation properly. At the helm stood Florence Sutro, chair of the Woman's Department of the MTNA. A talented pianist, the first woman to get her doctoral degree in music from the Grand Conservatory of New York, and the first woman law student of the University of the City of New York (now CUNY), Sutro was not one to sit idly by. But it seemed Rose had issues with Sutro. Years later, Rose wrote that she declined the position because Sutro was a complete stranger to her and had not consulted her.[2]

The committee announced a formal meeting in Chicago in January 1898, under the auspices of the Amateur Musical Club. In the circular sent to all the musical clubs inviting them to the Chicago meeting, Sutro used Rose's name as chair of the Executive Board, although she had clearly turned it down. Rose replied by sending a formal statement to all the clubs that had participated in the June convention, clarifying that she was not involved.

When Sutro sent out yet another announcement, again including Rose's name, Rose placed a notice in *The Etude* magazine:

> Mrs. Theodore Thomas desires to inform the press, the public, and the amateur musical clubs of America, that her name has been a second time fraudulently used in the circulars of the National Federation of Women's Musical Clubs, as the chairman of its Board, in spite of her published statement to the contrary and her indignant protest against its unauthorized use in the same connection last fall. Mrs. Thomas wishes to state emphatically that she is not, and never has been, connected with the Federation in any capacity whatsoever, and that the circulars issued by that Association signed with her name as president of its Board, are, so far as she is concerned, fraudulent.[3]

The battle lines were drawn.

More than one hundred women met in Chicago's Steinway Hall over three days in January 1898, undaunted by a tremendous snowstorm that halted trains and bore sixty-five-mile-per-hour winds.[4] A delegation was dispatched to Rose, asking her to become president. She declined but endorsed friend Alice Follett Uhl, wife of diplomat Edwin Uhl.

Rose wrote to Louise Bryan Dorr, chair of the Nominating Committee, explaining that her work with the orchestra took up all her spare time:

> But I want the Federation to be put into hands who will carry it out in the right way, and if this is done I will gladly work with them in every way I can without any office and help it to succeed. You know I really care nothing at all for the glory of being a prominent officer and I perfectly hate to have my name in the papers. I want to see the work done right, and under the right leaders I am just as ready to work amongst the rank and file as if I were on the Board. But under the wrong leaders I won't work in any capacity or come near the Federation at all.[5]

In a show of sisterly solidarity, Rose, Amy, and Zina all avoided the day of the vote. Rose's friend Uhl won in a landslide, beating out Sutro eighty-seven to twelve. Though Rose didn't attend the vote, she sent in her multipage plan for how the permanent organization should be structured. And she had no qualms about attending an informal meeting after the conference, once "the right leaders" had been put in place.[6]

The following month, *The Etude* magazine summarized the event: "Set in motion by Mrs. Theodore Thomas at the Columbian Exposition, a great wave of musical activity in the line of women's musical clubs has swept over the country." The article went on point out that over 225 women's clubs had been formed since the fair. "Mr. Thomas felt so strongly the great influence these clubs . . . would have on the musical culture of the country that he gave great help to the movement which Mrs. Thomas so ably carried out."[7]

At the next meeting of the National Federation of Musical Clubs, in New York in October 1898 (the word "Women's" had been removed from the name earlier that year), Rose was appointed honorary president and Theodore was made honorary member to thank them for their efforts at the 1893 World's Columbian Exposition.[8] The federation did all it could to promote women musicians. It published an annual list of members available for performances, had a library of circulating scores, suggested sample programs, offered educational guides, and ran a composition competition.[9]

Years later, Theodore said, "No other one influence in America had been so potent and far reaching for good results as had women's musical clubs." According to biographer Ezra Schabas, Theodore believed women deserved much of the credit for making Chicago the musical city that it was, in large part because of the education they received through their clubs.[10]

By the mid-1890s, Rose had relinquished her role as president of Chicago's Amateur Musical Club, but she remained very active in that local organization, as did its members in promoting the concerts of the Chicago Orchestra. For decades, women had served as patronesses of their local orchestras. The New York Philharmonic, early in its existence, offered free public rehearsals on Friday mornings. These occasions were opportunities for women to attend unescorted, something considered socially unacceptable for evening events. Out of this grew a cadre of "Symphonic Ladies" who worked as unofficial, unpaid public relations officers and fundraisers.[11] Similarly, Chicago's Amateur Musical Club encouraged its members—now numbering around two hundred—to attend symphony concerts, give financial support, and get out into the community to promote upcoming events, driving attendance to the Auditorium.

In 1895, an article in *Ladies' Home Journal* applauded Rose's role in the success of the orchestra: "One of the most potent factors in the success of Mr. Theodore Thomas in Chicago was, doubtless, the fact of his having married a Chicago woman. . . . As president [of the Amateur Musical Club] . . . , Mrs. Thomas is able to wield a great influence in the proper development and cultivation of music in Chicago, and she wields her power wisely."[12]

The National Federation of Musical Clubs grew quickly. What had started with just 76 clubs grew to 145 in the early 1900s, and by 1930, the federation included over 5,000 clubs, representing an estimated four hundred thousand members, as well as new junior clubs for children.[13] The club's stated goal was "to make America the music center of the world."[14]

Women's Philharmonic

1898

THROUGH THEIR CLUB WORK, THE Fays participated in a critical part of a national social movement. Rose's success with the National Federation of Musical Clubs represented a broadening of the women's sphere. Women in the late nineteenth century, no longer content with confining their existence to their homes, expanded their lives through clubs. Through these entirely acceptable forms of social gatherings, women learned to organize, manage, and network in ways that paved the way for increased opportunities in the near future.

Starting at the ground floor, when Chicago's Amateur Musical Club consisted of just a couple of dozen women, Rose nurtured that seedling until it bloomed into a national organization, providing education and social opportunities for thousands of women. Like the Fays, many women of the middle and upper classes had been schooled at home and were largely isolated from larger networks. Clubs helped increase their skills, education, sense of community, and autonomy, without challenging the men's public sphere.[1] As opposed to the early suffragists, clubwomen worked within acceptable territory, raising no eyebrows, drawing no opposition. And in so doing, they found a power in their sisterhood. It was a different approach than that of the suffragists, but getting women out into public was a vital step toward greater opportunity.[2]

Amy took on the issue of women in music, becoming a leading voice for more equality in the arts. She wrote frequently for music magazines and journals such as *The Etude* and *Musical Courier*, increasingly about the restrictions placed on female performers. "Women have been too much taken up with helping and encouraging men to place proper value on their own talent," she noted, "which they are too prone to underestimate and to think not worth making the most of. Their whole training, from time immemorial, has tended to make them take an intense interest in the work of men and to stimulate them to their best efforts." She went on to say that things were changing. "Women are beginning to realize that they, too, have brains and even musical ones. They are, at last, studying composition seriously, and will, ere long, forge out a path for themselves."[3]

However, some in the male-dominated music industry were less than eager to welcome women into the ranks. Female performers often ran up against male critics who concerned themselves more with a woman's appearance than her actual talent, as well as conductors reluctant to engage women instrumentalists. Amy wrote, "The men are so busy showing themselves off, you may depend they will not let the women in! It is ever so. Fortunately they are obliged to have women singers!"[4]

In this aspect, she ran headlong into Theodore, but here she laid blame at Rose's feet, accusing her of keeping Theodore to herself. "I think that Rose has a jealous nature and if she has a man at all, she owns him. It was so with Theodore Thomas, and I have always felt that if she had wanted to, she could have got me the engagement to play with him. . . . I am convinced she did not care to have him take an interest in me!"[5] But sister Kate took a different view, believing that Theodore did not engage Amy "because she was not a first class artist."[6] As for Rose, it must have been an uneasy situation to be married to a prominent conductor who, for whatever reason, refused to book her sister for engagements with his orchestra.

Like Zina, Amy spoke her mind when it came to inequality. She wrote a letter to *Musical Courier*, a weekly trade magazine, complaining that of the seventy-two participants at the Music Teachers National Association convention, only eight were women. She pointed out that men chaired all the roundtables and presented all the papers and that none of the instrumentalists performing were women.[7] In an article titled "The Woman Music-Teacher in a Large City," Amy bemoaned the difficulties for women piano teachers: "It is almost impossible for a woman to get a good position in the private fashionable schools in the city. They want a 'professor,' and the parents feel better satisfied when their daughters have lessons from a 'gentleman teacher.' If women teach in schools, it is usually as under-teachers, poorly paid."[8] Years earlier, her mother, Emily, similarly frustrated, had partially addressed this inequality by shortening what were normally hour-long private piano lessons to forty-five minutes.[9]

In 1898, Zina and Amy, living together on Fifty-Sixth Street in New York, acted on their frustrations and launched the Women's Philharmonic Society (WPS). As a letter in the April 1899 *Musical Courier* explained, "During the last week of July, 1898, while the MTNA was in session at the Waldorf-Astoria Hotel, Mrs. Fay Pierce [*sic*], sister of Miss Amy Fay, and Mrs. Theodore Thomas, though not herself a professional musician, became impressed with the feeling that it was an exceptionally favorable time to take the preliminary steps toward carrying out her long cherished plan of forming in New York a musical society for women."[10] A preliminary committee, including Amy, assembled to explore this possibility. Zina became the first president, serving from 1899 to 1902, followed by Amy, who held the position until 1914.[11]

The WPS grew rapidly. It consisted of numerous committees (vocal, piano, strings, composition) that each met twice a month for lectures and performances in a suite of rooms the society had rented in the new Carnegie Hall, which had opened in 1891. The WPS also formed a small orchestra and choir, which presented monthly musicales as well as four concerts each season. Instrumentation in the orchestra was unusual. There were no trombones or tubas, as those were still considered masculine instruments.[12] Unlike the Chicago Orchestra and other newly established resident orchestras based on a corporate model, the WPS ran on a club model. The performers paid into the organization rather than receiving payment for their performances. Their goals were self-improvement and social betterment, more socially acceptable for women than performing publicly for pay.[13]

The WPS gave young women a chance to perform before a welcoming audience, supported women composers and conductors, and provided scholarship opportunities for deserving students, both male and female. Scholarship applications were mailed to Amy's address, as she was responsible for sorting through them. Her mailman, who had a talented son, noticed the many envelopes and inquired about the scholarships. Amy volunteered to hear the young man play and, finding he had promise, placed him before the committee for consideration. The postman's son won the scholarship, and Amy became his teacher.[14]

Zina, true to form, launched the organization and then moved on, moving back to Chicago for a few years. For Amy, however, the WPS served as a nucleus for her musical efforts, providing not only opportunities to perform but also a social network of peers. Amy gave a paper on the Salzburg Mozart Festival at the first general meeting and was a frequent performer, speaker, and committee member. She wrote, "I never saw a Club in such a continued state of activity as this one, and there seems no let-up to it!"[15]

Amy had progressed in her own thinking about female musicians. Early in her career, her programs consisted of works by male composers, but as her work with the WPS progressed, she more often included pieces by women. In fact, she began to prefer working with women in general and turned down an engagement at a different club with the explanation, "I have no mind to work for men, however, which is always a thankless task!" Similarly, she wrote to Zina, "I suppose you would not enjoy working under a man!"[16]

This represented a definite evolution for Amy, who wrote in 1871 of seeing a woman composer conduct a symphony in Berlin: "That is quite a step for women in the musical line. . . . All the men were highly disgusted because she was allowed to conduct the orchestra herself. I didn't think myself that it was a very becoming position, though I had no prejudice against it. Somehow, a woman doesn't look well with a baton in her hand directing a body of men."[17]

Around that same time, Amy described a woman conducting as a "virago," a word that has since fallen out of the vocabulary, perhaps reflecting societal values, as it disparagingly depicts a woman who has strong masculine characteristics. Stating again that there were certain things that were unbecoming to a woman, Amy concluded that "this strong assertion of women is as distasteful to me as a man sewing baby clothes would be."[18]

Though she claimed to have no prejudice, Amy, like most people, had clearly been thoroughly indoctrinated in gender roles. In 1874, having enjoyed piano lessons with one of Deppe's assistants, a woman, Amy praised her teaching skills, which were based on Deppe's methods, writing, "Men should *create,* and women *perfect.*"[19] Even to Amy, a remarkably independent young woman at the time, custom dictated that men were the leaders and women the supporters.

But by the mid-1890s, Amy had modified her views on a woman's place, recognizing and bridling at the unnecessary restrictions placed on talented women. She began to do what she could to dismantle some of the obstacles in the music world. Society, too, was beginning to awaken to the unfair disparity, but at a slow, lurching pace filled with conflict, discomfort, and occasional hope.

Anti-Cruelty Society

1899–1904

IN 1899, THE SAME YEAR that Zina and Amy launched the Women's Philharmonic Society in New York, Rose started an initiative of her own in Chicago, one based on compassion. Communing with nature at Felsengarten in the summers, both Rose and Theodore came to despise harm to any living creature. When neighbors recommended Rose trap the abundant squirrels and chipmunks to prevent them from stealing birds' eggs, she instead manufactured a miniature dinner table out of a mushroom and a small log, hung it in a tree near a window, and kept it stocked with nuts or corn, enjoying the small animals instead of banning them.[1]

Similarly, Theodore, having finally succeeded at creating a scenic pond, was advised by friends to stock it with trout to add some variety to their diet. He responded, "What! First feed a creature, and then eat it?—I do not like that idea. I wish one could get on without this everlasting killing and eating of meat, but, since that is not practicable, let us at least not devour our friends!"[2]

In *Our Mountain Garden*, Rose drew connections between hunting and child labor:

> Let all unharmful creatures live and be happy, as is their right. In my opinion hunting for mere pleasure—or, as it is called, "sport"—is a relic of barbarism which is unworthy of the civilization of the twentieth century, and ought to be dropped. When

> one considers it honestly, what is it, after all? It is the deliberate enjoyment of the torture and murder of living creatures who are helpless to escape. . . . What wonder is it that when human beings find their pleasure thus, they do not hesitate to sacrifice the lives, and, what is worse, the souls of helpless children in mills, coal mines, and factories?[3]

At the time, children often worked twelve-to-fourteen-hour shifts in textile factories, cotton mills, and coal mines, as employers exploited their nimble fingers and small bodies. When Illinois established the Child Labor Act of 1903, it was ahead of the curve, though the legislation merely placed restrictions on the length of workdays (eight hours) and required that children also be enrolled in school. The National Child Labor Committee was formed in 1904 to consider the question, involving prominent Progressive leaders such as Jane Addams and Florence Kelley, but the Fair Labor Standards Act, establishing nationwide youth employment regulations, was not enacted until 1938. One of the arguments against suffrage held that factory owners feared that women voters would be more inclined to insist on protecting child workers.

Rose wrote, "At Felsengarten no living thing is harmed save as a last resort, when there is no other way of preventing it from doing harm. And so the wild creatures are so fearless and friendly that they come almost to our hands. When I see that 'winged jewel,' the ruby-throated humming-bird, poise apparently motionless in the air before me, and sip honey from the flowers in my hand, I marvel that any woman can endure to see it dead, transfixed and distorted on her hat."[4] The 1896 founding of the Massachusetts Audubon Society by Harriet Hemenway and Minna Hall—soon to be followed by societies in numerous other states and eventually a national organization (1905)—was driven in part by a backlash against the fashion of trimming extravagant hats with bird parts, including not just the feathers but sometimes the wings, heads, or entire bodies.

Rose took issue fur coats as well, writing, "I once saw a woman's cloak which contained the skins of a thousand gray squirrels. It made me quite ill to look at it and think of all the pretty creatures that had gone into its vast superfluities. A thousand painful deaths in one garment—I had as lief wrap myself in a shroud as wear such a ghastly robe as that."[5] Instead of wearing furs, Rose was fond of accessorizing her outfits with colorful pins; her collection included a butterfly, dog, bug, and silver owl.[6]

Harsher cruelties than fur coats and the millinery use of feathers could be found on the streets of Chicago near the turn of the century. Lame horses were seen on many street corners, being driven mercilessly, their flanks bearing scars from beatings. Anna Sewell's children's book *Black Beauty*, published in the United States in 1890, brought attention to the bleak lives of carriage horses.[7] Another book, Upton Sinclair's *The Jungle*, released in 1906, highlighted the horrors taking place in the Chicago stockyards. The numbers alone were staggering and the methods often inhumane. In 1900, the Union Stockyards slaughtered two hundred thousand hogs, fifty thousand cattle, thirty thousand sheep, and five thousand horses.

Animal cruelty was one of the issues the members of the Woman's Christian Temperance Union (WCTU) addressed through its Department of Mercy, established in 1890. Though the WCTU is known particularly for its work opposing abuse of intoxicating liquors, this apolitical group took on a broad array of issues having to do with family violence and animal cruelty, particularly after Evanston resident Francis Willard was appointed president. Other organizations, such as the state-based branches of the Society for the Protection of Cruelty to Animals and the American Anti-Vivisection Society, which opposed experimentation on animals, were popping up around the country as well.[8]

But for Rose, progress on reducing animal cruelty was moving too slowly in Chicago. By now no stranger to organizing, in January 1899, Rose invited her friends Kate Ellwood Allport, Eugenia Mason, and Frances Baker Gilbert to her home to meet with Dr. John G. Shortall of the Illinois Humane Society. She wanted to discuss what could be done about city animals' needless suffering. A second, larger meeting held two months later in the home of Genevieve Baldwin Winterbotham formally established the Anti-Cruelty Society of Chicago; bylaws were adopted, and Rose was elected president.[9] The society's mailing address was the Thomas home on Bellevue Place.

All women were welcome and encouraged to join, regardless of social status. Men could join as associate members. The goal was to start with women and add men if the work warranted it (which it did in short order). Rose stressed that they wished to work closely with the all-male Illinois Humane Society, but it seems there was little cooperation in the early years.

Whereas today the Anti-Cruelty Society (ACS) is known primarily for its work with dogs and cats, its first major concern was workhorses. The women of the ACS, having donned five-pointed silver stars on their lapels, stood at bridge inclines and other busy traffic spots and bravely confronted carriage drivers who were mistreating their horses. ACS members collaborated with the police and with Mayor Carter Harrison Jr. on this campaign. This was one point of difference with the WCTU and other early organizations, whose members avoided "unladylike" confrontations on the streets, choosing to argue their points rather than physically enforce them.[10]

Challenging a driver who had been maltreating a horse must have taken serious courage. In some cases, the horses were starving, with their ribs showing; in other instances, they were clearly lame or in need of horseshoes. The ACS provided guidance for its members on how to handle these situations: remain calm and dignified, show the membership star, suggest measures to remedy the situation, but be clear that legal action could follow if the drivers did not respond appropriately. In case of outright malice, the ACS representatives were advised to look for a police officer and ask him to take the offender into custody. If they were not able to locate a policeman, they wrote down the name on the wagon, the kind of horse, the vehicle license information, and names of witnesses so officials could follow up.[11] Punishing the drivers, rather than the employers who were pushing their workers into working longer hours and carrying heavier loads, was not always fair or effective.

When faced with a driver abusing a horse that had stopped, Rose's approach was to firmly admonish the driver, "You must not hit that horse again!" and then suggest gentler ways to get the animal moving. She carried lumps of sugar and apples in her pockets, and often that small kindness proved sufficient. Failing that, she suggested cramping the wheel to avoid slippage or lightening the load, all while lifting the horse's harness slightly and petting its neck. As a last resort, she prevailed on passing carriages to help by giving a gentle push at the back.[12]

The women of the ACS had quick results. By June 1899, just five months after the initial planning meeting, most major bridge crossings bore signs reading "Horse-beating is prohibited on this bridge and the inclines thereto. The police will see that this rule is enforced."[13]

By late January 1900, Rose reported that the stars they were deputized to wear proved useful: "In the majority of cases it is only necessary for us to show our stars and the drivers desist from the ill treatment. It is seldom that we are compelled to call on the police to aid us in the enforcement of our authority." She added that some members had even flashed their Chicago badges when visiting other cities, with good results.[14] Given that women had been unable to walk unescorted in public areas just a few decades earlier, the idea of one standing at a busy intersection, wearing a badge, and confronting men represented tremendous change. The volunteers maintained the moral superiority inherited from the Victorian age but had not yet moved into the salaried workplace.

The ACS took on other avenues of improving life for workhorses, including recommending a different type of horseshoe suitable for slippery pavements, stationing a large horse (Beauty) at the busy Rush Street bridge to help push tired equine teams up the incline, appealing to the fire department to lighten heavy trappings on its horses, and campaigning the mayor to obligate carriage companies to use only strong, healthy animals.[15] The society maintained a farm on the South Side of the city, named Horse Haven, as a retirement spot for sick and aged horses.

Soon Rose was able to report that the carriage horses were fattening up and that the policemen at the bridges were vigorously enforcing the laws against beating animals on the inclines. Newspaper reports carried stories of slick roads being fixed, drivers of injured horses being jailed or fined, and solitary ACS representatives bravely advocating for clearly overworked horses.

The ACS also took on poor conditions for horses in the work yards, such as that of the Chicago and Eastern Illinois Railway. Rose described the situation:

> A few weeks ago, the yard was covered with coal dust to a thickness of from eight to ten inches. I noticed that the horses bore

> whip marks, and calling upon Albert Young, President of the Teamsters' Union, I asked him where the horses received their lashings. He pointed out the condition of the coal yard at Fourteenth street and I made an investigation. I found great ruts in all the roads and also found that the pulling was extremely heavy on account of the large amount of coal dust. I made an appeal to an official of the company and now the yard is clean and newly paved.[16]

From saving Poe's cottage and Fraunces Tavern to their activities with the National Federation of Musical Clubs, the Women's Philharmonic Society, and the Anti-Cruelty Society of Chicago, the Fay sisters personified the critical roles women could play. None of these issues were overtly political or controversial, yet all helped challenge the boundaries of the women's sphere.

Compassion

1901–1904

ROSE'S ANTI-CRUELTY SOCIETY HAD THREE main goals: to suppress cruelty to animals, to educate the public about humane treatment, and to provide a refuge for strays.[1] Having gained confidence from their early successes with horses, and as automobiles steadily replaced horse-drawn carriages, the women of the ACS turned their attention to other creatures in need. The society was growing quickly in terms of volunteers, and it was able to open an animal shelter in 1904. Previously, the issue of stray animals had been handled by dogcatchers and city pounds, but they were often not treated in a humane fashion. Shelters were considered enough of a domestic space not to be unfeminine. The shelter at 459 East Division Street became the ACS's official headquarters.

One of its members, Ellen Butler Linn, provided enough money to operate the space for a year. It did not take long for the shelter to fill to capacity, as the starving alleyway dogs and cats were quickly snatched up and tended. The ACS purchased a motorcycle with a trailer cage to transport stray dogs. Getting them off the streets was a double success, not just for the safety of the animals but also for humans who feared rabies or bites.

Notably, the first manager of the shelter was a woman, Eva Copeland Schumann, who sent out weekly lists of the dogs and cats available for adoption. Dr. John J. Millar provided animals with a thorough veterinary exam; dogs and cats determined to be unfit for home life (whether because of physical ailments or temperament) were euthanized.[2] In the early years, over half of the small animals taken in were put to death. The society's founders felt strongly that humane euthanasia was preferable to slow starvation on the streets.

There were many facets to the work of the ACS, all operating simultaneously. Members installed troughs and four large Ensign fountains around the city to provide drinking water for workhorses. In a record heat wave during the summer of 1905, the ACS stationed a man with a watering hose in front of the shelter to water down horses. Representatives advocated for protective legislation and to raise the standard of duty of public officials. ACS members endeavored to break up cockfights, discouraged people from giving chicks at Easter, distributed nonslip shoe covers to horses, and lectured at public schools, women's clubs, and church groups on humane treatment of animals. In 1908, after the publication of Sinclair's *The Jungle*, they participated in a series of meetings with representatives from the meatpacking houses to discuss humane slaughter techniques.

The early annual reports reflect a much more rough-and-tumble ACS than we are familiar with today. They euthanized a large number of ailing animals, with photographs showing the proper, humane way to shoot a horse. Compassion took many different forms. It was not just about animals either. In those days before the establishment of state and local departments of children and family services, the ACS also responded to complaints of abuse against children or women. The 1913 annual report indicates it provided protective services to over 439 children. In that same year, members responded to 1,614 complaints of animal cruelty; succeeded in getting 521 old horses retired to farms and 133 mercifully killed; examined over 26,000 animals on streets and alleys; received over 800 dogs, finding homes for 250 of them; and took in 849 cats, of which 102 found homes.[3]

Rose became known as a local leader, advocating for humane treatment of all creatures. When organizers of a pet show at the Chicago Coliseum announced they would host a canary-catching contest in 1903, releasing birds for children to chase and catch, a friend dispatched a note via messenger to Rose. She promptly sent a delegation of women to demand the event not take place, "fearing that the canaries would be torn to pieces. The women threatened to have a hundred policemen in the hall, if necessary, to prevent liberation of the birds."[4]

In a presentation Rose wrote for the convention of the American Humane Association, taking place during the 1904 St. Louis World's Fair, she blamed inappropriate toys for encouraging cruelty in boys. Pointing out that boys were often given toy soldiers, popguns, or play whips as early toys, she suggested that a gentler alternative could be found outside: "Children are not by nature cruel, but it is easy to make them so by giving them toys which are to be employed in the killing or the hurting of innocent creatures. There is nothing better fitted for the wholesome development of the better traits in the character of a child than care for the protection of animals and the study of nature."[5] Rose's pacifist ideals ran in the face of popular culture. Americans had long loved violence as entertainment, as evidenced by the fact that at the turn of the century, Buffalo Bill Cody was one of the nation's most famous people. Cody, named for his aptitude for killing buffalo along the new railroad lines, performed his Buffalo Bill's Wild West show before millions of people, glorifying attacks on Native Americans and wildlife. Both Cody and sharpshooter Annie Oakley had been popular shows on or adjacent to the Midway Plaisance during the 1893 World's Fair.

In terms of teaching children more humane behavior, the women of the society flooded the city. Under the rallying cry of "Five thousand more members within two years," the membership established children's chapters throughout the city, some boasting several hundred on their rolls.[6] With names like the Robin Hood Chapter and the Children's Animal League, these junior humane societies educated children on proper care for animals and inspired thousands of youngsters to help gather strays and raise money for fountains and other projects.

Though busy with his orchestral work, Theodore proudly supported Rose's new venture. He wrote to her:

> I hope you have not taken in some old alley dog or cat to nurse!... The other day I saw a man maltreating his horse at a small way-station where the train stopped for a few minutes. I did not have time to get out, but I was so mad I pushed up the car window and

> roared at him, "If my wife was here you would stop that pretty quick!" He was so astonished at this surprising threat that he actually did stop, and my wrath evaporated in a hearty laugh, as the train moved on![7]

Secure in her husband's support, Rose pressed forth. The work that she and the other determined ACS volunteers undertook spread compassion at both large and small scales throughout Chicago.

Concert Hall

1901–1904

AMONG THE MANY TRIUMPHS WERE losses and heartbreak. On December 21, 1901,Rose was sitting with Norman at a concert conducted by Theodore when she was handed a telegram for her husband, informing him that his eldest son, Franz, had died in Pensacola, Florida. Born in 1865, Franz had suffered a fall as a young child that left him with permanent injuries and delicate health. Rose took the telegram backstage at intermission to share the sad news with Theodore. He absorbed the information but went on to stoically conduct the second half of the concert, ironically, Wagner's Funeral March from *Parsifal*. Following the concert, they went to a dinner the orchestra members gave in Theodore's honor that had been planned in advance, with the conductor saying nothing about his son's death. Rose and Theodore came home at about 3 a.m., when "his grief was finally released." Norman later wrote, "The men found out about the tragedy next day; but they said nothing to him—so that writer thinks. Such is the tradition of the stage. Private griefs do not cross the footlights."[1]

Theodore was an introvert whose musical talents had forced him into a public role. Despite all his musical accomplishments, he drew his greatest joy from his children. Six months after Franz's death, his youngest daughter, Marian, married Gale Carter in a small ceremony at 43 Bellevue. All four remaining Thomas children now had lives of their own. Two of them married into the same family: Son

Hector wedded Margaret Sturgis, and daughter Minna married Margaret's brother D'anford (their father was architectural critic Russell Sturgis). Hector became a New York City lawyer and the four-time mayor of his small town of Croton-on-Hudson.

Money was a continuing source of worry for Theodore. Because of several financial catastrophes—the failed Chicago concerts during the 1871 fire, a calamitous series for the Philadelphia Centennial Exposition, and the ill-fated attempt at an American Opera Company—he had essentially no savings. In fact, in 1876, he owed over $20,000 in debts, leading the sheriff to sell his possessions at auction. Fortunately, a friend bought them and later returned them to Theodore.[2]

With the Chicago position, he enjoyed a generous annual income, but a lifetime of gigging left him feeling as though he would never have enough money. He still worried about long-term stability and leaving something behind for Rose and his children. Though Theodore claimed to live a simple life, he had two summer homes, the Bellevue house, and a taste for fine cigars and rare wines. He had paid for his sons' college education. Dressed impeccably in well-tailored clothing, he always carried two crisp $50 bills in his pocket, not necessarily for spending but just to know he had them available. A careful, meticulous man, Theodore always washed his hands after handling money.[3]

But Theodore was dependent on the generosity of the trustees for his livelihood, and there was never a guarantee of another season, an uncertainty that wore on him. The size of the Auditorium continued to hold down subscription sales, and of the fifty-four original guarantors, twenty-two had died or moved, while others had suffered financial reverses. The orchestra could not be sustained by a small group of wealthy individuals indefinitely. Something needed to change.

Now approaching seventy, Theodore was worn out. Rose reported that after one particularly grueling season, he "was so tired that for a month he sat every day in his chair, moveless and inert, his head drooped forward in a kind of coma."[4] Finally, exhausted physically and spiritually, Theodore put forth an ultimatum: To survive long-term, the orchestra needed its own concert hall, and unless the trustees could raise an endowment to build and maintain a hall, he would resign.[5]

Norman approached the rest of the trustees again: It was time for the orchestra to become self-sustaining. In February 1903, the trustees issued a statement that they planned to build a permanent home for the orchestra, something smaller, a place where they could collect rental income instead of paying it out. The managers of the Auditorium discussed remodeling to better suit the orchestra's needs but determined that would not solve the problems. The trustees plunged ahead, with considerable opposition and backlash from fans of the Auditorium.[6]

Daniel Burnham stepped up once again, finding nine others, including Norman, to join him in each putting forth $10,000 toward the purchase of an old livery stable lot on Michigan Avenue, across from the Art Institute and just west of the Exposition Building where Theodore's summer night programs had taken place decades earlier. They paid $100,000 and mortgaged an additional $350,000. This generous committee offered to head a subscription drive to raise a total of $750,000, which would cover the price of the land as well as construction of a hall.

For Norman, who still had not recovered financially from the 1893 crash, making a pledge of this size must have been difficult, but the orchestra remained a top priority for him. In a February 1903 letter sent to the newspapers and widely circulated, the trustees made the stakes clear: raise this money to ensure the future of the organization or abandon the orchestra at the end of the season.[7] Norman also approached his fellow businessmen and community leaders both in person and via letter, as he had done initially, to cajole them into financial support.

Rose grew ever more concerned about her husband's health. A letter she wrote to Frances Glessner explained the emotional toll: "The strain & anxiety & uncertainty are simply killing to him, & he can't stand it any more. I have never seen him so nervous and upset as he has been all this last year."[8]

Efforts to entice large cornerstone donations from Chicago's wealthiest individuals largely failed. In a letter to a niece, Amy wrote that Norman was doubtful the fund drive would succeed and worried that the orchestra would fail: "It will be a terrible shame if all your Uncle's efforts and sacrifice to establish a first class orchestra permanently should come to naught."[9]

But then something astounding happened. The people of Chicago, from all walks of life, collectively saved the orchestra.[10] Word spread that Chicago was about to lose the orchestra, and suddenly, contributions—some a matter of cents, others thousands of dollars—began to roll in. Clubs, merchants, newspapers, universities, kindergarten associations, and other organizations—even an association of scrubwomen at one of the settlement houses who surely could not afford concert tickets—mustered subscribers, and bit by precious bit, the money rolled in. The orchestra contributed a week's combined salary, about $5,000. In the end, the subscription list contained over eight thousand names. Norman wrote, "Literally, the butcher, the baker, and the candlestick-maker were there."[11]

After years of scraping by and worrying, Theodore had his efforts rewarded by this citywide, grassroots endorsement. The total amounted to $650,000 (in today's dollars, over $23 million). With this public vote of confidence, the trustees borrowed the remainder and moved full speed ahead.

Daniel Burnham won the contract for designing the hall and followed guidelines written by Theodore. In 1897, at the behest of Russell Sturgis, Theodore had written an essay on the proper construction of music halls for the *Dictionary of Architecture*. But because the Chicago lot was fairly shallow, the ideal design of a shoebox-shaped hall, like Boston's Symphony Hall, had to be shortened and curved, more closely resembling New York's esteemed Carnegie Hall. The plans had a main hall, a chamber hall, a music library, and offices, including some that could be turned into classrooms in the event a musical university ever came to fruition.[12] Because of the tragic 1903 Iroquois Theatre fire in Chicago, which had resulted in over six hundred deaths, the plan followed strict new fire code regulations.

Perhaps Theodore pushed so hard for a permanent hall because he knew his time was limited. Doctors had warned Theodore that his heart might fail if he continued to conduct.[13] Over the summer of 1904, Rose watched his physical health rapidly decline. In addition to his heart issues, he had long suffered from catarrh (inflamed mucous membranes, resulting in chronic coughing and throat clearing), and he had gradually become deaf in his right ear and blind in one eye—maladies Rose helped him keep under wraps. As his hairline receded, he took to wearing a wig in public.[14]

Rose and Theodore retreated to Felsengarten, hoping for some much-needed physical and emotional recuperation. Of that 1904 summer, Rose wrote, "It was pathetic to see the old, sick lion, wandering slowly through the woods where he had been wont to roam in all the glory of abounding health and strength . . . but he seemed to feel the same deep and quiet and content that always pervaded his spirit at Felsengarten."[15]

Rose's *Our Mountain Garden* book about Felsengarten had been released by Macmillan that spring to good reviews, *The Kansas City Star* commenting, "[It] is one of the most charming books the season can bring to the lovers of nature."[16] *The Guardian* from London called it a "delightful little volume," and *The Outlook* from New York suggested that "a special pleasure awaits the reader."[17] The review in *The St. Louis Republic* emphasized the feminine aspect of the book: "Withal it is a fascinating story full of the sort of interest that always adheres to a spirited account of the making of a country home by a woman of talent and cultivation."[18]

The trip back to Chicago resembled a farewell tour. Theodore requested they stop in Boston, Fairhaven, and New York City so he could say goodbye to family and friends along the way. He even dispatched Rose to Mount Auburn Cemetery in Cambridge to pick out their burial plots.

Back in Chicago, he was dismayed to discover the hall unfinished; the orchestra had to start the season in the Auditorium. Once the new building neared completion, Theodore and Rose went to see it on a Friday afternoon. Two nuns preceded them into the hall. Rose, acknowledging her own superstitious nature, wrote, "It seemed a sinister omen that Thomas should make his first entrance into the hall in the wake of these black-robed figures."[19]

On December 7, 1904, Theodore finally conducted his orchestra for the first time in its permanent home. The opening piece during rehearsal was the overture to Wagner's *Tannhäuser*, but the orchestra had a surprise in store. Rose described what occurred in a letter to Burnham: "A curious little incident happened which added to his happiness, for it was an expulsion of affection from the Orchestra which he was not expecting. . . . All was in readiness and Mr. Thomas gave the signal to begin. But instead of the opening notes of the

Overture, a big fanfare burst from all parts of the stage—a greeting to him in his own musical home!"[20] This was most likely a tusch, a traditional musical tribute from an orchestra to a conductor, a brief, loud fanfare of unscripted sound offered by the ensemble only in the rarest moments of honor.

For *Tannhäuser*, Theodore turned the baton over to assistant conductor Frederick Stock so he could walk around the hall, listening from different vantage points. When he finally reached the upper gallery, he danced a short jig.[21] To Norman and other trustees seated in the hall, he exuberantly shouted, "Your hall is a success, gentlemen, a great success!" Following the rehearsal, he telegrammed Burnham, working in Manila at the time, "Hall a complete success. Quality exceeds all expectations."[22] Rose shared the news with Frances Glessner: "The acoustics are perfect—wonderful 'beyond the highest expectations, & too much be said in its praise'—so says the Mister, don't need to add a thing more!"[23]

Although Theodore was pleased with the sound in the hall, other conditions were not ideal. Pushing hard to get into the hall before the holidays, the orchestra held its first rehearsals while the plaster and cement were still damp, the doors and windows were not fully fitted, the heaters were not yet functional, and construction dust still hung in the air. Numerous members of the orchestra fell ill, including Theodore, who developed a cold.

On opening night, Wednesday, December 14, 1904, members of the orchestra wore carnations in their lapels and a wreath hung on the podium stand, both gifts from orchestra "mother" Frances Glessner. Manager George Adams extended a brief address of welcome, but Theodore said nothing, letting his baton speak for him. The Apollo Chorus sang the opening words from the march of Wagner's *Tannhäuser* overture in German, which translate as "Hail, bright abode, where song the heart rejoices," a fitting selection to christen a new hall. Richard Strauss's *Death and Transfiguration*, Beethoven's Fifth Symphony, and Handel's "Hallelujah Chorus" followed, in between cheers of triumph from the audience.

For Theodore, it represented the culmination of a lifetime of work. He wrote of the significance of the new hall: "Its permanency is secure, its home is built, and the object for which I have worked all my life is accomplished. The old saying, 'Better late than never,' comes to mind as I see in my seventieth year the realization of the dreams of my youth."[24]

The members of the orchestra understood what it all meant to Theodore. They wrote a tribute to be delivered at a banquet after the holidays, confirming, "Fifty years of honest work have not been wasted. You have come to your own, nobly striven for, nobly won. You are recognized and will be remembered for your self-sacrificing, courageous devotion to the highest in our noble art."[25] It was a thoughtful, touching encomium that Theodore would never hear.

Finale

1904–1905

WHAT HAPPENED NEXT HAPPENED QUICKLY.

With his well-trained ear, Theodore Thomas had always tinkered with moving sections and using sound boards to maximize the balance of his orchestra, even while in the Auditorium. But because of the delay in construction, he had insufficient time to experiment in Orchestra Hall. In retrospect, his delight at the first rehearsal appears premature, as acoustics work quite differently when a room is filled with patrons. Or perhaps his age-related hearing difficulties affected his judgment. In any case, critics' reviews were mixed. The front page of the *Chicago Tribune* on December 15, 1904, carried celebratory coverage of the inaugural concert, followed by an acoustic assessment of the hall: "For the first time since the Chicago orchestra has been heard it sounded common. That is an unpleasant thing to say, but the fact is incontrovertible. Whether Mr. Thomas by shifting his men can restore the balance is a question which, of course, he can answer better than can any one else in Chicago."[1]

Performing in an orchestra is a constant quest for perfection—to capture precisely what the composer intended and the music demands—among all its members, though the responsibility lies heaviest on the conductor. In the years before sound recording, often the conductor was the only member who had advance knowledge of the composition. Balancing the sound among the sections is a critical piece of the perfection puzzle. Despite his cold and nasty cough, Theodore pushed himself to attend rehearsals and concerts, desperate to find the ideal setup and have Orchestra Hall declared a success.

Theodore's cold turned into the flu, and his health worsened. His concert on Christmas Eve 1904 preceded a lovely evening with Rose. They enjoyed oysters in the shell roasted in their fireplace on Bellevue Place. Theodore seemed happy and congenial. But then, abruptly, he wilted and announced, "I am so tired, so tired, I must go to bed."[2] On Christmas Day, although Theodore was gravely ill, he still dreamed of better times. Once again underestimating his own wealth, he asked Rose, "Would you be content to live with me in the country on what we have?" She replied, "Yes, any place on anything so it is with you."[3]

As pneumonia set in and took its toll on Theodore's overworked body, news of his illness stretched throughout the city. On December 30, for the first time, he missed a concert because of illness. His children were notified, and those who could rushed to Chicago. Norman stayed close, as did Frances and John Glessner.

Theodore rallied briefly on January 3. Rose recalled, "A few hours before his death the lamp of life flickered up for a moment, and as I sat beside him he murmured: 'I have had a beautiful vision—a beautiful vision—' "[4] Later, Rose detailed those final hours in an introduction she wrote in the third person for George Upton's biography of Theodore:

> She little thought that these were to be his last words, but fearing he was tired she left him to rest, and went down-stairs to luncheon. He had given her at Christmas a little chime of silver bells, to be used to summon the family to meals. As he had been ill ever since Christmas Day these bells had not been used, for fear of disturbing him. To-day, however, he had seemed so much better that she thought perhaps he might like to hear his bells for once. So she stopped as she passed them, and played a little bugle-call which came into her head. Hardly had she finished when one of the family said, "do you know that you have just played 'Taps'—the call that is sounded over the graves of dead soldiers?" Struck with consternation at the sinister omen which she had unconsciously wrought, she rushed back to the bells

> and played another call which was engraved upon a metal plate above them. Afterwards she noticed that it was "Reveille"—the soldier's signal to arise. And thus it chanced that the last music heard by Theodore Thomas on earth was symbolical of death and the resurrection.[5]

At his bedside, in addition to Rose, were Norman and Theodore's two remaining sons, Hector and Hermann.[6] Theodore died quietly at 5 a.m. on Wednesday, January 4, 1905, at the age of seventy. Telephone operators at Chicago switchboards announced "Theodore Thomas is dead" before asking callers to whom they would like to be connected.[7]

Mourning

1905

YEARS EARLIER, THEODORE HAD SAID to Norman ruefully, "The work of a painter or sculptor lives—even of a poor one, but that of the greatest interpreter of music dies with him—forgotten like a smoked cigar."[1] Theodore's music, performed in front of audiences before the advent of radio or orchestral recordings, evaporated into the atmosphere of Orchestra Hall. But the orchestra he had so carefully shaped and the hall he had willed into existence remained.

The body of Theodore Thomas was arranged in his coffin at the 43 Bellevue home with his hands clasped over his heart, a single rose in one and his baton in the other—"his wife and his art," said Rose. Tucked in with Theodore was a wreath of pink roses from Rose and four palm leaves from his children.[2] A death mask had been made and presented to Rose.

Floral pieces and wreaths arrived at St. James Episcopal Church from all over the country for the funeral on the morning of January 6. Eight members of the orchestra served as pallbearers, followed by the trustees, who then took seats in the choir stalls. Honorary pallbearers included John Glessner, Marshall Field, and Cyrus McCormick; other close friends served as ushers. Representatives from the Cincinnati Music Festival attended as well.

A large wreath from the orchestra hung on one side of the closed casket; a smaller one from the trustees adorned the other side. There was no sermon, just the brief Episcopal funeral service led by two priests (one being Rose's maternal uncle John Henry Hopkins Jr.). An organist and a forty-piece woodwind and brass ensemble from the orchestra played a few simple Bach pieces for the processional and recessional. The church bells tolled, upon which members of the public, paying their respects outside of the church, removed their hats and silently bowed their heads.[3] A hearse transported Theodore's coffin to the receiving vault at Graceland Cemetery, trailed by the family and twenty carriages holding the members of the orchestra.

After the short service, Frances Glessner and other women stood on the steps leading up to the altar to protect the flowers, which they then brought to Orchestra Hall for the memorial concert that afternoon. The doorways and wall under the organ had been draped with black and purple, and the wreaths and flowers transported from the church service provided a somber but elegant setting. The orchestra, wearing crepe armbands, and the audience stood during the first number, a Bach chorale, which was followed by the first two movements of Beethoven's *Eroica* Symphony, *Siegfried's Funeral March* by Wagner, and Richard Strauss's tone poem *Death and Transfiguration.* Frederick Stock conducted without words, intermission, or applause.

At the conclusion of the concert, Rose, who had been sitting with Hector and Hermann in the Glessners' box, went down to the stage to thank the orchestra, giving each member a rose. The concert was repeated on Sunday afternoon, this time to a full house in the Auditorium to accommodate more people. Rose wrote later, "So great was the concourse of people who desired to attend that not only was it taxed to its utmost limit, but many thousands, unable to get in, stood silently in the wintry blasts of the streets without, while it was in progress."[4]

Theodore's death, coming right on the heels of the opening of the hall for which he had fought his entire life, shocked Chicago. The *Chicago Tribune* memorialized him thus: "Grand in his ideals, unswervingly honest and honorable in his career, splendid in musical gift, and noble in manliness of character, with a great loving heart behind his austere seeming, he has gone, and thousands will mourn for him."[5]

Rose received thousands of condolence letters, including tributes from famous composers and musicians from around the world, such as Richard Strauss, Arthur Nikisch, and Lilli Lehmann.[6] Tributes were held in seven different cities.

The New York Times summed up what Theodore had done for classical music in the United States: "It is hard to estimate the debt that this country owes to Theodore Thomas. It is the debt of a pupil to a teacher; or it is the debt of a people led out of a wilderness to the prophet who has shown them a sight of the promised land. To him more than to any other single force is due the present state of musical culture in this country."[7]

One week after Theodore's death, longtime orchestra supporter Charles Hamill died as well. These dual deaths immediately after the opening of Orchestra Hall seemed to be proof that the trustees had been correct in pushing for a permanent home. Had they waited any longer, it is possible the orchestra would not have survived these losses.

Wishing to leave Chicago as soon as possible, likely out of grief, Rose waded through piles of telegrams and letters while managing the logistics of temporarily closing up a house. She arranged for most of Theodore's music library, filled with Theodore's personal transcriptions and handwritten notes, to be given to the trustees—a gift, Norman wrote, whose "value can hardly be over estimated."[8] Some scores were earmarked for the archives at the Newberry Library. At the time, before mass printing of orchestral parts, this likely represented the largest music library in the country, consisting of scores and parts to more than thirty-five hundred works. Rose arranged for other items, such as loving cups and inscribed vases, to be donated to the Art Institute.[9]

In early February, thoroughly spent, Rose moved in with the Glessners for recovery. "She brought her little dog," Frances wrote. "She was perfectly worn out with all the hard work and anxiety she has gone through. I gave her the big corner room with a bright fire in it—and have left her alone as much as possible. She says it is the first rest she has had since October."[10] Norman and Lily were frequent visitors at the Glessners' during those weeks, providing quiet support for their grieving sister.

Back in 1893, at the World's Columbian Exposition, Rose and Theodore had become friends with art collector Isabella Stewart Gardner. At the opening of her now famous gallery in Boston in 1903, Isabella had entered on Theodore's arm. In a letter Rose penned to Isabella in February 1905, she wrote of her time healing in the Glessner house: "Mrs. Glessner is so dear and sweet, and does everything in the world to brighten for me these dark days, &, best of all, she lets me alone to come and go as I like, and does not change her own daily life at all on account of my presence, but enjoys her own social engagements outside or at home just as if I was not here, and lets me stay in my room or come down with the family according to my wish."[11]

In that same letter, Rose outlined the plans for laying Theodore to rest. Before his death, the couple had chosen Mount Auburn Cemetery in Cambridge as their final resting place. Theodore had requested that there be no funeral or ceremony at all, but Rose explained to Isabella that honoring his wish had not been feasible, given the public outpouring of grief upon his passing. She did insist, however, that Theodore's burial be private, explaining, "Otherwise some fool reporters will get hold of it and we will find a crowd of curiosity seekers, and news-mongers at the grave we do so much want to keep private and inviolate from such presence."[12]

Rose succeeded in her goal. In early March 1905, a quiet burial was held at Mount Auburn, attended only by Rose, Kate, Theodore's children, a clergyman, and Isabella. Rose stayed with Isabella at her gallery home on Fenway Court during this period.[13]

A poem Rose wrote during this time, titled "To Theodore Thomas 'My Morning Star,'" expresses her grief and the depth of her love for her departed husband:

> The morning star in glorious splendor 'rose
> Upon my life when all the sky was bright
> With dawning day—my happy day of love.
> Through love's long day, of fourteen winged years
> He shone with steadfast, tender beaming light
> My guide and beacon towards the better life.
> And when at length the evening hour drew nigh.
> He sank to rest in sunset's radiant glow,
> Leaving me shrouded in eternal night
> Save for the rainbow orbit which he traced
> In transit o'er my life. This shineth still
> Above the mist of melancholy tears —
> A bow of promise, love and energy.
> The arch on which my hope of heaven rests.[14]

Fugue
Together Again

Siblings

1905–1912

After Theodore's funeral, Rose traveled from Boston to New York, staying at Hector Thomas's apartment for a few months. Amy reported, "When she first came it almost made me cry to look at her, she had such a grief-stricken and desolate expression!"[1]

The Fays lived in a constant roundabout of mini-reunions among family members, as various siblings and their offspring visited New York, Chicago, Cambridge, Felsengarten, and Kate and Will's summer home on Fishers Island, New York. Lily had moved to New York with her family, adding her five members to the in-and-out gatherings.

Felsengarten was a key meeting spot for family. Because of the success of *Our Mountain Garden*, Rose's gardens had become quite famous. She organized the local White Mountain Garden Club to share tips and cuttings with other gardeners. She also opened her home on Saturdays to nearby friends, whom she called the "Neighborlies," during which time she served tea and read a book aloud for an hour. Afterward, the neighbors strolled in the garden and admired her latest blooms.

Whereas Rose had embraced her traditional role as Theodore's wife and chief supporter, content to bask in his large shadow, after his death she refused to slink quietly into the background. Determined to be independent, she learned to drive and became notorious for speeding down the country roads. Amy recounted Rose's aggressive driving in one of her letters, describing the experience as "another escape from death!"[2]

Clearly feeling that the best medicine for her sadness was to keep busy, Rose spent hours every day in her garden. In the summer of 1905, Amy reported, "She wears herself out, I think, with her everlasting work. Never is she idle for five minutes, and she works like a man in the garden."[3] In what amounted to a labor of love, Rose began sifting through Theodore's letters and papers and writing his biography. Little mattered more to Rose than shaping a lasting narrative of her husband's life and work and ensuring that his legacy endured.

To her friend Margaret Sherman Burnham (wife of Daniel Burnham), Rose confessed:

> Alas, this world is a dreary place to me now without the companionship of the great and true to whom every act was the outcome of love, humanity and devotion to that which was noble, high and pure. But I fill my days with incessant work—as he would have done had he lost me—and surround myself with loving hearts for whom I can do some small services, and who in turn give me all the comfort that friendship and sympathy can bestow. And so the days pass, and I have achieved at least a certain acquiescence in the blow which fate has dealt me.[4]

The biography of Theodore turned into a family effort. Amy assisted with translations of German documents, and no doubt Norman, who had been so closely involved with and admiring of Theodore, provided information on the organization of the orchestra and a careful reading of the text. In 1906, Rose returned to Chicago and moved into an apartment with Norman at 79 East Twentieth Street, as the Bellevue Place house held too many memories for her to bear.

Zina had also recently returned to Chicago and was recruited to read the manuscript aloud so Rose could hear how it sounded. A restless soul, Zina had moved frequently, perhaps a trait instilled during her childhood, when the family relocated every few years. Even during her short time in Chicago, she listed 1014 North State Street, 6 Washington Place, and 4434 Champlain Avenue among her addresses. Kate's middle daughter, Amy Fay Stone, an aspiring actress, stayed with Zina and reported:

> Aunt Zina and I are having a beautiful time together, despite the fact that we are a trifle crowded. Her unmethodical way of living—of getting up and going to bed at any hour and of eating meals only when she happens to feel hungry—suits me down to the ground, and I find her "household" a much easier one to fit into than Aunt Rose's. Then I also find her so interesting to talk to that I never tire of her society, and on her side, I think it is a relief for her to have someone at whom to shoot off all her theories after they have been so long bottled up.[5]

The manuscript reading must have been bittersweet for Zina, who was wrestling with a novel she had been working on for almost two decades. Zina referred to her work in progress as "the gospel of womanhood," no insignificant undertaking. She complained about her slow headway and confessed her feeling of "disgrace" to Kate, writing, "All the life and energy have gone out of me and I hate the thing so that I can barely go and work upon it. The truth is, I undertook a task above my talent."[6] The once unstoppable Zina was beginning to succumb to self-doubt. Amy, always her sister's greatest cheerleader, urged her on: "You are a natural born queen! And ought to have a realm, and it is too bad you have not one."[7]

In Chicago, Zina applied for a patent for a new apartment design intended to improve fireproofing as well as efficiency.[8] But she was slowing down. Rheumatism began to limit her outings and undertakings. Forty years after the publication of her first *Atlantic Monthly* articles on cooperative housekeeping, Zina had faded into the background, replaced by more current voices. Author Charlotte Perkins Gilman took up the mantle of housekeeping reform in her popular books *Women and Economics* and *The Home: Its Work and Influence*. A spirited public speaker and talented novelist (her short story *The Yellow Wallpaper* became a classic), Gilman expressed many of the same suggestions Zina had in terms of collective housework, but in a softer, more accessible manner. Zina later accused Gilman of stealing her ideas.[9] Taking things one step further, Gilman proposed a feminist apartment hotel for working mothers, including on-site domestic workers who would handle the cooking and cleaning, as well as a childcare facility.[10]

One of the voices protesting these radical new ideas was none other than Laura's. After being almost entirely incapacitated for two decades, she finally rallied under the care of daughter Madeline, a nurse living in Saranac Lake, New York. Madeline found a private home for her mother nearby, and here Laura truly recovered, finding enjoyment in writing poems, playing piano, and painting watercolors. Her son Nelson wrote of the transformation, "At the age of 70, she had renewed the vigor of her youth."[11]

Notwithstanding her gratitude for Madeline's professional training, which had facilitated her own recovery, Laura believed women should be content tending to the home and caring for their children. She served as an outspoken adversary to anyone challenging that traditional role. Following Gilman's proposal for an apartment hotel, Laura submitted a four-page letter to *The New York Times* in which she warned that this "Feminist Paradise Palace" would lead to "the decay of the gentle graces, the tender charms of the women, that poets have sung and painters have pictured, and instead we shall have a set of keen, cold calculators having money as their only standard of value."[12]

Though Zina's earlier writings had inspired new discussions and ideas, she had fallen behind. The many social initiatives undertaken during the Progressive era included new approaches to education, efficiency, and immigration. Once an outspoken trailblazer, Zina had merely watched as Chicago leaders Jane Addams and Ellen Gates Starr founded Hull House in 1889 to provide education, housing, and support services for immigrants. The settlement house also offered opportunities for single women to make a living without getting dragged down by domestic duties.[13]

Similarly, the founding mothers of suffrage—Anthony, Stanton, Stone, and Mott—had died or been replaced by new leaders, such as Alice Paul, Carrie Chapman Catt, and Ida B. Wells, and the fight continued. Zina still believed in separate houses of legislation for men and women, with no crossover between the two. She was not alone; millions of women continued to feel that men should solely bear the responsibility of voting. The deeply inculcated value system of women being chiefly helpmates and caregivers was taking time to shake. Over fifty years of advocacy had thus far resulted only in a handful of Western states allowing women voting rights.

Amy, however, seems to have grown supportive of the suffragists' efforts. Perhaps she was annoyed—as many single teachers, nurses, and factory workers were—at the indignities of taxation without representation. She wrote to Zina about witnessing a parade of twenty thousand suffragists (Amy's estimate; the reported numbers vary). Frustrated that she could not persuade Rose to go, Amy watched the "lovely" and "quite impressive" sight alone. She described their banners, white garments, colored scarves, and jaunty straw hats, telling Zina, "They had been instructed to be dignified in their demeanor and to keep their eyes looking straight before them, which they did. Consequently there was a sense of perfect propriety." Newspaper reports indicate that, in fact, some of the marchers were spit on and attacked. But Amy was left with the impression that the men watching were "more inclined for, than against!" She summed it up by saying, "[It] made a great moral affect and I think achieved a victory."[14] In her buoyant description, Amy made no mention of the contingent of Black women dressed in black and yellow who marched separately or of the banners honoring the 146 garment makers, mostly women and girls, who had perished in the horrific Triangle Shirtwaist Factory fire the previous year.

After the financial highs of the 1880s and 1890s, finances had become a worry for many of the siblings, primarily because Norman's business ventures continued their downward spiral. Following his early success with the telephone and utility companies, he had never fully recovered from the 1893 crash. His typewriter business suffered a series of worker strikes and lawsuits, ultimately going bankrupt in 1909.

Rose wrote to her friend Frances Glessner, "Norman's business calamity means ruin for almost our whole family, for he supported, or helped to support most of them, & therefore I shall personally not only lose what I have in the Typewriter Company, but it will fall to me to take care of those who have formerly looked to him for assistance. Under these circumstances, you can understand that it is imperative for me to cut off every dollar of superfluous expenses that I can, & first & foremost I must give up even my modest entertaining, & my Fortnightly & other club memberships."[15] After Theodore's death, Rose had to make her money last, the opportunity for new income now gone.

In flusher years, Norman had provided $50 monthly allowances to each of his single sisters. But that practice had ended, and the mantle of helping the family financially fell to Rose. For Zina, who had publicly advocated for financial independence for women, being reliant on her brother and later her sister must have been galling. Amy, in her letters to Zina, vacillated between gratitude for Rose's generosity and resentment.[16] To Rose, Amy joked, referencing a drought in New York but also providing a jab, "I was just thinking that other day that *you* must be feeding on *nice, juicy* asparagus, as I was chewing on some dry old hay stalks."[17] A divide was growing between the siblings who were financially strapped and those who helped provide for them.

Back East Once More

1910–1917

MAY 1910 FOUND ROSE, NORMAN, and Amy hobnobbing with U.S. President William Howard Taft and First Lady Helen H. Taft at the opening of the Cincinnati May Festival. Theodore had founded the festival in 1873 and continued as music director until his death. Following President Taft's remarks, in which he referred to Theodore as "the greatest musical leader the country has known,"[1] festival trustees unveiled a large bronze statue of Theodore, by sculptor Clement Barnhorn, at the podium.

Amy wrote of the event in a letter to Kate:

> I don't know when I have enjoyed anything so much as Rose and Norman and I had such pleasant little family meetings at our meals in the Grand Hotel. Rose was treated like a princess, and no doubt she told you how she was given the seat of honor between the president and the governor! The calm and tranquil way in which she walks over the hearts of the swells everywhere fills me with admiration mingled with awe! But she was just the same as a child, when she conquered Edith Longfellow, who was the swellest girl in Cambridge, you remember![2]

Amy, always low on cash, had been able to attend because the ladies of her club had collected money for her travel.

Despite Amy's complaints about lack of money, she repeatedly managed to charm her way into exciting travel opportunities, such as an exciting trip to South America a few years earlier. Kate's eldest daughter, twenty-eight-year-old Pauline, had become engaged to Arthur Loring Jackson. The wedding was to take place in Peru, as Arthur worked as an executive for the Chicago-Bolivian Rubber Company, part of the scramble for cheap rubber for automobile tires in the early 1900s. Pauline's father, Will, was battling pneumonia, so Amy volunteered to be the family representative while Kate stayed home to tend to her husband. Much as Amy had enjoyed six years in Germany on Uncle Storey's dime, she now traveled to South America at Kate and Will's expense.

Accompanied by a colleague of Arthur's, Pauline and Amy sailed to Panama, with a wedding cake carefully packed in one of their trunks. They landed in Colon, then took a three-hour train trip to Panama City, on the other side of the isthmus, the canal not yet having been constructed. The travel party arrived in Lima twenty days after departing from New York. The wedding took place in an intimate ceremony at the home of the American minister to Peru. Newlyweds Pauline and Arthur continued on for ten days via steamer, train, boat (over Lake Titicaca), and mule to Sorata, Bolivia.[3] Having fulfilled her duties as "best woman," Amy made the return trip from Lima unescorted. She did her best to learn Spanish, reporting back to her family, "Everyone went into great shrieks of laughter over it when I began to try to talk, but they enjoyed my efforts so much, I kept on."[4]

Before Pauline's wedding, Rose had taken it upon herself to inform the new bride what to expect in terms of sex in a surprisingly blunt letter to her niece: "To the average man, it is the most important thing in his whole life, and his most supreme joy. To the average woman, it is of no importance at all, and to many simply a bore. Nevertheless, it is not wise for a woman to let her husband see that. It is better for her to feign a warmth she does not really feel than ever to meet him with indifference and coldness." Rose went on to suggest rubbing on a little Vaseline before going to bed. "The whole marriage relation is only the law of nature, it runs through all things that have life, whether plants, animals, or human beings. Looked at in the right spirit, it is a wonderful, beautiful, and perfectly pure relation, and it is only the vices and evil practices of odd men and women which have weighted it with evil associations."[5] Whereas Emily had viewed sex as merely for procreation and Zina seemed to find it abhorrent, Rose considered intercourse a service to her husband. Her candid letter represents a far more relaxed attitude toward sexuality than the rigid attitudes of the Victorian era.[6]

After returning from South America, Amy had only a few months in New York before embarking on another underwritten trip, this time to Europe as a companion for Sarah Hershey Eddy. Sarah's husband of twenty-five years, organist Clarence Eddy (who had performed at Rose and Theodore's wedding), had abandoned her after falling in love with her cousin. Sarah invited Amy to keep her company at the Eddys' château in Chatou, a suburb of Paris. She also rented an apartment in Paris and provided a Steinway for Amy's use during the visit.

Amy dutifully reported all her adventures back to her siblings in letters, as she had done so many years earlier. On the voyage to Europe, she performed in the saloon on board and was delighted when a few ladies asked her if she was "*The* Amy Fay." She also witnessed a burial at sea after a twenty-two-year-old Russian man died of consumption. Having been granted permission to attend the funeral ceremony, Amy described the touching moments when the corpse slipped silently into the sea, the "waves coming up to meet it."[7]

In Brussels, Amy stopped to visit to her old beau, Camille Gurickx. Clearly, there was still affection and attraction there—"after all, one does not replace the old loves"—though he had since married and had a child. They enjoyed a lovely visit, each performing a piece for the other on the piano. While she must have experienced some longing, Amy took a noble view of the situation, writing to Zina that Camille was very successful as a professor at the Royal Conservatory and that New York would have been a "poor exchange" for him. She granted, "His wife, too, suits him a great deal better than I would have done so it is all right. He was stirred up at seeing me again, though, and possibly had some regrets."[8]

To Amy's delight, Sarah Eddy footed the bill for tickets to the Wagner Festival in Berlin, where Amy visited with old friends and her former professor from Cambridge, John Knowles Paine. She also reconnected with her cousin Lillie de Hegermann and spent two enjoyable days with her. Lillie seemed happy for the company, as her husband, the Danish minister to the United States, and children had remained at home in Denmark.

Though Amy must have experienced ongoing disappointment that her brother-in-law Theodore Thomas had not helped her performance career beyond that first concert at the Sanders Theatre, she seemed to thrive in her chosen way of life. She wrote to Kate in 1910, "I have now lived in New York for twenty years and have such a nice circle of friends and acquaintances that I am in a whirl all the while, and experience the greatest difficulty in getting time to write or practice."[9] Her battle with nerves seemed to be in the past, no longer an issue once she focused on her Piano Conversations and performances before less critical audiences. She was clearly well liked among her peers. A 1910 article in the *Musical Observer* stated, "No club woman and no musician in New York is more universally beloved than is Miss Amy Fay."[10]

Norman and Rose moved to New York City, sharing an apartment to make it more affordable. Of the city, Amy wrote, "The enormous skyscrapers really *darken* the air, and hang over one with threatening mien . . . what will become of humanity, for there is a constant river of human beings *pouring* through Broadway *now*."[11] Zina also left Chicago for New York once again, prompting Amy to write that she could not help "regretting that splendid city is to know our family no more!"[12]

Memoirs of Theodore Thomas was published by Moffat, Yard and Company in 1911. Rose dedicated the book to Norman, "the best and truest friend of Theodore Thomas, and the chief promoter of his art."[13] *The Nation* raved that the book was "the most important, the most interesting, the most instructive, the most romantic book ever published on music in America."[14] The *Boston Evening Transcript* was more circumspect, calling it an "adequate and highly sympathetic account by his widow" and leaving the official biographies of Theodore to be written by men.[15] It was not uncommon for widows of famous men to take on the task of writing their husband's memoirs, though they were rarely considered analytical accounts. But friend Daniel Burnham enthused, "Nothing could be better and nothing more surely brings back the essential of the man! The thing has tone and this shows that he was married to a woman who had the soul of an artist as well as he."[16] Russian conductor and composer Wassily Safonoff had high praise as well, saying the book "enchanted me with its charming liveliness, sincere feeling and touching simplicity and love for our noble art."[17]

The family's decision to leave Chicago was validated when, in March 1913, the Orchestral Association offended Rose deeply. Following Theodore's death, the Chicago Orchestra had been renamed the Theodore Thomas Orchestra. However, fearing a different ensemble might claim the name and therefore the prestige of representing the city musically, the trustees adopted the new name Chicago Symphony Orchestra, founded by Theodore Thomas.

Rose wrote to the trustees, with copies of her letter to newspapers, protesting this injustice and expressing her concern that the latter part of the name would surely be dropped in time. Furthermore, Rose reminded them that she had donated Theodore's massive music library to the Orchestral Association with the unstated understanding that the ensemble would bear his name.[18] The Orchestral Association was not to be swayed, however, and the name change went through. Rose's prediction eventually proved correct.

In a letter to John Glessner, Rose succinctly expressed her most fervent desire: "I could not endorse it, because the one and only thing I cared for in life was that the name of Theodore Thomas should go down to posterity on that orchestra."[19]

Rose quickly learned that as a widow, she carried considerably less clout than she had as Theodore's spouse. Whereas once she had enjoyed complete backstage freedom, now even getting seats sometimes proved difficult. A letter from conductor Serge Koussevitzky indicates that the management (likely Boston Symphony Orchestra) refused to honor Rose's request for tickets to his concert.[20] She faced a similar situation years later when she was unable to secure tickets for a program including a composition by John Alden Carpenter, who stewed, "How could they have treated you like that at Symphony Hall! I could kill them all for it, with a smile. Next time, whenever that may be, I'll take you there hand in hand."[21]

Putting distance between her and Chicago, then, was good. But Rose found New York City too noisy, so in 1914, she and Norman moved to Cambridge, renting a home from the Longfellow family on a quiet cul-de-sac at 2 Willard Court.[22] They filled the home with sixteen bookcases containing works by friends Henry Wadsworth Longfellow, Oliver Wendell Homes, and Ralph Waldo Emerson, as well as William Shakespeare, Charles Dickens, Edgar Allan Poe, the Brontë sisters, and a war library of over one hundred volumes. An oil portrait of Bishop Hopkins hung in the dining room. In her bedroom, alongside the sewing machine, typewriter, radio, Brownie camera, and opera glasses, Rose had a .32-caliber pistol.[23] Whether this was for self-protection or left over from Theodore's time is unknown.

Soon Zina moved to Cambridge too, taking rooms in a house just blocks away at 36 Hawthorne Street, after first protesting, "You would be spared seeing an old dame who now has a big waist and hobbles about the rooms."[24] Over fifty years had passed since Zina had begun her married life with Charley in Cambridge. Charley died in Milford, Pennsylvania, in April 1914 with second wife, Juliette, still at his side. The couple was destitute, unable to afford food or medical care. Though his contributions in the fields of logic, statistics, and metaphysics were indisputably brilliant, the scandal of his relationship with Juliette while still married to Zina had ruined his reputation. Zina's lofty dreams for her former husband had not materialized, contributing to her overall feeling of failure. Despite their difficult years together, Zina retained her high opinion of Charley's intellect, publicly referring to him late in her life as "brilliant and profound."[25]

Norman, Rose, and Zina lived within just a few blocks of each other. Also nearby on Hawthorne Street were Kate and Will, who had retired from Champion Iron. The siblings and younger generations were slipping in and out of one another's homes, staying for a few weeks, a few months, or sometimes even longer, their lives intersecting over and over.

A Symphonic Study

1918–1919

Zina's book *New York: A Symphonic Study, in Three Parts* finally saw publication in 1918, but it was hardly a success. She had struggled to find a publisher and eventually found one in the Neale Company, though she had to pay part of the publication cost herself.[1] Part novel, part philosophical diatribe, the rambling manuscript represented her frustrations over the lack of progress for women and her evolving thoughts over the course of the twenty years it had taken to produce. In her prelude, she explained her goal in writing, saying it "has been the underlying motive of my whole life—to rescue my own sex from profanation and ruin." She called out in frustration: "O Waiting Women of the World! Sisters Beloved! AWAKE! UNITE! You have everything to gain. You have nothing to lose but your chains."[2]

After an introductory fictional interlude, Zina expanded on her earlier *Democratic Party* essay and outlined an entire charter for a new political party wherein the American people would uphold the Sisterhood of Woman equally with the Brotherhood of Man. Some ideas were of an ordinary sort: She argued for term limits, equitable taxes, restoring the Bible to public schools, school board reform, and access to playgrounds for all children.

Published just months before the Eighteenth Amendment outlawed liquor, Zina's book spelled out her own ideas about alcohol. Since the Bible allowed wine, Zina did too, much as her bishop grandfather had not condemned slavery. But she felt everyone should sign a temperance pledge that they would use alcohol to brighten and not inebriate. Her perfect society included replacing saloons with "Refreshment Rooms" that offered mild beverages, had dancing and card-playing supervised by proper chaperones, and closed promptly at 11:30. The weekly day of rest should be on Saturday, not Sunday, to align with the Jewish sabbath.

Though *New York: A Symphonic Study* was meant to be her manifesto, her strong negative opinions on Catholics, Blacks, and immigrants provided something to offend everyone. As always, Zina was blunt. Foreigners could apply for naturalization only after they had been in the country twenty-one years and mastered English, nor were they to be in positions of moral influence such as police officers or teachers. Zina was not alone in her fear of immigrants gaining too much power; the nativist movement still had many followers. She demanded the expulsion of all "Asiatics" from the country because of what she perceived to be their condescending attitudes toward women, and she called for the prosecution of Mormon polygamists. Zina suggested public hangings for rapists, pornographers, and pedophiles. She decried the use of nude models and near nudity onstage and in newspapers.

All her life, religion had been a source of comfort for Zina, an absolute right. And late in life, Zina had become a Congregationalist, indicating she still grappled to find religious answers. In the prelude to her book, she wrote that what she found in the Bible was "at once perfectly beautiful, beautifully perfect, and utterly, absolutely, infinitely satisfying."[3] She went on to offer her own interpretation of aspects of the Bible, postulating that the Holy Ghost had been a woman.

After twenty years of work, the reception of her published book, her manifesto, was a profound disappointment. Amy celebrated and cheered Zina's persistence, writing, "I am delighted it is out! Never say die!"[4] But others were less enthused. Niece Amy Fay Stone said, "The first part is tremendously interesting, but after she got to page 500 and something, I think she ought to have stopped and called that one book, and then started another for the other things she wanted to get out of her system."[5] Zina's final offering, so long in the making and meant to cement her legacy in women's reform, was met with scant interest, further proof that she had been left on the sidelines.

Now eighty-two, Zina's crippling rheumatism had become so painful she was barely able to walk or hold a book. Her younger siblings worried about her, took her to doctors, and helped with expenses. In 1917, Kate wrote to a daughter that she had to give up her symphony tickets to cover Zina's medical payments, though this seems unlikely, given the Stones' comfortable existence.[6] The siblings shared the burden of shuttling her from one facility to another, searching for any solution.[7] Zina, in pain and depressed, was not always gracious about the help. In a letter to Amy, Zina stated, "I don't feel that Rose & Kate are my sisters anymore. They are society swells."[8]

While Kate and Rose had well-appointed households, numerous china services, sterling silver dinnerware, and Persian rugs, Zina and Amy lived in rented rooms with few belongings of value. Kate's diamond earrings were appraised at $1,000 in 1928 (equivalent to $18,000 in 2025), and she owned a Steinway grand piano. Rose's Steinway was more modest, an upright, but her collection of fine jewelry rivaled Kate's. Theodore had outfitted her well with a variety of valuable rings, including sapphire, ruby, diamond, and pearl.[9] Zina and Amy, on the other hand, were always on the search for cheaper lodgings, moving every few years whenever a better opportunity presented itself.

The more well-to-do siblings were supporting those less financially comfortable. Whereas Kate and Will were the wealthiest of the family, particularly after Will retired from Champion Iron and sold his shares quite profitably, the sisters' resentment fell primarily on Rose. A few years earlier, Kate and Zina had tried to persuade her to use the $25,000 Norman had given her as a wedding gift as a buy-in for Laura's son Nelson Smith (then in his early forties and a father of two) to go into business. But Rose was reluctant to part with her nest egg, answering that her duty was to keep what she had to provide for herself, Zina, Amy, Norman, and Lily, if needed.[10] She doled out her money carefully, always concerned it would not be enough. That Rose occasionally traveled to the warmer climate in Florida to stay with friends added to her sisters' animosity.

Amy had problems of her own. After a successful teaching and performing career, she began losing her memory and, with it, first her livelihood and eventually her cheery demeanor. The siblings persuaded her, despite Amy's strong resistance, to move to the Cambridge area so they could help look after her. In a letter to a daughter, Kate complained that Amy would often appear unannounced and play the piano for hours, "till I felt as if I could not endure it another moment. She can't know how badly she plays." She continued, "Amy says the same things over and over and while I am awfully sorry for her and wish to heavens there was anything I could do for her, that does not make the situation any easier to bear and Rose gets in greatest despair over it."[11]

In the summers, Rose brought Amy with her to Felsengarten until she was unable to care for her there anymore. Amy, likely bitterly aware that her productive days were behind her, railed against the restrictions she felt Rose placed on her. Laura worried, "If only Amy does not become violent, as I fear she may. She hates Rose so bitterly—no such esclandre has yet happened in our family, but with five generations of insanity behind it, it wouldn't surprise me if Amy went as some of the others have done."[12] Amy lived with Rose and Norman briefly in 1919, but the tensions were more than anyone could bear.

It did not help that Norman's career had fizzled out. After the typewriter fiasco, he had various minor misadventures with a printing press invention, an airplane manufacturing company, and an electrical power company. He did, however, find satisfaction in writing. His first foray consisted of a well-received four-part series for *The Outlook* magazine in 1909, in which he dispensed his hard-won business advice in a charming, casual style. In 1912, he published his first book, *Big Business and Government*, through Moffat, Yard and Company.

Always interested in the newest gadgets and inventions, Norman became interested in aviation. When in France to sell his typewriter business, Norman had attended an aviation meet, where he met several aviators. His calling card appears in the Wright brothers' archives, indicating he at least attempted to connect with them. He even began investigations into manufacturing Bleriot airplanes, but patent restrictions held by the Wright brothers prevented him from doing so.[13]

Rose shared Norman's fascination with aviation, in 1914 sending Orville Wright a photograph of terns in flight, for which he appeared grateful, responding, "The picture is most interesting because it shows the birds with wings and legs extended in almost every conceivable direction. I think that there is no question but that birds use both the movements of the wings and the legs in maintaining equilibrium. One rarely sees a picture showing the various positions of the birds' wings as shown in the picture you sent me."[14]

While summering at Felsengarten, Rose had the opportunity to go up in an airplane to see the White Mountains from above. Her niece Madeline dates this as 1908–9; if true, that would be remarkably early. A local friend, William Dickson, a vice president of U.S. Steel and an amateur poet, recorded the event in a rollicking five-page rhyme titled "How Rose Arose." These lines from the poem make clear his affection for Rose, allude to her reckless driving, and indicate that she was able to fly around a cliff known locally as the Old Man of the Mountain:

> She's an all-a-round sport and has run a Tin Lizzie
> In a manner that's made all the countryside dizzy.
> She has hypnotized every susceptible male,
> Else the rest of her life she'd have spent in a jail.
> But breaking of speed laws and bursting of tires
> And wrestling with air-pumps and wrenches and pliers,
> Had at last become irksome: she wanted some thrills
> This coasting down valleys and climbing up hills
> Was all very well, Rose remarked with a sigh;
> (Here's the secret—our Rosie was pining to fly.)[15]

Old Age

1920

LAURA MATILDA FAY SMITH WAS the first of the adult siblings to die, passing on July 3, 1920, at the age of seventy-nine. A delivery boy from the bakery, coming in with bread, found her "sitting on the floor beneath an open window, leaning back against the wall, her eyes closed and hands crossed over her chest, a perfectly cozy position with no appearance of suffering."[1]

Hers had not been an easy life. The most conservative of all the sisters, Laura had embraced the Victorian ideal of True Womanhood, refusing to embrace change even when the toil of her domestic duties overwhelmed her. Her body was buried in the Pine Ridge Cemetery at Saranac Lake.[2]

Remarkably, five months earlier, Zina had said her goodbyes to Laura. Laura had come to visit Zina for her eighty-fourth birthday and, when parting, mentioned they might not see each other again, a sentiment familiar to aging siblings. In a prescient letter to Laura the next day, thanking her for the visit, Zina philosophized:

> No two people could have been more unlike than our dear parents. Mama all nerves and Papa without any. Mama all self-confidence, Papa all self-distrust. Mama all blazing gifts, Papa quiet consistent talent—and so throughout. It is not surprising if one or more of their children have been unable to achieve unity with themselves—as, for instance, myself. I have always been at

> cross purposes and so my life is a failure. I am often so crushed with the retrospect of my shortcomings and negatives that words cannot express it. I feel like those winter trees so overloaded with snow that their branches break. You, dearest, were always so loving and loyal to my unworthy self! God bless you for all those years of unfaltering affection, and in a brighter life, help me to return it. Fare thee well, Mama's little ray of sunshine! You have gone smiling through the world, may you go smiling out of it.[3]

There were, however, also family moments to celebrate. Several of Lily's and Kate's children married and had offspring of their own, bringing grandchildren into the fold and many more opportunities for family gatherings. And in the multigenerational back-and-forth, in-again-out-again relationships of the family, there was one major surprise in 1922, when Norman, age seventy-four, finally shed his bachelor status and married. His bride, Lillian Hale, had recently graduated from Radcliffe, earning a degree in French in 1920. She was a talented painter, though only for her own enjoyment. The sisters expressed concern over the couple's thirty-plus-year age difference, particularly when Lillian had a miscarriage the following year. Kate wrote to her daughter Margot: "Imagine their having a baby. I confess I was rather disgusted about it since Norman is 74 and she 41."[4]

While the older siblings were on the decline, Rose had fully hit her stride. She maintained her friendships with many musicians and added other famous people to her guest book and list of correspondents, including Oscar-winning actor George Arliss, whom she met through his work with the National Anti-Vivisection Society of Chicago; ornithologist Bradford Torrey; and John Pershing, general of the U.S. Armies, with whom she discussed a possible new leader for the Army Band. She met polar explorers Roald Amundsen and Robert Peary when they lectured on their most recent adventures.

One of the greatest events of Rose's life happened in September 1922, on the occasion of her seventieth birthday, when she was honored in Los Angeles by the National Federation of Musical Clubs. Unaware of the grand festivities being staged, Rose had planned to go visit Kate's daughter Margot in San Francisco after attending part of the conference. However, the events unrolled over a four-day period and were beyond Rose's wildest expectations.

A centerpiece of the visit was a luncheon on Rose's birthday at the Ambassador Hotel, with composer, novelist, and film director Rupert Hughes serving as toastmaster, a welcome address by the Los Angeles mayor, and performances by two small choirs. Three days later, members of the Los Angeles Philharmonic performed a concert in her honor at the Hollywood Bowl. She received a bouquet of flowers and a standing ovation, accolades usually bestowed on Theodore but not Rose.

A local reporter offered this description on the front page of the *Los Angeles Evening Express*: "The years have been gracious to her, for she looks hardly past 50, not the septuagenarian. There burns a wonderful light in her eyes. They are smiling eyes, radiating eyes, eyes that have seen a vision, which still hold this image, yet also far-seeing eyes."[5] The visit also offered Rose her first radio spot, as she went on KHJ Radio to thank the organizers for their hospitality and talked about the bright musical future for California.[6]

On the train back to Massachusetts, Rose wrote apologetically to Margot, explaining why she hadn't appeared for her planned visit: "You did not know what a distinguished old auntie you had—and neither did I! It seems, however, that the musical clubs all over America celebrated my birthday each in its own town, and when Los Angeles captured me in person, not only the musical clubs of Southern California, but the Chamber of Commerce, the Artistic and Literary Men's Club, the Orpheus Club, and the Symphony orchestra, entertained me as a guest of honor." After a description of the events, Rose concluded, "[I] heard the most surprising account of my own achievements and national importance—until this trip quite unknown to me but delightfully flattering to my vanity."[7]

Back in Cambridge, Zina's condition rapidly deteriorated, her rheumatism so debilitating that her brother and sisters decided to move her to a nursing facility in Watertown. In the spring of 1923, Zina suffered a series of small strokes that affected her speech, limiting her ability to communicate clearly, something that must have been tremendously difficult for this determined woman.[8] But at eighty-seven, her strength was failing, and perhaps she was simply too tired to care.

Harriet Melusina Fay Peirce died quietly on April 28, 1923, with family at her bedside. At a time when it was unbecoming for women to be outspoken, Zina had been a force, challenging society's mores through her own unceasing drive for success. Only twenty when her beloved, admired mother died, Zina dedicated her life to redefining a woman's role, surely a noble undertaking. Her bitterness and disappointment—exacerbated by a difficult, probably abusive marriage—only increased over the years, as the women's movement grew in directions other than those she had suggested. Zina clearly felt she had failed, but her efforts were beneficial in challenging the norms, broadening the conversation, and investigating options. Though she explored the edges of gender discrimination, Zina was unable to fully break out of her belief in a separate sphere for women. Zina's solutions to problems often involved the exclusion of other parties, such as immigrants, different races, and those less fortunate. She was a complicated individual, and in the end, her xenophobia worked against her hopes for mass acceptance of her ideals.

Zina had surely undervalued her contributions to her siblings. Following Emily's death, Zina held the household together. After moving to Cambridge, she served as the driving force behind getting her siblings out of St. Albans and more fully educated. She likely placed Rose into Longfellow's school. She submitted Amy's letters for publication, leading to *Music-Study in Germany* and the piano career that followed. Zina probably was also the impetus behind several of her sisters' marriages: Laura's husband, Frank, had been a friend of Zina's, and her boardinghouse played a vital role in the relationships with Theodore Thomas and Lily's husband, Harry Wilmerding. Zina, the eldest sister, orchestrated their lives.

It had been Zina's wish to be cremated, and Norman and his new wife, Lillian, scattered her ashes on top of Fairfield Hill in St. Albans, which had views of both the mountains and the bay.[9] Her accomplishments merited an obituary in *The Boston Globe*, which noted, "She was one of the earlier supporters of cooperative housekeeping and had written articles upon that subject. She was instrumental in having preserved in New York the Edgar Allan Poe House and an old tavern where George Washington is said to have made his farewell address."[10]

Zina's interest in historical preservation had been but one aspect of the Fay siblings' patriotism. After Kate and Rose went to hear flying ace Eddie Rickenbacker speak when he came to Boston,

Kate wrote, "Rose is so deeply interested in everything concerning aviation in particular and the war in general."[11] Rose devoted countless volunteer hours to the Soldiers' and Sailors' Club of Boston, a free clubhouse where servicemen could relax when off duty. Rose served as hostess, hat checker, or just a friendly ear for the soldiers who came to visit. In her capacity as volunteer with the club, she became friends with Lieutenant Colonel Paul-Jean-Louis Azan, an officer sent by the French government to teach methods of modern trench warfare at the Harvard officers' training unit. Azan was so impressed by Rose that he extended an invitation to her to visit him at Tlemcen, Algeria, then a French colony.

So in 1924, at age seventy-two, Rose embarked by herself on a cruise that included France, Italy, Spain, Greece, Egypt, Constantinople, and Palestine.[12] When the ship arrived in Oran, Algeria, she was escorted by a guard of honor inland to Tlemcen. Though no descriptive records of her adventure remain, Norman reported that she had the time of her life.[13]

Rose believed strongly in the power of music to unite and to instill patriotism. At a 1927 convention of the National Federation of Musical Clubs, held in Chicago, she spoke passionately about the connection between the two. Extending a particularly warm welcome to the delegates from the South, who had not been present at the 1893 World's Columbian Exposition, Rose said, "Fighting to bring back seceded States is not at all the same thing as preventing them from wishing to secede, and it is my firm conviction that the NFMC can do this better than any other agency, because it draws together the women from every State and section of our great country . . . opening our Hearts as hostesses and guests, uniting us through Song and Symphony and holding us together in one great sisterhood. . . . So long as this continues among our women, our men will never draw the sword against each other again."[14]

Once again working safely within the women's sphere, Rose impressed on attendees the power they possessed: "I believe the Federation has a mission which is even greater and more important than creating a propaganda for good music—it is that of creating a nation-wide propaganda of love, sympathy, good fellowship and unity among American women."[15]

Coda

1925–1946

AMY'S CONDITION HAD BEEN GETTING progressively worse; she first experienced memory issues and then worsening dementia. By 1925, she lived in the same care facility where Zina had died. Kate reported that Amy spent her days "sitting in her rocking chair by the window doing nothing." Sadly, Kate told her daughter, "She just sits there with nothing to occupy her, as she seems incapable of doing anything—she is just fading away by slow degrees."[1]

In the end, Amy died much like Zina had, just slipping away. On February 28, 1928, Amelia Müller Fay died, her music done. *The Boston Globe* ran a brief obituary of Amy.[2] In contrast to Zina, Amy had known real success in her lifetime, having chosen a career over a traditional woman's role. Though her failed romances may have caused initial disappointment, there is no indication she regretted opting for music over marriage. Through her writings, teaching, and club work, she paved a smoother path for future female musicians to follow. In almost direct opposition to Zina's trajectory, it was likely Amy's positive outlook and friendly persona that enabled her to make the most of her musical talent.

Norman arranged for twin gravestones for Amy and Zina to be placed near Theodore's gravesite in Mount Auburn Cemetery (though Zina had been cremated). The inscription on the tombstones reads, "They were lovely and pleasant in their lives, / And in their death they were not divided."

Norman also immortalized Amy in a poem he read to the Hopkins clan:

> The rhythm, emotion, insistent refrain,
> The master-musician that beat in her brain.
> Humor, wit, sweetness she had; and her gold
> Ripple-hair many a fairy-tale told.
> . . . .
> Farewell, loved artist! Memory goes a-roaming
> Back to dim parlors and midsummer gloaming,
> Whence unseen keys and showy fingers roll
> Billows of melody over thirsty soul.
> Ballade, Prelude, Fugue, Appassionata—
> Of all the beautiful inamorata—
> How is thy charm delicious to remember,
> As a flame of youth burns down to old-age ember!
> Though thou are past that ultimate dark portal,
> Still dost thou leave us love and art, immortal![3]

Katherine Maria Fay Stone followed just a few months later, dying on May 29, 1928. Kate's interment took place in Mount Auburn Cemetery alongside her husband, Will, who had died in 1921, and not far from her father, Charles. Beautiful, charming, and reserved, Kate was remembered fondly by her three daughters and six grandchildren as an elegant and gentle matriarch. Kate never seemed to question her boundaries as a wife and mother. Perhaps she had a more introverted personality, or maybe her economic status left little incentive to advocate for change. She was determined, however, to provide educational opportunities for her daughters that had not been available during her own childhood.

A few months after Kate's death, Rose went to visit Lily's daughter Katherine in New York and came down with the flu. She grew steadily worse until February, when her friend William Dickson arranged for an ambulance to drive her back to Cambridge.[4] Rose Emily Fay Thomas died in her Cambridge home, surrounded by family and friends, on April 19, 1929, Patriots' Day. Exactly 154 years earlier, her ancestor Samuel Prescott had completed his Midnight Ride.

To honor Rose's volunteer work with the Soldiers' and Sailors' Club, she was awarded a military funeral, only the fourth woman in the United States to be granted one, and the first from New England. Her pallbearers were representatives of the U.S. Army, Navy, and Marine Corps, in full military dress. The service took place at Christ Church in Cambridge, Rose's casket completely covered in flowers. A brass choir from the Boston Symphony Orchestra played a Bach chorale and the "Ode to Joy" from Beethoven's Ninth Symphony.

Following the service, her funeral party brought Rose's casket to Mount Auburn Cemetery. As an army trumpet player sounded "Taps," her body was lowered into the ground next to her beloved Theodore and near Zina and Amy. Remarkably, Rose, who had been sent away at age four to live with a different family after her mother's death, never shared Zina's bitterness, instead always moving forward with an eye toward how to help.

By 1930, only two Fay siblings remained: Norman and Lily. Norman, eighty-two, living in Cambridge with his wife, Lillian, honored Rose by writing an eleven-page biography for the National Federation of Musical Clubs. A copy eventually found its way to the Library of Congress.

Norman had been busy writing books on various business topics. The foreword of *Labor in Politics, or Class versus Country,* privately printed at a university press in 1920, spoke directly to new women voters, underscoring their importance as voters for the family. Norman appealed to the women keenly alive to their new powers and responsibilities: "The women should have their say in matters so nearly concerning the family; and it is particularly desirable that their conscience and intelligence should be wide awake *now,* at the beginning of their political power. . . . No duty rests more squarely upon the new women-voters than the defence of the family; first by their own right thinking, and afterwards by its enactment into law."[5] It is ironic that in this family of six daughters and one son, the only written statement that remains concerning the Nineteenth Amendment was authored by the male.

Charles Norman Fay died on April 7, 1944, at the age of ninety-six, having outlived his considerably younger wife, Lillian, by two years. He had spent his last few years residing in the Harvard Faculty Club.

Without a doubt, his greatest contribution, historically speaking, was his work in establishing the Chicago (Symphony) Orchestra. An ardent believer in the arts, Norman served as the driving force behind Theodore's decision to start over once again in Chicago.[6] Furthermore, Norman's consistent pressure on the Chicago business community to put their money behind their new ensemble kept the orchestra afloat when it otherwise might have floundered. The Chicago Symphony Orchestra honored him with performances of a Bach chorale and the "Ode to Joy" from Beethoven's Ninth Symphony.

Norman and Lillian were buried in side-by-side graves in Mount Auburn Cemetery, near Theodore, Rose, Amy, and Zina. Norman's grave features a writing pen; Lillian's bears a palette to honor her passion for painting.

That left just Lily, the youngest sibling. After her husband, Harry, died in 1917, Lily moved into an apartment in Manhattan, New York. Here, at the tail end of a quiet life devoted to her family, Lily finally found her public voice, advocating for natural spaces in the city and combating traffic congestion. She was elected a delegate to the Parks Conservation Association, a role that would have pleased her activist sister Zina.[7] Lillian Valeria Fay Wilmerding died on June 16, 1946, at the age of ninety. She was buried in Greenwood Cemetery in Brooklyn, New York, alongside Harry.

The siblings now all having passed, the mantle fell to the nieces, nephews, and new generations to carry on the Fay name and traits. Many of the descendants demonstrated considerable abilities in the skills so abundant in that first generation, particularly in writing and the arts. It is noteworthy that most of the women descendants went on to attend college, an opportunity that had not been available to Zina, Laura, Kate, Amy, Rose, and Lily.

THE FAY WOMEN WERE CAUGHT in between the Victorian era of True Womanhood, when it was considered unbecoming for women to speak up or rock the boat, and the Progressive era, when women were afforded opportunities for higher education, voting rights, public roles, and a wider range of employment. The sisters approached these boundaries in different ways, each according to her personality. And each met with measures of success and failure, depending on her efforts, expectations, and circumstances. Through it all, they were Fays, proud of their ancestry, and they were sisters, lifting one another up as needed and providing support, despite occasional complaints and skirmishes.

A final description of the family comes from Laura, who wrote just before her death, "The Fays had a curious temperament. They were at heart ambitious, but unwilling to pursue their ambitions. They were undemonstrative yet very sensitive—which was evidenced by their extreme consideration for others, and their great respect for public opinion. They were generous to a degree, and yet thrifty and self-denying. Deeply religious, yet tolerant of the creeds of others, and with the dignity that goes with a self-respect that never asserted itself."[8]

Throughout their lives, Zina, Amy, and Rose made valuable contributions to society in the areas of women's reform, improved education for women, music education and women in music, the humane movement, and historical preservation. Perhaps Amy's charm and Rose's gentle compassion allowed them to achieve more success in their fields than did Zina's exclusionary tactics, but every effort was integral to the overall expansion of their spheres and helped move these reforms forward for women and society. And each woman carved a path uniquely her own.

Appendix

Acknowledgments

Notes

Bibliography

Index

Appendix

FAMILY

Zina

Zina continues to inspire scholars interested in domestic feminism, meriting numerous dissertations on her contributions and chapters in several books on the topic. Over a century later, Dolores Hayden wrote in *The Grand Domestic Revolution*, "A woman of extraordinary talent and energy, Peirce displayed great agility in exploiting the weak points of industrial capitalism or consumer cooperation, traditional conceptions of the home or bourgeois feminism. She merged radical ideas of industrial cooperation and conservative approaches to the separateness of women's work because she was seeking a practical economic basis for women's economic self-determination."[1] Her ex-husband, Charles Sanders Peirce, despite his lack of economic or academic success during his lifetime, is broadly considered one of our country's most brilliant philosophers and a founder of the field of pragmatism, alongside his friend William James.

Amy

Amy's eloquent descriptions of Franz Liszt and other prominent musicians in *Music-Study in Germany* are still quoted by modern biographers, her words remaining fresh and lyrical over a century later. Liszt biographer Alan Walker wrote that Amy rendered all other writers "speechless" with her "irreplaceable" prose: "Miss Fay's descriptions of her lessons with Liszt are so famous that they have become part of the folklore surrounding his classes, and it is almost impossible to think of them at all except through her eyes. Her observations are riveting, and widely accessible."[2]

In addition to her collection of letters in *Music-Study in Germany*, Amy's life has been documented in a biography by Margaret McCarthy, who also published a compilation of Amy's letters from 1879 to 1916, as well as numerous articles about her contribution to music education. In 1995, musical historians Robert Dumm and Karen Shaffer summed up Amy's life thus: "As a performer, writer, lecturer, teacher and clubwoman, this extraordinary woman won a significant place in music history for boldly advancing the place of women in music and the place of music in American society."[3]

Rose

The organizations Rose launched, the Anti-Cruelty Society of Chicago and the National Federation of Music Clubs, are still going strong (documented later in this appendix). These groups continue to foster compassion and fellowship, as well as to provide education.

After Rose's death, her friends in Bethlehem, the "Neighborlies," wrote tributes to her, one declaring, "Mrs. Thomas had a genius for friendship. She made and held friends by her own unselfish friendliness. She had devoted friends in every walk of life, of various social station, and of all ages. She was intensely interested in life and in people. She did not grow old in spirit, because her sympathies were always young. She was charitable, liberal, and progressive, yet strong in her convictions and steadfast in her principles. Her mind was appreciative of the finest and noblest things. She was an artist in feeling and expression; and her heart was pure gold."[4] John Glessner, husband of Rose's dear friend Frances, gave her what many still considered "the greatest praise that can be given a woman. She was a good helpmeet for her husband."[5] Rose, traditional in her beliefs about marriage, might have agreed with Glessner's remark. Despite her own considerable accomplishments, being Theodore's wife was the role she most relished.

ORGANIZATIONS

Chicago Symphony Orchestra

The organization founded by Norman and shaped musically by Theodore Thomas is today broadly recognized as one of the finest orchestras in the world. Theodore's commitment to perfection and refined ensemble playing remain hallmarks of the institution. Some historians indicate the orchestra's famous rich, robust brass sound was shaped by its early years in the cavernous Auditorium.[6] Were it not for his relationship with Rose and Norman's persistence, Theodore likely never would have agreed to take on a new orchestra in Chicago. Surely, one would have eventually been founded, but without Theodore at the helm, the ensemble would have borne a different signature sound and ethic.

The orchestra's 2022–23 annual report lists operating expenses for the year as $77 million. It is difficult to comprehend how Theodore ran his own orchestra single-handedly for so many years, managing not only the conducting but also the hiring/firing, programming, advertising, booking, and operational details (particularly of the extensive train tours). Today the Chicago Symphony Orchestra Association employs over 120 administrative members, including specialists in education, donor relations, archival collections, marketing, and artistic administration. The ensemble now numbers 106 members, up from 60 at its founding. Though the orchestra is moving closer to gender parity (in 2024, 36 percent of the musicians were women), the lower brass remains a male bastion, and the organization has not yet had a female music director. In 2020, Marin Alsop was named chief conductor of the orchestra at its summer residency in Ravinia Festival. The first African American musician was hired in 2002. The string section was once almost entirely of German descent, but now many members are of Asian heritage, reflecting exceptional educational institutions abroad.

Theodore's Orchestra Hall, remodeled in 1997 at a cost of $110 million, has been renamed Symphony Center. The women's locker room, greatly enlarged during the renovation, had to be augmented again a few years later. Theodore's name is still on the facade of the building, which is designated a national historic landmark.

Helping ensure a future for the organization is the Theodore Thomas Society, a planned giving program for donors leaving money to the orchestra in their estates. Retiring orchestra members receive a Theodore Thomas Medal.

Anti-Cruelty

The Anti-Cruelty Society of Chicago, now just Anti-Cruelty, recently celebrated its 125th anniversary. It runs two separate shelters in Chicago. According to the 2022 Annual Report, 4,263 animals were adopted in one year. Though exact figures are not available, the number of animals rescued over 125 years must be staggering. In addition, Anti-Cruelty continues its education efforts and community outreach. In 2022, 6,276 dog/cats were spayed or neutered, 145,046 animal meals were distributed for families struggling to feed their pets, and volunteers offered over 61,000 hours of free labor. Anti-Cruelty's planned giving program is called the Rose Fay Thomas Society.

National Federation of Music Clubs

The nationwide organization that Rose first suggested in 1893 and all three sisters helped found in 1898 is now the largest nonprofit organization in the country dedicated to music education and performance in the United States. Over ninety thousand members are involved in programs, competitions, community outreach, and education. It is chartered by the U.S. Congress. Continuing Rose's belief in the unifying power of music, in 1949, the NFMC was the first music organization accredited a nongovernmental organization of the United Nations as a participant in its Department of Public Information (now the Department of Global Communications). The NFMC offers over $750,000 in scholarship money to young composers, performers, educators, and music therapists. Rose is still considered the godmother of the organization. Contributors of more than $1,000 become Rose Fay Thomas Fellows and receive bronze medallions bearing Rose's likeness.

Amateur Musical Club of Chicago

The women's musical club that Amy and Rose helped champion continues to foster musical appreciation and education in Chicago. Now called the Musicians Club of Women, the nonprofit organization offers performance opportunities for its members through monthly classical concerts. Its scholarship programs award $50,000 annually for talented artists.

Woman's Education Association/Fay House/Radcliffe College

Though Zina was involved only at its inception, the WEA went on to help form Radcliffe and Simmons Colleges and a chemical lab for women at MIT; provide educational fellowships, cooking classes, nursing programs, and traveling libraries; and offer summer programs at what eventually became the Marine Biological Laboratory at Woods Hole.[7] Its members also pushed for the establishment of nursery schools and kindergartens and initiated reform in the local public schools.

After purchasing the Fay House from Aunt Maria Fay in 1885, the Society for the Collegiate Instruction of Women ran classes out of the former home for many years, colloquially known as the Harvard

Annex. Thus the Fay House, containing classrooms, offices, a library, and a botanical laboratory, became the initial building owned by Radcliffe, one of the nation's first elite women's colleges. Chartered as the all-women Radcliffe College in 1894, it was and still is a fitting use of a site that had hosted so many spirited discussions.[8] Aside from a few years during World War II, women did not gain access to Harvard undergraduate classes until the 1970s. Other colleges, similarly concerned about coeducation, launched parallel women's institutions, such as Barnard for Columbia in 1889 and Pembroke for Brown in 1891. In many cases, it was not until 1972, when Title IX outlawed gender discrimination, that the segregated admissions regulations were lifted.[9]

With enough time, some things come full circle. In 2000, the Captain Jonathan Fay Prize, established in 1907 by Uncle Storey to honor an outstanding female senior at Radcliffe, was suspended as administrators deliberated about how to proceed. Because of Radcliffe's 1999 merger with Harvard, it had become unfair to give the $5,000 prize exclusively to women. Henceforth, both men and women are considered eligible for the award.

SITES

The Fay home still stands on South Main Street in St. Albans, Vermont. The family church, St. Luke's Episcopal, whose construction was overseen by Charles, has been in continuous operation with an active congregation. The stained-glass window to honor Emily, the pulpit Sophronia donated in Charles's honor, and the baptismal font given by Maria Fay are all well kept and enjoyed.

Felsengarten, in the White Mountains of New Hampshire, is a private family home. The Chicago home at 43 Bellevue has been converted to condominiums. Zina and Charley's former home on Arrow Street in Cambridge features a historical marker that mentions Zina but not Charley.

In 2021, the administration at the Rock Point School in Burlington, Vermont, took down a portrait of its founder, Bishop John Henry Hopkins, to protest his attitudes toward the institution of slavery and hung a Black Lives Matter banner right below the engraved "Bishop Hopkins Hall."[10] The current Episcopal bishop of Vermont is an African American woman, appointed in 2019.

Similarly, various sites named after Zina's teacher, Louis Agassiz, have been renamed because of his scientific racism, though over a dozen species of animals still bear his name, as well as several mountain peaks, a glacial lake, a crater on Mars, and an asteroid.

WOMEN'S REFORM

In the first installment of Zina's *Atlantic Monthly* articles about cooperative housekeeping, she wrote, "I have come to the conclusion that entirely too much is expected of women."[11] Over 150 years later, the statement still rings true. America Ferrera's impassioned speech in the *Barbie* movie rang true to millions of women attempting to uphold societal expectations in terms of motherhood, career, and physical appearance. It is still an impossible combination.

Though the sisters would surely be amazed at the many opportunities available to today's women, it continues to be a difficult road. While the domestic ideal of True Womanhood has been left behind, the guilt of abandonment still resides in many women.

Parity is still elusive. According to the World Bank in 2024, globally, women earn an average of 77 cents for every dollar earned by men. For rural women of color, it is even less. The same report shows that, on average, compared with their male counterparts, women spend 2.4 more hours per day on unpaid household and childcare work and enjoy only 64 percent of the legal protections.[12]

Progress toward parity has been achingly slow. The Equal Rights Amendment, introduced in 1923, which would ensure wage equality and equal representation, has still not been adopted as of 2025, notwithstanding President Biden's declaration. With issues like reproductive rights and bodily autonomy questions on the table, equal rights for women is once again—or, rather, still—up for discussion. In what could be a giant leap backward, legislation proposed in 2025 may make it more difficult for married women to vote.

Considerable work remains to be done on many fronts. Diverse voices and assorted techniques will be required to further break down the gender spheres and improve opportunities for women. May we take inspiration from the Fay sisters and each do our part, using our personal strengths, personalities, and beliefs.

Acknowledgments

ROSE SURELY WOULD HAVE UNDERSTOOD what it took to write this book. A biographer herself, she wrote of her experiences writing Theodore's memoirs, "It has been no easy matter to piece together—from programmes and prospectuses, from the scrap-books of friends, from old magazine articles and musical encyclopedias, and from a hundred other nondescript sources—the continuous narrative of his life."[1] Rose turned to family and friends for help; I too have many people to thank.

I am indebted to Sylvia Wright Mitarachi, Kate's granddaughter. Sylvia was a talented writer who undertook to write Zina's biography. An essayist and editor for *Harper's Bazaar,* and author of *A Shark-Infested Rice Pudding,* Sylvia was a graduate of Bryn Mawr College and did much of her research while a fellow at the Bunting Institute at Radcliffe College. She died in 1981, her manuscript not yet complete. Her files and drafts at the Schlesinger Library were an invaluable resource; it almost felt like cheating to have all this material already organized. The depth of her research into Zina was simultaneously inspiring and humbling. Thanks to Sylvia's widower, Paul Mitarachi, and Barbara Kapp for sharing their time and stories, and to Fay descendants Chris King and David Fay Smith for the photographs. I hope Sylvia would be pleased with this effort to tell the sisters' stories, though surely her version would have been more lyrical.

I owe a debt of gratitude to the incredible staff at the Schlesinger Library, who handled my many requests with grace. Time and again they went above and beyond, particularly during the COVID shutdown. My days spent at Schlesinger were filled with delightful discovery—including a lock of Amy's hair—dampened only by the news of the overturning of *Roe v. Wade* on my final day there. It felt surreal to be in a center of women's history on such a historic day. We went right from there to a march on the commons, careening from the past to the present. May the future hold better.

Alongside Sylvia Wright Mitarachi, I must acknowledge writer Margaret William McCarthy. Her research into Amy Fay and her efforts to document Amy's contributions to music education and women in music were critical to this book. Not only did Sister Margaret gather and publish Amy's American letters, but she also wrote numerous articles and a book about Amy's life. We often feel we are speaking into a void. Margaret, I heard you. Thank you.

Bill Tyre, executive director at the Glessner House in Chicago, provided Frances Glessner's journals, which were research gold, as well as photographs from Felsengarten and other materials. His knowledge of Chicago history is deep and wide; I have benefited from many of his Zoom events and newsletters. The Glessners and Thomases were closely intertwined, and I hope Bill feels that I did the story justice. His opinion matters to me.

Ellie Carlson, domestic historian extraordinaire, informed me on Victorian housekeeping practices, helped me date photographs, and as always, made me laugh. Her talents and her friendship are such gifts.

In St. Albans, I am grateful to Deacon Jim at St. Luke's Episcopal Church, for his patience and kindness, and to Simon Walter at the St. Albans Museum. My gratitude also goes to Frank Villella at the Chicago Symphony Orchestra, Tracy Elliott at Anti-Cruelty, Linda Hermann at the Bethlehem Heritage Society, and Kate Hanson Plass at the Longfellow House. Archive staff at the Art Institute of Chicago, Newberry Library, Chicago History Museum, Evanston History Center, Massachusetts Historical Society, Peirce Edition Project at Indiana University, University of Michigan, University of Vermont, Rijksmuseum, and Houghton Library all provided helpful material. Archivists are such remarkable people; instead of eye rolls, they responded with encouragement. The librarians at the Elmhurst Public Library were able to track down materials from all corners with the aid of the interlibrary loan system, and I am grateful. Thanks to Sara Barrena at the Universidad de Navarra and Brianna Sanchez at Texas Tech's Institute for Studies in Pragmaticism for help with photographs.

Waves of insecurity and uncertainty are not uncommon in a project like this. I appreciate the many readers of *Edith: The Rogue Rockefeller McCormick* who encouraged me to write another book, to keep at it, to tell these women's stories. Your kind words rang in my ears, helping me stay at the keyboard despite my doubts.

I am appreciative of the support of my women's roundtable group from Biographers International. Our monthly Zooms these last few years have been a lifeline, a source of both knowledge and inspiration. In particular, Theresa Kaminski gently pointed me toward useful sources and shared some of her voluminous knowledge of women's history.

Sylvia Frank Rodrigue at Southern Illinois University Press is the type of editor all writers should be fortunate enough to work with. She always knows how to improve a manuscript while simultaneously offering encouragement. Her expertise, both historical and editorial, is invaluable. The readers involved in the peer-review process provided excellent suggestions to make this book better. SIU Press has such a talented staff, and I am grateful for their improvements all along the way, from permissions to editing, production, design, and marketing. Special callouts to Joyce Bond, for her eagle-eyed copyediting and fact-checking, and to Galen Schroeder, for careful indexing. *Sisters of Influence* was in good hands.

While in the process of writing her novel, Zina often begged out of social engagements with family and friends, explaining that she needed to work on her book. To my own friends, badly neglected while I worked on this manuscript, thank you for your understanding and patience.

In the end, this story is about family. It is about how siblings are there for each other, no matter what the circumstances. I am so fortunate to have my own siblings, Claudia and Peter, who, along with their families, provide support and serve as reminders of what it means to be a Friederici. My family is my center.

To Jim and the past and present members of the orchestra: My hat is off to you for your never-ending quest for perfection. Surely Theodore would be proud.

To Annie, thanks for your many days in the archives with me, photographing hundreds of letters; for your constructive comments; and for your constant support. To Greg, your belief in this project helped buoy me when I wavered in my confidence. May the two of you always be there for each other, no matter where life might take you. I'll be cheering you on from home.

Notes

CHARLES AND EMILY

1. Sylvia Wright Mitarachi, "The Life of Melusina Fay Peirce," 1990, Mitarachi Papers, Series 1.1, 3, Schlesinger Library, Radcliffe Institute for Advanced Study, Harvard University.

2. Margaret William McCarthy, *Amy Fay: America's Notable Woman of Music* (Warren, MI: Harmonie Park, 1995), 4–6.

3. Laura Fay Smith, "Charlotte Emily Hopkins," Mitarachi Papers, Series 2.

4. Smith, "Charlotte Emily Hopkins."

5. Mitarachi, "Melusina," Series 1.1, 1.

6. Mitarachi, "Melusina," Series 1.1, 2.

7. Charlotte Emily Fay Poems, Mitarachi Papers, Series 2.

8. "Child Mortality Rate (Under Five Years Old) in the United States, from 1800 to 2020," Statista, June 2019, https://www.statista.com/statistics/1041693/united-states-all-time-child-mortality-rate/.

9. Mitarachi, "Melusina," Series 1.1, 5.

10. Charlotte Emily Fay Poems.

11. Mitarachi, "Melusina," Series 1.1, 7–8.

CHURCHES AND CHILDREN

1. Stephen Elliott, "Montpelier Institute," Archives of the Diocese of Georgia, http://archives.georgiaepiscopal.org/?page_id=1031.

2. Elliott, "Montpelier Institute."

3. Smith, "Charlotte Emily Hopkins."

4. Khalil Gibran Muhammad, "The Barbaric History of Sugar in America," *New York Times*, August 14, 2019.

5. Charles Fay to Harriet Howard Fay, May 29, 1844, Stone-Jackson Family Papers, 1819–54, Massachusetts Historical Society.

6. Charles Fay to Harriet Howard Fay, May 29, 1844.

7. R. E. Hood, "From a Headstart to a Deadstart: The Historical Basis for Black Indifference Toward the Episcopal Church, 1800–1860," *Historical Magazine of the Protestant Episcopal Church* 51, no. 3 (September 1982): 278.

8. Deaths, *Burlington Weekly Free Press*, October 4, 1844, 3.

9. Charlotte Emily Fay Poems.

10. Smith, "Charlotte Emily Hopkins."

11. W. S. B. Mathews, ed., *A Hundred Years of Music in America: An Account of Musical Effort in America During the Past Century* (Chicago: G. L. Howe, 1889), 137.
12. Mitarachi, "Melusina," 14.
13. Emily Fay to Melusina Hopkins, October 28, 1848, Mitarachi Papers, Series 3.
14. C. Norman Fay to cousin Emily, May 3, 1930, Mitarachi Papers, Series 2.
15. Erika Janik, *Marketplace of the Marvelous: The Strange Origins of Modern Medicine* (Boston: Beacon, 2014), 132.
16. C. Norman Fay to cousin Emily, May 3, 1930.
17. Smith, "Charlotte Emily Hopkins."
18. Charlotte Emily Fay Poems.
19. Smith, "Charlotte Emily Hopkins."
20. *Reflections: The Bicentennial of St. Albans, Vt., 1788–1988* (St. Albans, VT: St. Albans Historical Society, 1988), 26.
21. Mitarachi, "Melusina," 30.
22. John D'Emilio and Estelle B. Freedman, *Intimate Matters: A History of Sexuality in America* (Chicago: University of Chicago, 1997), 58.
23. Emily Fay to Mrs. Houghton, March 10, 1853, Mitarachi Papers, Series 3.

MAPLESHADE

1. Mitarachi, "Melusina," Series 1.1, 72.
2. Smith, "Charlotte Emily Hopkins."
3. Emily Fay to Amelia Hopkins, October 1848, Stone-Jackson Family Papers, 1819–54.
4. C. Norman Fay to cousin Emily, May 3, 1930.
5. Sylvia Mitarachi with Pauline Stone and Amy Fay Stone, Mitarachi Papers, Series 3.
6. Smith, "Charlotte Emily Hopkins."
7. Judge Fay to Joseph Storey Fay, May 9, 1866, Fay family correspondence, March–December 1840, Fay-Mixter Family Papers, 1775–1962, Massachusetts Historical Society.
8. Charles Fay, Account Book, 1855–61, unpublished, private collection.
9. Fay, Account Book, 1855–61.
10. Fay, Account Book, 1855–61.
11. Amy Fay to Zina Fay, February 12, 1860, Fay Family Papers, Series 1.
12. Mitarachi, "Melusina," Series 1.2, 106.
13. Charles Norman Fay, "Memoir of Rose Fay Thomas," unpublished manuscript, Cambridge, 1939, Library of Congress.
14. Emily Fay to Melusina Hopkins, November 17, 1854, Mitarachi Papers, Series 3.

15. Charles Fay account book, 1855–61.
16. Emily Fay to Melusina Hopkins, October 28, 1848, Mitarachi Papers, Series 3.
17. Mitarachi, "Melusina," Series 1.1, 9.
18. Emily Fay to Melusina Hopkins, November 22, 1848, Mitarachi Papers, Series 3.
19. Melusina Fay Peirce, *Co-operative Housekeeping*, ed. Amanda Webster (McLean, IL: Elderfly, 2020), 85.
20. Emily Fay to Melusina Hopkins, October 28, 1848.
21. Emily Fay to Melusina Hopkins, July 21, 1844, Mitarachi Papers, Series 3.
22. Emily Fay to Zina Fay, November 28, 1854, Mitarachi Papers, Series 2.
23. Mathews, *Hundred Years,* 137.
24. Emily Fay to Melusina Hopkins, March 25, 1849, Mitarachi Papers, Series 3.

SEPARATION

1. Emily Fay to Zina Fay, November 14, 1854, Mitarachi Papers, Series 2.
2. Emily Fay to Zina Fay, November 17, 1854, Mitarachi Papers, Series 2.
3. Emily Fay to Zina Fay, January 10, 1855, Mitarachi Papers, Series 2.
4. Emily Fay to Zina Fay, December 6, 1854, Mitarachi Papers, Series 2.
5. Emily Fay to Zina Fay, January 9, 1855, Mitarachi Papers, Series 2.
6. Christina Hopkinson Baker, *The Story of Fay House* (Cambridge, MA: Harvard University Press, 1929), 102.
7. Baker, *Fay House*, 74.
8. Emily Fay to Zina Fay, December 6, 1854.
9. Barbara Welter, "The Cult of True Womanhood: 1820–1860," *American Quarterly* 18, no. 2, pt. 1 (Summer 1966): 152.
10. Emily Hopkins Fay to Zina Fay, January 17, 1855, Mitarachi Papers, Series 2.
11. Mitarachi, "Melusina," Series 1.1, 55.
12. Mitarachi, "Melusina," Series 1.1, 63.
13. Mitarachi, "Melusina," Series 1.1, 75.
14. Charlotte Emily Fay Poems.
15. C. Norman Fay to cousin Emily, May 3, 1930, Mitarachi Papers, Series 2.
16. Smith, "Charlotte Emily Hopkins."
17. Mitarachi, "Melusina," Series 1.1, 78.
18. Rose Fay Thomas to Amy Stone, July 10, 1901, Mitarachi Papers, Series 2.
19. Amy Fay to Zina Fay, December 24, 1859, Fay Family Papers, Series 1.
20. Melusina Fay Peirce, "Co-operative Housekeeping: IV," *Atlantic Monthly*, February 1869, 162.

SCATTERING

1. "Buried by Bishop Hopkins, Mrs. C. Emily Fay," *Union Register*, September 21, 1856.

2. Smith, "Charlotte Emily Hopkins."

3. *Parish Administrator Manual*, 2013, St. Luke's Episcopal Church, St. Albans, VT, 21.

4. *Parish Administrator Manual*, 21.

5. S. Margaret William McCarthy, *More Letters of Amy Fay: The American Years, 1879–1916* (Detroit: Information Coordinators, 1986), xv.

6. Charles Fay account book, 1855–61.

7. "The Death of Henry Selden," *St. Albans Weekly Messenger*, July 15, 1858, 1.

8. U.S. Census Bureau, 1860 Census, Rochester and St. Albans.

9. Charles Fay account book, 1855–61.

10. Frances Murray, "Henry Rogers Selden," Historical Society of the New York Courts, 2007, https://history.nycourts.gov/figure/henry-rogers-selden/.

11. Fay, "Memoir of Rose Fay Thomas."

12. Mitarachi, "Melusina," Series 1.1, 84.

13. Mitarachi, "Melusina," Series 1.1, 100.

14. Mitarachi, "Melusina," Series 1.2, 101–2.

15. Christoph Irmscher, *Louis Agassiz: Creator of American Science* (New York: Houghton Mifflin, 2013), 285.

16. Zina Peirce to Kate Stone, September 18, 1909, Mitarachi Papers, Series 2.

17. Mitarachi, "Melusina," Series 1.2, 115.

18. *Parish Administrator Manual*.

19. Laura Fay to Zina Fay, March 13, 1860, Mitarachi Papers, Series 2.

20. Mitarachi, "Melusina," Series 1.1, 87–96.

21. Melusina Müller Hopkins to Caspar Hopkins, October 1, 1858, Hopkins Family Papers, 1800–1932, box 2, University of Michigan, William L. Clements Library.

22. Charles Fay to Zina Fay, February 7, 1860, Mitarachi Papers, Series 2.

23. Lucy Allen Paton, *Elizabeth Cary Agassiz: A Biography* (Boston: Houghton Mifflin, 1919), 51.

24. Mitarachi, "Melusina," Series 1.2, 102.

25. L. de Hegermann-Lindencrone, *In the Courts of Memory, 1858–1875* (New York: Harper and Brothers, 1911; POD, Monee, 2022), 1.

26. "An Account of the Early Formation of the Woman's Education Association," Woman's Education Association (WEA) Records, 1871–1935, Massachusetts Historical Society.

27. Paton, *Elizabeth Cary Agassiz*, 47–48, 38–39; "Address of the Chairman, Thomas Wentworth Higginson," *Proceedings of the Cambridge Historical Society* 2 (1906–7): 77, https://historycambridge.org/wp-content/uploads/2017/06/Proceedings-Volume-2-1906-1907.pdf.

28. Mitarachi, "Melusina," Series 1.2, 104.

29. 175th Anniversary Brochure, St. Luke's Episcopal Church, St. Albans, VT.

30. Union Church Parish Records, St. Luke's Episcopal Church.

31. Michelle Arnosky Sherburne, *Abolition & the Underground Railroad in Vermont* (Charleston, SC: History Press, 2013), 50.

32. 175th Anniversary Brochure.

33. Sherburne, *Abolition*, 96–97.

34. John Henry Hopkins, *The Life of the Late Right Reverend John Henry Hopkins* (New York: F. J. Huntington, 1873; POD, Alpha Editions, 2021), 335.

35. "Address of the Chairman," 78.

"I DO"

1. Paul K. Conkin, *Puritans & Pragmatists: Eight Eminent American Thinkers* (New York: Dodd, Mead, 1968; Bloomington: Indiana University Press, 1976), 193.

2. Joseph Brent, *Charles Sanders Peirce: A Life* (Bloomington: Indiana University Press, 1993), 37.

3. Ralph Barton Perry, *The Thought and Character of William James* (Cambridge, MA: Harvard University Press, 1948), 69.

4. Brent, *Peirce*, 40–41.

5. Charles Sanders Peirce journal, January 19, 1861, Mitarachi Papers, Series 2.

6. Mitarachi, "Melusina," Series 1.2, 129.

7. Charles Sanders Peirce journal, December 27, 1861.

8. Brent, *Peirce*, 61.

9. "Account of the Early Formation."

10. Kenneth Lane Ketner, *His Glassy Essence: An Autobiography of Charles Sanders Peirce* (Nashville: Vanderbilt University Press, 1998), 241.

11. Charles Jerome Hopkins program notes, Fay Family Papers, Series 4.

12. Mitarachi, "Melusina," Series 1.1, 66.

13. Zina Fay to Charles Jerome Hopkins, June 7, 1856, Mitarachi Papers, Series 2

14. Mitarachi, "Melusina," Series 1.1, 29–31.

15. Charles Jerome Hopkins journal, July 22, 1862, Mitarachi Papers, Series 2.

16. Roger Ward, *Peirce & Religion: Knowledge, Transformation and the Reality of God* (Lexington Books, 2018), 1.

17. Brent, *Peirce*, 62.

18. Norma Pereira Atkinson, "An Examination of the Life and Thought of Zina Fay Peirce, an American Reformer and Feminist" (PhD diss., Ball State University, 1983), 23.

19. Charles Jerome Hopkins journal, June 25, 1863.

20. Charles Jerome Hopkins journal, October 16, 1862.

21. Charles Jerome Hopkins to Zina Peirce, May 5, 1867.

22. Mitarachi, "Melusina," Series 1.2, 153.

NEW HORIZONS

1. Fay, "Memoir of Rose Fay Thomas."

2. Lawrence Goldstone, *Drive! Henry Ford, George Selden, and the Race to Invent the Auto Age* (New York: Ballantine, 2016), 338.

3. Ida Husted Harper, *The Life and Work of Susan B. Anthony* (Indianapolis: Bowen-Merrill, 1899), 1:432–45.

4. Goldstone, *Drive!*, 23.

5. Fay, "Memoir of Rose Fay Thomas."

6. Mitarachi, "Melusina," Series 1.1, 171.

7. Nicholas Basbanes, *Cross of Snow: A Life of Henry Wadsworth Longfellow* (New York: Knopf, Doubleday, 2020), 353.

8. "The Secret," Henry Wadsworth Longfellow Family Papers, 1768–1972 (bulk dates 1825–1950), Series 3, Edith Longfellow Dana Papers, 1857–1949, Longfellow House Washington's Headquarters, Cambridge, MA.

9. Henrietta Dana Skinner, *An Echo from Parnassus: Girlhood Memories of Longfellow and His Friends* (New York: J. H. Sears, 1928), 87.

10. Skinner, *Echo*, 95.

CAMBRIDGE

1. *Reflections: Bicentennial of St. Albans*, 7.

2. Brent, *Peirce*, 61.

3. Charles Jerome Hopkins journal, September 13, 1863.

4. Michelle Arnosky Sherburne, *The St. Albans Raid: Confederate Attack on Vermont* (Charleston, SC: History Press, 2014), 56–75.

5. William Warner White, Vermont, U.S. Wills and Probate Estate Files, Wheeler, Horace-Wightman, Adah, 1850–1920 (1862).

6. Amy Fay to Zina Peirce, April 1870, Fay Family Papers, Series 1.

7. Madeline Smith, "Portraits of My Aunts," n.d., 14, Schlesinger Library.

8. Smith, "Portraits," 15.

9. Charles Jerome Hopkins journal, September 25, 1863.

10. Charles Jerome Hopkins journal, May 10, 1863.

11. Charles Jerome Hopkins journal, May 10, 1863.

12. "Note and Lock of Hair, Originals Removed from 1866–1869," Mitarachi Papers, Series 3.

13. Mitarachi, "Melusina," Series 1.2, 167.

14. Andrew Hilen, ed., *The Letters of Henry Wadsworth Longfellow*, vol. 6, *1875–1882* (Cambridge, MA: Harvard University Press), 2358.

15. Skinner, *Echo*, 177–78.

16. Mitarachi, "Melusina," Series 1.2, 183.

17. Memories of the Golden Wedding, 24–25, Fay Family Papers, Series 4.

18. Memories of the Golden Wedding, 36.

19. Hopkins, *John Henry Hopkins*, 359.

REFORM

1. Zina Peirce to Benjamin Mills Peirce, March 10, 1863, Mitarachi Papers, Series 2.

2. Mitarachi, "Melusina," Series 1.3, 215.

3. Mitarachi, "Melusina," Series 1.3, 216.

4. Melusina (Zina) Fay Peirce, letter to the editor, *New York World*, July 11, 1864.

5. Charles Jerome Hopkins journal, May 10, 1863.

6. Lindal Buchanan, *Regendering Delivery: The Fifth Canon and Antebellum Women Rhetors* (Carbondale: Southern Illinois University Press, 2005), 1.

7. Lisette Nadine Gibson, "A Homely Business: Melusina Fay Peirce and Late-Nineteenth-Century Cooperative Housekeeping," in *Separate Spheres No More: Gender Convergence in American Literature, 1830–1930*, ed. Monika M. Elbert (Tuscaloosa: University of Alabama Press, 2000), 189.

8. Ruth Schwartz Cowan, *More Work for Mother: The Ironies of Household Technology from the Open Hearth to the Microwave* (New York: Basic Books, 1983), 18.

9. Mitarachi, "Melusina," Series 1.1, 186.

10. Dolores Hayden, *The Grand Domestic Revolution: A History of Feminist Designs for American Homes, Neighborhoods, and Cities* (Cambridge, MA: MIT Press, 1981), 78.

11. Gibson, "Homely Business," 188.

12. Harriet Beecher Stowe, "A Model Village," *The Revolution* 1 (April 2, 1868), 1.

13. Melusina Fay Peirce, "Co-operative Housekeeping: I," *Atlantic Monthly*, November 1868, 521.

14. Peirce, "Co-operative Housekeeping: II," *Atlantic Monthly*, December 1868, 693.

15. Peirce, "Co-operative Housekeeping: III," *Atlantic Monthly*, January 1869, 30.

16. Peirce, "Co-operative Housekeeping: V," *Atlantic Monthly,* March 1869, 297.
17. Peirce, "Co-operative Housekeeping: I," 519.
18. Hayden, *Grand Domestic,* 68–69.
19. Peirce, "Co-operative Housekeeping: V," 287–94.
20. Sara M. Evans, *Born for Liberty: A History of Women in America* (New York: Free Press, 1997), 136.
21. "Co-operative Housekeeping," *New York Times,* December 17, 1869, 4.
22. E. J. Cutler to Zina, December 11, 1868, Mitarachi Papers, Series 2.
23. Mitarachi, "Melusina," Series 1.3, 211.

COOPERATION

1. "Co-operative Housekeeping," *Cambridge Chronicle* 24, no. 28 (July 10, 1869), 1.
2. Susan Strasser, *Never Done* (New York: Pantheon, 1982), 195.
3. *New York World,* October 22, 1869.
4. Peirce, "Co-operative Housekeeping: V," 287.
5. Mitarachi, "Melusina," Series 1.3, 228–29.
6. McCarthy, *Amy Fay,* 18.
7. Mitarachi, "Melusina," Series 1.1, 27.
8. Hayden, *Grand Domestic,* 79.
9. "Co-operative Housekeeping," *Cambridge Chronicle.*
10. Mitarachi, "Melusina," Series 1.3, 4.
11. Suzanne M. Spencer-Wood, "A Survey of Domestic Reform Movement Sites in Boston and Cambridge, ca. 1865–1905," *Historical Archaeology* 21, no. 2 (1987): 15.
12. Mitarachi, "Melusina," Series 1.3, 3.
13. Mitarachi, "Melusina," Series 1.3, 7.
14. Hayden, *Grand Domestic,* 82.
15. Peirce, *Co-operative Housekeeping,* ed. Amanda Webster, 176, 183.

EUROPEAN INTERLUDE

1. "U.S. Passport Applications, 1795–1925," digital image, s.v. "Zena Fay Peirce" (October 15, 1870), Ancestry.com.
2. Zina Fay Peirce to Benjamin Peirce, Appendix No. 16, "Reports of Observations upon the Total Solar Eclipse of December 22, 1870," *United States Coast Survey Report for 1870,* 13, https://www.unav.es/gep/ZinaInformeG3.html.
3. Benjamin Peirce, Appendix No. 16a, "Report on the Eclipse of the Sun on the 22d of December, 1870," *United States Coast Survey Report for 1871,* 69, https://www.unav.es/gep/apendice16a.pdf.
4. Mitarachi, "Melusina," Series 1.3, 1.

5. Peirce, *Co-operative Housekeeping*, ed. Amanda Webster, 5.
6. Hayden, *Grand Domestic*, 82.

EDUCATION

1. "Account of the Early Formation."
2. Peirce, "Co-operative Housekeeping: V," 290.
3. Woman's Education Association (WEA) first report, WEA Records.
4. WEA first report.
5. "An Account of the Early Formation of the Woman's Education Association," WEA Records 1871–1935, box 1, folder 3, History of WEA, Massachusetts Historical Society.
6. Jennifer C. Madigan, "The Education of Girls and Women in the United States: A Historical Perspective," *Advances in Gender and Education* 1 (2009): 11–13.
7. Edward H. Clarke, *Sex in Education; or, A Fair Chance for Girls* (Boston: James R. Osgood, 1875; Project Gutenberg ebook, 2006).
8. Brent, *Peirce*, 106–11.
9. Melusina Fay Peirce, "Foreign Sketches," *Boston Post*, August 18, 1877.
10. Baker, *Fay House*, 116.
11. Margaret A. Nash, *Women's Education in the United States, 1780–1840* (New York: Palgrave Macmillan, 2005), 115.
12. Brent, *Peirce*, 89–90.
13. "Account of the Early Formation."
14. Spencer-Wood, *Survey*, 15.
15. Evans, *Born for Liberty*, 142.

DISCORD

1. Melusina Fay Peirce, "The Externals of Washington," *Atlantic Monthly*, December 1873, 701–16.
2. Amy Fay to Charles Fay, May 31, 1874, Fay Family Papers, Series 1.
3. Amy Fay to Charles Fay, May 31, 1874.
4. Amy Fay to Charles Fay, May 31, 1874.
5. Amy Fay to Sophronia Fay, March 1, 1873, Fay Family Papers, Series 1.
6. Mitarachi, "Melusina," Series 1.3, 9.
7. Amy Fay to Zina Peirce, November 23, 1871, Fay Family Papers, Series 1.
8. D'Emilio, *Intimate Matters*, 56.
9. Mitarachi, "Melusina," Series 1.2, 187.
10. Conkin, *Puritans*, 196.
11. Hayden, *Grand Domestic*, 82.
12. Brent, *Peirce*, 99–100.
13. Brent, *Peirce*, 100.
14. Brent, *Peirce*, 101.
15. Perry, *William James*, 143.

16. "Charles Sanders Peirce," Peirce Edition Project: Writings of Charles S. Peirce, Indiana University Indianapolis, accessed December 12, 2024, https://peirce.iupui.edu/peirce.html.

17. Brent, *Peirce*, 149.

18. Brent, *Peirce*, 105.

19. Mitarachi, "Melusina," Series 1.3, 31.

20. Brent, *Peirce*, 148–49.

21. Brent, *Peirce*, 82.

OPINIONS

1. Zero [Melusina Fay Peirce], *The Democratic Party: A Political Study, by a Political Zero* (Cambridge, MA: J. Wilson and Son, 1875).

2. Zero, *Democratic Party.*

3. Zero, *Democratic Party.*

4. Zero, *Democratic Party.*

5. Zero, *Democratic Party.*

6. Melusina Fay Peirce, *New York: A Symphonic Study, in Three Parts* (New York: Neale, 1918), pt. 3, 41.

7. Zero, *Democratic Party.*

8. Zero, *Democratic Party.*

9. "Married Happiness," *Statesman,*" November 16, 1877.

10. "Silent Husbands," *Statesman,*" [?] 28, 1877.

11. George Eliot to Harriet Melusina Fay Peirce, September 14, 1866, George Eliot Letters, 1954, 383–84.

12. Eliot to Peirce, September 14, 1866.

13. Mitarachi, "Melusina," Series 1.3, 220.

14. Z. F. Peirce, "George Eliot," *Boston Advertiser*, January 27, 1877.

15. Peirce, "George Eliot."

16. Laura Fay Smith, "An Appeal," *St. Albans Daily Messenger*, March 9, 1874, 3.

17. Mitarachi, "Melusina," Series 1.3, 8.

18. Brent, *Peirce*, 111.

GERMANY

1. Elam Douglas Bomberger, "The German Musical Training of American Students, 1850–1900" (PhD diss., University of Maryland–College Park, 1991), 8.

2. McCarthy, *Amy Fay*, 26.

3. McCarthy, *Amy Fay*, 30.

4. Amy Fay, *Music-Study in Germany, from the Home Correspondence of Amy Fay* (Chicago: Jansen, McClurg, 1880; Okitoks, 2017), 31.

5. McCarthy, *Amy Fay*, 31.

6. Mitarachi, "Melusina," Series 1.3, 10.

7. Amy Fay to Zina Peirce, May 10, 1870, Fay Family Papers, Series 1.
8. Amy Fay to Zina Peirce, May 16, 1870, Fay Family Papers, Series 1.
9. Brent, *Peirce*, 78.
10. Mitarachi, "Melusina," Series 1.3, 13.
11. McCarthy, *Amy Fay*, 34.
12. McCarthy, *Amy Fay*, 37.
13. Fay, *Music-Study*, 37.
14. Fay, *Music-Study*, 98.

LETTERS HOME

1. Fay, *Music-Study*, 45.
2. Fay, *Music-Study*, 19.
3. Amy Fay to Laura Smith, December 2, 1874, Fay Family Papers, Series 1.
4. Amy Fay to Rose Fay, October 2, 1871, Fay Family Papers, Series 1.
5. Fay, *Music-Study*, 16.
6. Fay, *Music-Study*, 41.
7. Fay, *Music-Study*, 44.
8. Amy Fay to Zina Peirce, November 23, 1871, Fay Family Papers, Series 1.
9. Bomberger, "German Musical Training," 285.
10. Fay, *Music-Study*, 76.
11. Bomberger, "German Musical Training," 261, 268.
12. McCarthy, *Amy Fay*, 43.
13. Amy Fay to Zina Peirce, May 21, 1873, Fay Family Papers, Series 1.
14. Fay, *Music-Study*, 88.
15. McCarthy, *Amy Fay*, 50.

CAMBRIDGE ENCORE

1. "Musical Matters," *Buffalo Courier*, January 22, 1876, 4.
2. McCarthy, *Amy Fay*, 91.
3. "Musical," *Boston Globe*, February 17, 1876, 4.
4. "Music and the Drama," *Buffalo Commercial*, February 5, 1876, 4.
5. Hilen, *Letters of Longfellow*, February 25, 1877, 6:248.
6. Zero [Melusina Fay Peirce], "Musical Days in Weimar." *Boston Daily Advertiser*, April 28, 1876.
7. Amy Fay to Zina Peirce, November 25, 1871, Fay Family Papers, Series 1.
8. Amy Fay to Zina Peirce, July 22, 1874, Fay Family Papers, Series 1.
9. McCarthy, *Amy Fay*, 66.
10. McCarthy, *Amy Fay*, 70.

CHICAGO

1. Donald L. Miller, *City of the Century: The Epic of Chicago and the Making of America* (New York: Simon & Schuster, 1996), 178.

2. Mark Clague, "Building the American Symphony Orchestra," in *American Orchestras in the Nineteenth Century*, ed. John Spitzer (Chicago: University of Chicago Press, 2012), 29–39.

3. McCarthy, *Amy Fay*, 76.

4. U.S. Census Bureau, 1880 Census, Chicago.

5. Miller, *City of the Century*, 414.

6. Sally Sexton Kalmbach, *The Jewel of the Gold Coast: Mrs. Potter Palmer's Chicago* (Chicago: Ampersand, 2009), 39–55.

7. "Music: The Leading Event of the Week," *Chicago Tribune*, February 9, 1879.

8. McCarthy, *More Letters*, 3.

9. McCarthy, *More Letters*, 7.

10. "Thomas Will Wed," *Chicago Tribune*, February 13, 1890, 1.

11. Melusina Fay Peirce, "John Talbot Donoghue, a Memorial Tribute," Mitarachi Papers, Series 2.

12. Charles Norman Fay, "The Stock Exchange and the Trusts," pt. 2 of "Plain Tales from Chicago," *Outlook* 91 (March 1909): 591.

13. George P. Upton, "The Piano Recitals of the Week," review of recital by Amy Fay (piano), Hershey Hall, Chicago, *Chicago Tribune*, May 18, 1879, 5.

14. McCarthy, *Amy Fay*, 80.

15. McCarthy, *More Letters*, 9.

16. McCarthy, *Amy Fay*, 79.

17. Howard Pollack, *John Alden Carpenter: A Chicago Composer* (Urbana: University of Illinois Press, 1995), 10.

18. "A Telephonic Feat," *Burlington Weekly Free Press*, January 30, 1880, 3.

19. Charles Fay to Kate Stone, April 4, 1881, Stone-Jackson Family Papers.

20. Anna-Lise P. Santella, "Modeling Music: Early Organizational Structures of American Women's Orchestras," in Spitzer, *American Orchestras*, 53.

21. Karen J. Blair, *The Torchbearers: Women & Their Amateur Arts Associations in America, 1890–1930* (Bloomington: Indiana University Press, 1994), 6.

22. Blair, *Torchbearers*, 24.

23. Alan Walker, *Franz Liszt: The Final Years, 1861–1886* (Ithaca, NY: Cornell University Press, 1997), 235.

CLUBS

1. *Chicago Blue Book of Selected Names of Chicago and Suburban Towns for the Year Ending 1890* (Chicago: Chicago Directory Company, 1889), https://archive.org/details/chicagobluebook01890chic; *Fortnightly Annual Program Book*, Fortnightly of Chicago Records, Newberry Library, Chicago.

2. Blair, *Clubwoman*, 5.

3. Santella, "Modeling Music," 54.

4. Evans, *Born for Liberty*, 140.
5. Amy Fay, "The Amateur Musical Clubs," *Etude* 5, no 12 (December 1887): 180.
6. Fay, "Amateur Musical Clubs."
7. McCarthy, *Amy Fay*, 97.
8. Mathews, *Hundred Years*, 141.

CHAMELEON

1. U.S. Census Bureau, 1880 Census, Chicago.
2. Amy Fay to Zina Peirce, July 21, 1874, Fay Family Papers, Series 1.
3. Charles Fay to Kate Stone, August 18, 1881, Stone-Jackson Family Papers.
4. Hilen, *Letters of Longfellow*, December 25, 1876, 6:214.
5. C. Norman Fay to Thomas Edison, June 21, 1882, Thomas Edison Papers, Rutgers University Collection, https://edisondigital.rutgers.edu/document/D8252K.
6. Fay, "Memoir of Rose Fay Thomas."
7. Amy Fay to Laura Smith, October 7, 1870, Fay Family Papers, Series 1.
8. Charles Fay to Kate Stone, April 4, 1881, Stone-Jackson Family Papers.
9. Daniel MacDonald and Yasemin Dildar, "Married Women's Economic Independence and Divorce in the Nineteenth- and Early-Twentieth-Century United States," *Social Science History* 42, no. 3 (Fall 2018): 611.
10. Vitaly Kiyushchenko, "In the Net of Abductions (On Juliette Peirce's Identity)," *Russian Journal of Communications* 3, no. 1–2 (2010): 126.
11. David E. Pfeifer, "A Singular Love Affair—Charles and Juliette Peirce," *Cognitio* 16, no. 1 (2015): 137–52.
12. Brent, *Peirce*, 123.
13. Peirce, *Co-operative Housekeeping*, ed. Amanda Webster, 189.
14. Zina Peirce to Kate Stone, February 3, 1910, Mitarachi Papers, Series 2.
15. Mitarachi, "Melusina," Series 1.3, 12–13.

FAMOUS FRIEND

1. Ezra Schabas, *Theodore Thomas: America's Conductor and Builder of Orchestras, 1835–1905* (Urbana: University of Illinois Press, 1989), 228.
2. Rose Fay Thomas, *Memoirs of Theodore Thomas* (New York: Moffat, Yard, 1911; POD, Benediction Classics, 2009), 250.
3. Charles Edward Russell, *The American Orchestra and Theodore Thomas* (Westport, CT: Greenwood, 1927), 194.
4. George Upton, ed., *Theodore Thomas: A Musical Autobiography* (New York: Da Capo, 1964), 20.
5. Upton, *Theodore Thomas*, 22–23.
6. Upton, *Theodore Thomas*, 25, 50.

7. Lawrence W. Levine, *Highbrow Lowbrow: The Emergence of Cultural Hierarchy in America* (Cambridge, MA: Harvard University Press, 1988), 113.
8. Russell, *American Orchestra*, 153.
9. Schabas, *Theodore Thomas*, 46.
10. Upton, *Theodore Thomas*, 60.
11. Upton, *Theodore Thomas*, 226–27.
12. Schabas, *Theodore Thomas*, 257.
13. Thomas, *Memoirs*, 251.
14. Theodore Thomas to Melusina Fay Peirce, June 30, 1883, Theodore Thomas Papers, Newberry Library.
15. Thomas, *Memoirs*, 252.
16. Melusina Fay Peirce, *Chicago Evening Journal*, July 22, 1882.
17. Melusina Fay Peirce, *Chicago Evening Journal*, August 5, 1882.
18. Thomas, *Memoirs*, 16.
19. Upton, *Theodore Thomas*, 250.
20. Upton, *Theodore Thomas*, 233.

FAMILY DYNAMICS

1. Peirce, *Co-operative Housekeeping*, ed. Amanda Webster, 207–8.
2. "Brief Notices," *Chicago Tribune*, March 22, 1884, 9.
3. Hayden, *Grand Domestic*, 84, 85.
4. Hayden, *Grand Domestic*, 84.
5. McCarthy, *Amy Fay*, 103.
6. McCarthy, *Amy Fay*, 105.
7. Margaret William McCarthy, "Amy Fay's Reunions with Franz Liszt," *Journal of the American Liszt Society* 24 (July–December 1988): 23–32; Fay, *Music-Study*, 87–88.
8. McCarthy, *More Letters*, 11.
9. "National Opera," *InterOcean*, June 6, 1886, 8.
10. Norman Fay to Samuel May, November 20, 1888, *Harvard College Class Book*, Class of 1829, 352, "Margaret McCarthy Material for Amy," Mitarachi Papers, Schlesinger Library.
11. Laura Smith to Zina Peirce, March 20, 1920, Mitarachi Papers, Series 2.
12. "Pleasant Matrimonial Events," *Chicago Tribune*, June 13, 1889, 6.

WEDDING

1. Schabas, *Theodore Thomas*, 174.
2. Thomas, *Memoirs*, 325–27.
3. Thomas, *Memoirs*, 31.
4. "Thomas Will Wed," *Chicago Tribune*, February 13, 1890, 1.
5. Fay, "Memoir of Rose Fay Thomas."
6. Russell, *American Orchestra*, 193.
7. Thomas, *Memoirs*, 488–90.

8. "Theodore Thomas Wedded," *InterOcean*, May 8, 1890, 6.

9. "Mr. and Mrs. Thomas," *Chicago Tribune*, May 8, 1890, 1.

10. "Mr. and Mrs. Thomas," 1.

11. Schabas, *Theodore Thomas*, 179.

ORCHESTRA

1. Rose Fay Thomas to Pauline Jackson, July 14, 1905, Mitarachi Papers, Series 2.

2. Charles Norman Fay, "The Theodore Thomas Orchestra," *Outlook* 94, no. 4 (January 22, 1910): 159.

3. Thomas, *Memoirs*, 353.

4. Thomas, *Memoirs*, 372.

5. Fay, "Theodore Thomas Orchestra," 160.

6. Mary Wallace Davidson, "John Sullivan Dwight and the Harvard Musical Association Orchestra," in Spitzer, 264.

7. Levine, *Highbrow Lowbrow*, 122.

8. Clague, "Building," 29.

9. Clague, "Building," 52.

10. Schabas, *Theodore Thomas*, 181.

11. Thomas, *Memoirs*, 355.

12. Thomas, *Memoirs*, 356–57.

13. Santella, "Modeling Music," 77.

WORLD'S FAIR

1. World's Columbian Exposition, *Dedicatory and Opening Ceremonies of the World's Columbian Exposition* (Chicago: Stone, Kastler & Painter, 1893), 133.

2. Thomas, *Memoirs*, 382.

3. World's Columbian Exposition, *Dedicatory and Opening Ceremonies*, 153.

4. Thomas, *Memoirs*, 386–87, 390.

5. Thomas, *Memoirs*, 390.

6. Upton, *Theodore Thomas*, 235.

7. Fay, "Theodore Thomas Orchestra," 164.

8. Schabas, *Theodore Thomas*, 203.

9. Philo Adams Otis, *The Chicago Symphony Orchestra: Its Organization, Growth and Development, 1891–1924* (Chicago: Clayton F. Summy, 1924), 50.

10. Otis, Chicago Symphony Orchestra, 50.

11. Schabas, *Theodore Thomas*, 206.

12. Zina Fay Peirce, "We Are a Musical People," letter to the editor, *The Sun*, December 29, 1875, Mitarachi Papers, Schlesinger.

13. Rose Fay Thomas to Daniel Burnham, May 19, 1893, Daniel Burnham Papers, Art Institute of Chicago.

14. Frances Glessner journal, August 1893 insert, Glessner House, Chicago.
15. Lucile Parrish Ward, *A Musical Legacy of 100 Years* (Greenville, SC: A Press, 1995), 26–27.
16. Ward, *Musical Legacy*, 29.
17. Ward, *Musical Legacy*, 30.
18. Ward, *Musical Legacy*, 28.
19. Sondra Wieland Howe, *Women Music Educators in the United States* (Lanham, MD: Scarecrow, 2014), 67.
20. Thomas, *Memoirs*, 417.
21. Otis, *Chicago Symphony Orchestra*, 53.
22. Miller, *City of the Century*, 535.

STRUGGLING

1. Charles Norman Fay, "The Ten Percent Margin," pt. 3 of "Plain Tales from Chicago," *Outlook* 91 (April 1909): 638.
2. Smith, "Portraits," 7.
3. Smith, "Portraits," 16.
4. Thomas, *Memoirs*, 423.
5. Fay, "Theodore Thomas Orchestra," 164.
6. Glessner journal.
7. Harvard College Class of 1869, *Eleventh Report of the Class of 1869 of Harvard College, June, 1919: 50th Anniversary* (Cambridge, MA: Riverside, 1919), 89, accessed March 15, 2025, https://archive.org/details/11threport clas1869harvuoft/page/88/mode/2up.
8. Glessner journal, March 4, 1893.
9. Thomas, *Memoirs*, 418.
10. Glessner journal, June 3, 1894.
11. Theodore Thomas to William Rainey Harper, February 26, 1901, Office of the President, Harper, Judson and Burton Administrations Records, University of Chicago Special Collections.
12. Rose Fay Thomas to Frances Glessner, May 3, 1892, Glessner journal.
13. Thomas to Glessner, May 3, 1892.
14. Glessner journal, April 15, 1893.
15. Rose Fay Thomas to Frances Glessner, n.d., Glessner journal.
16. Karen Ahlquist, "Performances to 'Permanence': Orchestra Building in Late Nineteenth-Century Cincinnati," in Spitzer, 171.
17. Glessner journal, October 21 and November 26, 1893.
18. Barbara Miller Solomon, *In the Company of Educated Women* (New Haven, CT: Yale University Press, 1985), 59.
19. Theodore Thomas to John Glessner, December 25, 1893, Glessner journal.
20. Glessner journal, December 25, 1893.

FELSENGARTEN

1. Glessner journal, September 29, 1893.

2. Rose Fay Thomas to Frances Glessner, September 12, 1894, Glessner journal.

3. Thomas, *Memoirs*, 436–37.

4. Schabas, *Theodore Thomas*, 219.

5. Otis, *Chicago Symphony Orchestra*, 419.

6. Rose Fay Thomas, *Our Mountain Garden* (New York: Macmillan, 1904; POD, Forgotten Books, 2012), 31.

7. Upton, *Theodore Thomas*, 256–57.

8. Thomas, *Memoirs*, 488.

9. Rose Fay Thomas to Margot Garrad Wright, September 15, 1916, Mitarachi Papers, Series 3.

10. Thomas, *Our Mountain Garden*, 18.

11. Thomas, *Our Mountain Garden*, 21.

12. Thomas, *Our Mountain Garden*, 25.

13. Thomas, *Our Mountain Garden*, 115.

14. Thomas, *Our Mountain Garden*, 117.

15. Thomas, *Our Mountain Garden*, 70.

16. Thomas, *Our Mountain Garden*, 136.

17. Thomas, *Memoirs*, 451.

18. Thomas, *Our Mountain Garden*, 488.

19. Thomas, *Our Mountain Garden*, 107.

BUSY LIVES

1. Smith, "Portraits," 11.

2. Thomas, *Memoirs*, 432, 434.

3. Thomas, *Memoirs*, 435.

4. Glessner journal, May 12, 1895.

5. Thomas, *Memoirs*, 452.

6. Miller, *City of the Century*, 349.

7. Evans, *Born for Liberty*, 135.

8. Marc Callis, "The Beginning of the Past: Boston and the Early Historic Preservation Movement, 1863–1918," *Historical Journal of Massachusetts* 32, no. 2 (Summer 2004): 121–23.

9. "Fraunces's Tavern Site," *New York Times*, December 5, 1900, 5.

10. Women of the Revolutionary War: The Preservation Movement, Fraunces Tavern Museum, accessed January 30, 2025, frauncestavernmuseum.org/wrw-preservation-movement.

11. Hayden, *Grand Domestic*, 218; "Evanston Co-operative Scheme," *Chicago Tribune*, December 9, 1890, 6.

12. Hayden, *Grand Domestic*, 72.

13. Amy Fay to Rose Fay Thomas, March 28, 1895, Fay Family Papers, Series 1.

14. McCarthy, *More Letters*, 84.

FEDERATION

1. Ward, *Musical Legacy*, 38.
2. Ward, *Musical Legacy*, 47.
3. Ward, *Musical Legacy*, 47.
4. "City in Grip of Ice," *Chicago Tribune*, January 26, 1898, 3.
5. Ward, *Musical Legacy*, 47–48.
6. Ward, *Musical Legacy*, 54.
7. Ward, *Musical Legacy*, 71–72.
8. Ward, *Musical Legacy*, 73–74.
9. Christine Ammer, *Unsung: A History of Women in American Music*, 2nd ed. (Portland, OR: Amadeus Press, 2001), 304.
10. Schabas, *Theodore Thomas*, 227.
11. Ammer, *Unsung*, 303.
12. Mrs. Hamilton Mott, "Mrs. Theodore Thomas," *Ladies Home Journal* 15 (August 1895): 3.
13. Blair, *Torchbearers*, 52.
14. Blair, *Torchbearers*, 49.

WOMEN'S PHILHARMONIC

1. Karen J. Blair, *The Clubwoman as Feminist: True Womanhood Redefined, 1868–1914* (New York: Holmes & Meier, 1980), 4.
2. Blair, *Clubwoman*, 5.
3. Amy Fay, "Women and Music," *Music* 18 (October 1900): 505–7.
4. McCarthy, *More Letters*, 103.
5. McCarthy, *More Letters*, 139.
6. Kate Fay Stone to Margot Garrad Wright, October 13, 1919, Mitarachi Papers, Series 3.
7. Amy Fay, "Women and the Music Teachers' Association," *Musical Courier* 46, no. 24 (June 17, 1903): 30.
8. Amy Fay, "The Woman Music Teacher in a Large City," *Etude* 20, no. 1 (January 1902): 14.
9. Mitarachi, "Melusina," Series 1.1, 12.
10. Louise Gage Courtney, "The Women's Philharmonic Society of New York," *Musical Courier* 26 (April 1899): 12.
11. McCarthy, *Amy Fay*, 116.
12. Ammer, *Unsung*, 126.
13. Santella, "Modeling Music," 69.
14. "Helping Musicians," *New York Tribune*, October 24, 1909.
15. McCarthy, *More Letters*, 76.

16. McCarthy, *More Letters*, 81, 76.

17. Fay, *Music-Study*, 42.

18. Amy Fay to Zina Peirce, December 18, 1872, Fay Family Papers, Series 1.

19. Fay, *Music-Study*, 118.

ANTI-CRUELTY SOCIETY

1. Thomas, *Our Mountain Garden*, 84–85.

2. Thomas, *Our Mountain Garden*, 88.

3. Thomas, *Our Mountain Garden*, 189.

4. Thomas, *Our Mountain Garden*, 189–90.

5. Thomas, *Our Mountain Garden*, 196–99.

6. Rose Fay Thomas Estate Appraisal and Inventory, Fay Family Papers, Series 4.

7. Janet M. Davis, *The Gospel of Kindness: Animal Welfare & the Making of Modern America* (New York: Oxford University Press, 2016), 64–65.

8. Davis, *Gospel of Kindness*, 51–55.

9. *Kindness in Action*, Anti-Cruelty Society Golden Anniversary booklet, March 6, 1949, Archives of Anti-Cruelty, Chicago.

10. Davis, *Gospel of Kindness*, 52.

11. Anti-Cruelty Society Annual Report, 1913, Anti-Cruelty Society Papers, Chicago History Museum.

12. "She Feeds Stray Cats," *InterOcean*, April 20, 1902, 44.

13. "Horse Beating Prohibited, *InterOcean*, June 1, 1899, 10.

14. "Stars Prevent Cruelty," *Chicago Tribune*, January 29, 1900, 9.

15. About Anti-Cruelty, accessed January 30, 2025, anticruelty.org/about; "Pity Fire Engine Horses," *Chicago Tribune*, March 9, 1904, 4; untitled article, *Chicago Tribune*, April 27, 1901.

16. "Horses Are Picking Up," *Chicago Tribune*, April 16, 1902, 2.

COMPASSION

1. About Anti-Cruelty, anticruelty.org/about.

2. "Stray Dogs and Cats Befriended," *Chicago Tribune*, January 15, 1905, 18.

3. Anti-Cruelty Society Annual Report, 1913.

4. "Canary Rush Is Forbidden," *Chicago Tribune*, January 25, 1903, 37.

5. "Toys Teach Art of Cruelty, Declares a Chicago Woman," *Chicago Tribune*, November 5, 1904, 3.

6. Untitled article, *Chicago Tribune*, November 8, 1903, 6.

7. Thomas, *Memoirs*, 486–87.

CONCERT HALL

1. Fay, "Memoir of Rose Fay Thomas."

2. Thomas, *Memoirs*, 108.

3. Thomas, *Memoirs*, 331–32.
4. Russell, *American Orchestra*, 255.
5. Thomas, *Memoirs*, 511.
6. Thomas, *Memoirs*, 512.
7. "Crisis in Big Orchestra," *Chicago Daily Tribune*, February 13, 1903, 1.
8. Rose Fay Thomas to Frances Glessner, May 2, 1904, Glessner journal.
9. McCarthy, *More Letters*, 70.
10. Russell, *American Orchestra*, 293.
11. Fay, "Theodore Thomas Orchestra," 166.
12. Thomas, *Memoirs*, 529.
13. Fay, "Theodore Thomas Orchestra."
14. Schabas, *Theodore Thomas*, 246.
15. Thomas, *Memoirs*, 530–31.
16. "A Summertime Paradise," *Kansas City Star*, June 7, 1904, 9.
17. Book flyer, Thomas Papers.
18. "Books of Fact," *St. Louis Republic*, June 11, 1904, 6.
19. Thomas, *Memoirs*, 535.
20. Rose Fay Thomas to Daniel Burnham, December 8, 1904, Burnham Papers.
21. Russell, *American Orchestra*, 299.
22. Thomas, *Memoirs*, 535.
23. Rose Fay Thomas to Frances Glessner, December 1904 insert, Glessner journal.
24. Upton, *Chicago Symphony Orchestra*, 107.
25. Thomas, *Memoirs*, 538.

FINALE

1. "Orchestra Hall Is Dedicated," *Chicago Tribune*, December 15, 1904, 1–2.
2. Thomas, *Memoirs*, 542.
3. Glessner journal, January 8, 1905.
4. Thomas, *Memoirs*, 543.
5. Upton, *Chicago Symphony Orchestra*, 112–3.
6. "Death Comes to Maestro Thomas," *Chicago Tribune*, January 5, 1905, 4.
7. Schabas, *Theodore Thomas*, 253.

MOURNING

1. Charles Norman Fay, "Theodore Thomas: An Appreciation," Chicago Symphony Orchestra program notes, January 2–3, 1941, 25, Rosenthal Archives of the Chicago Symphony Orchestra.
2. Glessner journal, January 8, 1905.
3. "Music's Tribute Paid to Thomas," *Chicago Tribune*, January 7, 1905, 14.

4. Thomas, *Memoirs*, 544.
5. Thomas, *Memoirs*, 558.
6. Thomas, *Memoirs*, 544.
7. "Theodore Thomas," *New York Times*, January 5, 1905.
8. Fay, "Theodore Thomas Orchestra," 167.
9. Glessner journal, January 8, 1905.
10. Glessner journal, February 5, 1905.
11. Rose Fay Thomas to Isabella Stewart Gardner, February 12, 1905, Glessner House.
12. Thomas to Gardner, February 12, 1905.
13. Margot Garrad Wright to Pauline Stone Jackson, May 6, 1905, Fay Family Papers, Series 4.
14. Rose Fay Thomas poems, Mitarachi Papers, Series 2.

SIBLINGS

1. McCarthy, *More Letters*, 71.
2. McCarthy, *Amy Fay*, 125.
3. McCarthy, *More Letters*, 79.
4. Rose Fay Thomas to Margaret Sherman Burnham, September 5, 1905, Burnham Papers.
5. Mitarachi, "Melusina," Series 1.3, 12–29.
6. Zina Peirce to Kate Stone, November 18, 1910, Mitarachi Papers, Series 2.
7. McCarthy, *More Letters*, 75.
8. Melusina Fay Peirce apartment patent, Fay Family Papers, Series 4.
9. Peirce, *New York*, pt. 3, 15–16.
10. Hayden, *Grand Domestic*, 198.
11. W. Nelson Smith, "Mrs. Laura Fay Smith," *Vermont Standard*, September 16, 1920, 2.
12. Laura Fay Smith, "That Feminist Paradise Palace," *New York Times*, April 25, 1915, 21.
13. Erin C. Tarver and Shannon Sullivan, eds. *Feminist Interpretations of William James* (University Park: Pennsylvania State University Press, 2015), 82.
14. Amy Fay to Zina Peirce, 12 May 1912, Fay Family Papers, Series 1.
15. Rose Fay Thomas to Frances Glessner, December 18, 1908, Glessner journal.
16. McCarthy, *More Letters*, 117.
17. Amy Fay to Rose Fay Thomas, May 25, 1911, Fay Family Papers, Series 1.

BACK EAST ONCE MORE

1. "2000 Line Banks of Canal to See Taft and Festival Gowns," *Cincinnati Post*, May 4, 1910, 1–2.

2. Amy Fay to Kate Stone, May 30, 1910, Fay Family Papers, Series 1.

3. "Spent Christmas Day in La Paz," *Boston Evening Transcript*, January 1, 1903.

4. Amy Fay to Pauline Jackson, January 4, 1903, Fay Family Papers, Series 1.

5. Rose Fay Thomas to Pauline Jackson, October 3, 1902, Mitarachi Papers, Series 2.

6. Evans, *Born for Liberty*, 161.

7. McCarthy, *More Letters*, 44–45.

8. McCarthy, *More Letters*, 52.

9. McCarthy, *Amy Fay*, 131.

10. "Miss Amy Fay," *Musical Observer* 4, no. 9 (September 1910): 18.

11. McCarthy, *More Letters*, 115.

12. Amy Fay to Rose Fay Thomas, April 3, 1912, Fay Family Papers, Series 1.

13. Jennis Irene Mix, "Musical Comments and Current Events," *Pittsburgh Daily Post*, December 17, 1911, 9.

14. Book flyer, Thomas Papers.

15. "The Christmas Bookstalls," *Boston Evening Transcript*, December 13, 1911, 24.

16. Daniel Burnham to Rose Fay Thomas, December 21, 1911, Thomas Papers.

17. Wassily Safonoff to Rose Fay Thomas, July 31, 1908, Thomas Papers.

18. "Thomas' Widow Loses Fight for Orchestra Name," *InterOcean*, March 6, 1913, 1.

19. Glessner journal, March 9, 1913.

20. Serge Koussevitzky to Rose Fay Thomas, December 12, 1927, Theodore Thomas guest book, Thomas Papers.

21. John Alden Carpenter to Rose Fay Thomas, 1928, Thomas Papers.

22. *Cambridge Directory, 1926–27* (Boston: W. A. Greenough, 1927), https://archive.org/details/cambridgedirecto1926unse/mode/2up, 806.

23. Rose Fay Thomas estate appraisal and inventory, Fay Family Papers, Series 4.

24. Zina Peirce to Kate Stone, November 18, 1910, Mitarachi Papers, Series 2.

25. Peirce, *New York*, pt. 3, 99.

A SYMPHONIC STUDY

1. Atkinson, "Examination," 172.

2. Peirce, *New York*, pt. 1, 5; pt. 2, 107.

3. Peirce, *New York*, pt. 1, 7.

4. McCarthy, *More Letters*, 155.

5. Amy Fay Stone to Kate Stone, June 20, 1918, Fay Family Papers, Series 2.

6. Kate Stone to Margot Garrad Wright, August 16, 1917, Fay Family Papers, Series 3.

7. Kate Stone to Margot Garrad Wright, December 3, 1917, Fay Family Papers, Series 3.

8. Zina Peirce to Amy Fay, February 9, 1914, Fay Family Papers, Series 1.

9. Katherine Fay Stone and Rose Fay Thomas estate appraisals and inventory, Fay Family Papers, Series 4.

10. Zina Peirce to Kate Stone, September 19, 1911[?], Mitarachi Papers, Series 2.

11. Kate Stone to unidentified daughter, November 18, 1919, Fay Family Papers, Series 3.

12. Laura Smith to Zina Peirce, March 20, 1920, Mitarachi Papers, Series 2.

13. Harvard College Class of 1869, *Eleventh Report*, 89.

14. Orville Wright to Rose Fay Thomas, October 28, 1914, Thomas Papers.

15. William Dickson, "How Rose Arose," January 1921, Mitarachi Papers, MC567, Series 6.9.

OLD AGE

1. Kate Stone to Margot Garrad Wright, July 5, 1920, Fay Family Papers, Series 3.

2. Stone to Wright, July 5, 1920.

3. Zina Peirce to Laura Smith, February 24, 1920, Mitarachi Papers, Series 2.

4. Kate Stone to Margot Garrard Wright, April 5, 1923, Fay Family Papers, Series 3.

5. Bruno David Ussher, "Wife of Thomas, Noted Orchestra Leader, Is Feted," *Los Angeles Evening Express*, September 5, 1922, 1.

6. "Local Pianist Assists Mrs. Thomas in KHJ Radio Program," *Santa Ana Register*, September 9, 1922, 5.

7. Rose Fay Thomas to Margot Garrard Wright, September 9, 1922, Fay Family Papers, Series 3.

8. Kate Stone to Margot Garrard Wright, April 5, 1923, Fay Family Papers, Series 3.

9. Kate Stone to Margot Garrard Wright, June 28, 1923, Fay Family Papers, Series 3.

10. "Mrs. Melusina Fay-Peirce Dies in Watertown, Aged 87," *Boston Globe*, April 29, 1923, 11.

11. Kate Stone to unidentified daughter, March 1919, Fay Family Papers, Series 3.

12. "U.S. Passport Applications, 1795–1925," digital image, s.v. "Rose Fay Thomas" (January 1924), Ancestry.com.

13. Fay, "Memoir of Rose Fay Thomas."

14. Ward, *Musical Legacy*, 342.
15. Ward, *Musical Legacy*, 341.

CODA

1. Kate Stone to Amy Fay Stone, December 29, 1925, Fay Family Papers, Series 2.
2. "Miss Fay, Composer, Dead in Watertown," *Boston Globe*, February 29, 1928, 25.
3. McCarthy, *Amy Fay*, 133.
4. Fay, "Memoir of Rose Fay Thomas."
5. Charles Norman Fay, *Labor in Politics, or Class versus Country: Considerations for American Voters*, 4th ed. (Cambridge: University Press, 1921), xiii–xiv.
6. Jessica C. E. Gienow-Hecht, *Sound Diplomacy: Music and Emotions in Transatlantic Relations, 1850–1920* (Chicago: University of Chicago Press, 2009), 109–28.
7. "'Preserve the Parks' Her Motto," *Times Union*, August 11, 1925, 51.
8. Laura Smith to Zina Peirce, March 20, 1920, Mitarachi Papers, Series 2.

APPENDIX

1. Hayden, *Grand Domestic*, 88.
2. Walker, *Franz Liszt*, 234.
3. Robert Dumm and Karen A. Shaffer, "Amy Fay, American Pianist: Something to Write Home About," *Maud Powell Signature* 1, no. 2 (Fall 1995): 29.
4. Grace Wilson and Lincoln Adams, "Tributes to the Memory of Mrs. Theodore Thomas," newspaper clipping, May 9, 1929.
5. John Glessner, "Tributes to the Memory of Mrs. Theodore Thomas," newspaper clipping, May 9, 1929.
6. Pollack, *John Alden Carpenter*, 104; Schabas, *Theodore Thomas*, 257.
7. "The Work of a Volunteer Organization for the Benefit of the Public Schools," WEA Records, 6.
8. Baker, *Fay House*, 116.
9. Nash, *Women's Education*, 115.
10. Maleeha Syed, "Rock Point School Takes Down Portrait of Bishop Who Argued Slavery Was Not a Sin," *Burlington Free Press*, May 27, 2021.
11. Peirce, "Co-operative Housekeeping: I," 33.
12. World Bank, *Women, Business and the Law 2024* (Washington, DC: World Bank, 2024), https://doi.org/10.1596/978-1-4648-2063-2.

ACKNOWLEDGMENTS

1. Thomas, *Memoirs*, viii.

Bibliography

NOTE

Zina's writings on cooperative housekeeping exist in multiple formats. *The Atlantic Monthly* articles are listed according to the issue in which they appeared. As for her books, for reference purposes in the endnotes, I used a condensed volume incorporating both versions (1870 and 1884), edited by Amanda Webster and released in 2020.

MANUSCRIPTS AND UNPUBLISHED SOURCES

Archives of Anti-Cruelty, Chicago

Art Institute of Chicago

  Burnham, Daniel. Papers.

Chicago History Museum

  Anti-Cruelty Society Papers.

Fay, Charles. Account Book, 1855–61. Unpublished. Private collection.

Glessner House, Chicago

  Gardener, Isabella Stewart. Letters.

  Glessner, Frances. Journals.

Indiana University Indianapolis

  Peirce Edition Project: Writings of Charles S. Peirce.

Library of Congress

  Fay, Charles Norman. "Memoir of Rose Fay Thomas." Unpublished manuscript. Cambridge, MA, 1939.

Longfellow House Washington's Headquarters, Cambridge, MA

  Henry Wadsworth Longfellow (1807–1882) Family Papers, 1768–1972.

Massachusetts Historical Society, Boston

  Fay-Mixter Family Papers, 1775–1962.

  Stone-Jackson Family Papers, 1836–1955.

  Woman's Education Association (WEA) Records, 1871–1935.

Newberry Library, Chicago

  Fortnightly of Chicago Records, 1869–2018.

  Musicians Club of Women Papers, 1891–2019.

  Thomas, Theodore. Papers, 1852-1926.

Rosenthal Archives of the Chicago Symphony Orchestra
Fay, Charles Norman. "Theodore Thomas: An Appreciation." Chicago Symphony Orchestra program notes. January 2–3, 1941.
Schlesinger Library, Radcliffe Institute for Advanced Study, Harvard University
Fay Family Papers, 78-M105–96-M100.
Mitarachi, Sylvia Wright. Papers.
Mitarachi, Sylvia Wright. "The Life of Melusina Fay Peirce." MC567, Series 1. Unpublished typescript, 1990. Series 1.1: pp. 1–100; Series 1.2: pp. 101–200; Series 1.3: pp. 201 to end (numbering is erratic in later portions).
Mitarachi, Sylvia Wright. Supporting materials for "The Life of Melusina Fay Peirce." MC567, Series 2–4. (*Note:* These often overlap with the Fay Family Papers.)
Smith, Madeline. "Portraits of My Aunts." Unpublished manuscript.
St. Luke's Episcopal Church, St. Albans, VT
175th Anniversary Brochure.
Parish Administrator Manual, 2013.
Union Church Parish Records.
University of Michigan, William L. Clements Library
Hopkins Family Papers.
University of Vermont Special Collections
Hopkins and Canfield Families Papers.

PUBLISHED WORKS

"Address of the Chairman, Thomas Wentworth Higginson." *Proceedings of the Cambridge Historical Society* 2 (1906–7). https://historycambridge.org/wp-content/uploads/2017/06/Proceedings-Volume-2-1906-1907.pdf.

Ahlquist, Karen. "Performances to 'Permanence': Orchestra Building in Late Nineteenth-Century Cincinnati." In Spitzer, *American Orchestras,* 156–74.

Ammer, Christine. *Unsung: A History of Women in American Music.* 2nd ed. Portland, OR: Amadeus, 2001.

Anderson, Ruth. "Rose Fay Thomas." *Music Clubs Magazine* 99, no. 1 (Autumn 2019): 10–11.

Atkinson, Norma Pereira. "An Examination of the Life and Thought of Zina Fay Peirce, an American Reformer and Feminist." PhD diss., Ball State University, 1983.

Baker, Christina Hopkinson. *The Story of Fay House.* Cambridge, MA: Harvard University Press, 1929.

Bakker, Jan. "Another Dilemma of an Intellectual in the Old South: Caroline Gilman, the Peculiar Institution, and Greater Rights for Women in the Rose Magazines." *Southern Literary Journal* 17, no.1 (Fall 1984): 12–25.

Barry, Kathleen. *Susan B. Anthony: A Biography.* New York: New York University Press, 2020.

Basbanes, Nicholas. *Cross of Snow: A Life of Henry Wadsworth Longfellow.* New York: Knopf, Doubleday, 2020.

Beecher, Catharine E. *A Treatise on Domestic Economy, for the Use of Young Ladies at Home and at School.* New York: Marsh, Capen, Lyon, and Webb, 1841.

Beecher, Catharine E., and Harriet Beecher Stowe. *The American Woman's Home.* New York: J. B. Ford, 1869.

Blair, Karen J. *The Clubwoman as Feminist: True Womanhood Redefined, 1868–1914.* New York: Holmes & Meier, 1980.

Blair, Karen J. *The Torchbearers: Women & Their Amateur Arts Associations in America, 1890–1930.* Bloomington: Indiana University Press, 1994.

Bomberger, Elam Douglas. "The German Musical Training of American Students." PhD diss., University of Maryland–College Park, 1991.

Brent, Joseph. *Charles Sanders Peirce: A Life.* Bloomington: Indiana University Press, 1993.

Buchanan, Lindal. *Regendering Delivery: The Fifth Canon and Antebellum Women Rhetors.* Carbondale: Southern Illinois University Press, 2005.

Callis, Marc. "The Beginning of the Past: Boston and the Early Historic Preservation Movement, 1863–1918." *Historical Journal of Massachusetts* 32, no. 2 (Summer 2004): 118–37.

Cambridge Directory, 1926–27. Boston: W. A. Greenough, 1927. https://archive.org/details/cambridgedirecto1926unse/mode/2up.

Chicago Blue Book of Selected Names of Chicago and Suburban Towns for the Year Ending 1890. Chicago: Chicago Directory Company, 1889. https://archive.org/details/chicagobluebook01890chic.

Clague, Mark. "Building the American Symphony Orchestra." In Spitzer, *American Orchestras*, 25–52.

Clarke, Edward H. "Sex in Education; or, A Fair Chance for Girls." Boston: James R. Osgood, 1875. Project Gutenberg eBook.

Cohen, Ruth Schwartz. *More Work for Mother: The Ironies of Household Technology from the Open Hearth to the Microwave.* New York: Basic Books, 1983.

Conkin, Paul K. *Puritans & Pragmatists: Eight Eminent American Thinkers.* New York: Dodd, Mead, 1968; Bloomington: Indiana University Press, 1976.

Courtney, Louise Gage. "The Women's Philharmonic Society of New York." *Musical Courier* 26 (April 1899): 12.

Davidson, Mary Wallace. "John Sullivan Dwight and the Harvard Musical Association Orchestra." In Spitzer, *American Orchestras*, 247–68.

Davis, Janet M. *The Gospel of Kindness: Animal Welfare and the Making of Modern America*. New York: Oxford University Press, 2016.

de Hegermann-Lindencrone, L. *In the Courts of Memory, 1858–1875*. New York: Harper and Brothers, 1911; POD, Monee, 2022.

D'Emilio, John, and Estelle B. Freedman. *Intimate Matters: A History of Sexuality in America*. Chicago: University of Chicago, 1997.

Douglass, Frederick. *Autobiographies*. New York: Literary Classics, 1994.

Dumm, Robert, and Karen A. Shaffer. "Amy Fay, American Pianist: Something to Write Home About." *Maud Powell Signature* 1, no. 2 (Fall 1995): 4–8, 29.

Dutcher, L. L. *The History of St. Albans, VT: Civil, Religious, Biographical and Statistical*. St. Albans, VT: Stephen E. Royce, 1872; POD.

Eliot, George, and Gordon Sherman Haight. *The George Eliot Letters Journal*. New Haven, CT: Yale University Press, 1954.

Evans, Sara M. *Born for Liberty: A History of Women in America*. New York: Free Press, 1997.

Ewen, Barbara Ellen. "The Education of Ellen Emerson." *Discover Concord*, September 15, 2022, 20–21.

Fay, Amy. "Music in New York." *Music* 18 (December 1900): 179–82.

Fay, Amy. *Music-Study in Germany, from the Home Correspondence of Amy Fay*. Chicago: Jansen, McClurg, 1880; Okitoks, 2017.

Fay, Amy. "The Woman Music Teacher in a Large City." *Etude* 20, no. 1 (January 1902): 14.

Fay, Amy. "Women and Music." *Music* 18 (October 1900): 505–7.

Fay, Amy. "Women and the Music Teachers' Association." *Musical Courier* 46, no. 24 (June 17, 1903): 30.

Fay, Charles Norman. *Labor in Politics, or Class versus Country: Considerations for American Voters*. 4th ed. Cambridge, MA: University Press, 1921.

Fay, Charles Norman. "Plain Tales from Chicago." 3 pts. *Outlook* 91 (January–April 1909): 548–52; 591–94; 626–42.

Fay, Charles Norman. "The Theodore Thomas Orchestra." *Outlook* 94, no. 4 (January 22, 1910): 159–69.

Fay, Orlin P. *Fay Genealogy: John Fay of Marlborough and His Descendants*. Cleveland: J. B. Savage, 1898; POD, Higginson Books.

Geer, Ashley. "The 1893 Chicago World's Columbian Exposition and the Emergence of the Women's Music Club Movement." Master's thesis, Florida State University, 2011.

Gibson, Lisette Nadine. "A Homely Business: Melusina Fay Peirce and Late-Nineteenth-Century Cooperative Housekeeping." In *Separate Spheres No More: Gender Convergence in American Literature, 1830–1930,* edited by Monika M. Elbert, 179–202. Tuscaloosa: University of Alabama Press, 2000.

Gienow-Hecht, Jessica C. E. *Sound Diplomacy: Music and Emotions in Transatlantic Relations, 1850–1920*. Chicago: University of Chicago Press, 2009.

Goldstone, Lawrence. *Drive! Henry Ford, George Selden, and the Race to Invent the Auto Age*. New York: Ballantine, 2016.

Greenleaf, William. *Monopoly on Wheels: Henry Ford and the Selden Automobile Patent*. Detroit: Wayne State University Press, 2011.

Harper, Ida Husted. *The Life and Work of Susan B. Anthony*. Vol. 1. Indianapolis: Bowen-Merrill, 1899.

Harvard College Class of 1869. *Eleventh Report of the Class of 1869 of Harvard College, June, 1919: 50th Anniversary*. Cambridge, MA: Riverside, 1919. https://archive.org/details/11threportclas1869harvuoft/mode/2up.

Hayden, Dolores. *The Grand Domestic Revolution: A History of Feminist Designs for American Homes, Neighborhoods, and Cities*. Cambridge, MA: MIT Press, 1981.

Hilen, Andrew, ed. *The Letters of Henry Wadsworth Longfellow*. Vol. 6, *1875–1882*. Cambridge, MA: Harvard University Press.

Hoffman, Joan Bentley. "Rose Fay Thomas." In *Women Building Chicago 1790–1990: A Biographical Dictionary*, edited by Rima Lunin Schultz and Adele Hast, 875. Bloomington: Indiana University Press, 2001.

Hood, R. E. "From a Headstart to a Deadstart: The Historical Basis for Black Indifference Toward the Episcopal Church 1800–1860." *Historical Magazine of the Protestant Episcopal Church* 51, no. 3 (September 1982): 278.

Hopkins, John Henry. *The Life of the Late Right Reverend John Henry Hopkins, First Bishop of Vermont, and Seventh Presiding Bishop*. New York: F. J. Huntington, 1873; POD, Alpha Editions, 2021.

Horowitz, Joseph. "A Life in Limbo: Laura Langford and Brooklyn's Seidl Society." *Journal of the Gilded Age and Progressive Era* 13, no. 1 (January 2014): 80–92.

Horowitz, Joseph. "Music and the Gilded Age: Social Control and Sacralization Revisited." *Journal of the Gilded Age and Progressive Era* 3, no. 3 (July 2004): 227–45.

Howe, Sondra Wieland. *Women Music Educators in the United States*. Lanham, MD: Scarecrow, 2014.

Irmscher, Christoph. *Louis Agassiz: Creator of American Science*. New York: Houghton Mifflin, 2013.

Janik, Erika. *Marketplace of the Marvelous: The Strange Origins of Modern Medicine.* Boston: Beacon, 2014.

Kalmbach, Sally Sexton. *The Jewel of the Gold Coast: Mrs. Potter Palmer's Chicago.* Chicago: Ampersand, 2009.

Katz, Mark. "Making America More Musical Through the Phonograph, 1900–1930." *American Music* 16, no. 4 (Winter 1998): 448–76.

Ketner, Kenneth Lane. *His Glassy Essence: An Autobiography of Charles Sanders Peirce.* Nashville: Vanderbilt University Press, 1998.

Kiryushchenko, Vitaly. "In the Net of Abductions (On Juliette Peirce's Identity)." *Russian Journal of Communications* 3, no. 1–2: 123–46.

Levine, Lawrence W. *Highbrow Lowbrow: The Emergence of Cultural Hierarchy in America.* Cambridge, MA: Harvard University Press, 1988.

Levy, Ronald. "Bishop Hopkins and the Dilemma of Slavery." *Pennsylvania Magazine of History and Biography* 91, no. 1 (January 1967): 56–71.

MacDonald, Daniel, and Yasemin Dildar. "Married Women's Economic Independence and Divorce in the Nineteenth- and Early Twentieth Century United States." *Social Science History* 42, no. 3 (Fall 2018): 601–29.

Mathews, W. S. B., ed. *A Hundred Years of Music in America: An Account of Musical Effort in America During the Past Century.* Chicago: G. L. Howe, 1889.

McCarthy, Margaret William. "Amy Fay: The American Years." *American Music* 3, no. 1 (Spring 1985): 52–62.

McCarthy, Margaret William. *Amy Fay: America's Notable Woman of Music.* Warren, MI: Harmonie Park, 1995.

McCarthy, Margaret William. "Amy Fay's Reunions with Franz Liszt." *Journal of the American Liszt Society* 24 (July–December 1988): 23–32.

McCarthy, Margaret William, ed. *More Letters of Amy Fay: The American Years, 1879–1916.* Detroit: Information Coordinators, 1986.

McColley, Robert. "Classical Music in Chicago and the Founding of the Symphony, 1850–1905." *Illinois Heritage Journal* 78 (Winter 1985): 289–302.

McCrea, Roswell Cheney. *The Humane Movement: A Descriptive Survey.* New York: Columbia University Press, 1910; POD, Andesite.

Miller, Donald L. *City of the Century: The Epic of Chicago and the Making of America.* New York: Simon & Schuster, 1996.

Mott, Mrs. Hamilton. "Mrs. Theodore Thomas." *Ladies Home Journal* 15 (August 1895): 3.

Nash, Margaret A. *Women's Education in the United States 1780–1840.* New York: Palgrave Macmillan, 2005.

Otis, Philo Adams. *The Chicago Symphony Orchestra: Its Organization, Growth and Development, 1891–1924.* Chicago: Clayton F. Summy, 1924.

Paton, Lucy Allen. *Elizabeth Cary Agassiz: A Biography.* Boston: Houghton Mifflin, 1919.

Peirce, Melusina Fay. "Co-operative Housekeeping." *Atlantic Monthly* 22, no. 133–? (1868–69).

Peirce, Melusina Fay. *Co-operative Housekeeping*. Edited by Amanda Webster. McLean, IL: Elderfly, 2020.

Peirce, Melusina Fay. *Co-operative Housekeeping: How Not to Do It and How to Do It; A Study in Sociology*. Boston: J. R. Osgood, 1884.

Peirce, Melusina Fay [Mrs. C. F. Peirce]. *Co-operative Housekeeping: Romance in Domestic Economy*. Edinburgh: John Ross, 1870.

Peirce, Melusina Fay. *New York: A Symphonic Study, in Three Parts*. New York: Neale, 1918.

Perry, Ralph Barton. *The Thought and Character of William James*. Cambridge, MA: Harvard University Press, 1948.

Pfeifer, David. E. "A Singular Love Affair—Charles and Juliette Peirce." *Cognitio* 16, no. 1 (2015): 137–52.

Pfeiffer, Judith. "Amy Fay and Her Teachers in Germany." PhD diss., University of Memphis, 2008.

Plante, Ellen M. *The American Kitchen: 1700 to the Present, from Hearth to Highrise*. New York: Facts on File, 1995.

Plante, Ellen M. *Women at Home in Victorian America: A Social History*. New York: Facts on File, 1997.

Pollack, Howard. *John Alden Carpenter: A Chicago Composer*. Urbana: University of Illinois Press, 1995.

Reeves, William D. *From Tally-Ho to Forest Home: The History of Two Louisiana Plantations*. Bloomington: Author House, 2006.

Reflections: The Bicentennial of St. Albans, Vt., 1788–1988. St. Albans, VT: St. Albans Historical Society, 1988.

Ross, Ishbel. *Crusades and Crinolines: The Life and Times of Ellen Curtis Demorest and William Jennings Demorest*. New York: Harper & Row, 1963.

Russell, Charles Edward. *The American Orchestra and Theodore Thomas*. Westport, CT: Greenwood, 1927.

Santella, Anna-Lise P. "Modeling Music: Early Organizational Structures of American Women's Orchestras." In Spitzer, *American Orchestras*, 53–77.

Schabas, Ezra. *Theodore Thomas: America's Conductor and Builder of Orchestras, 1835–1905*. Urbana: University of Illinois Press, 1989.

Sherburne, Michelle Arnosky. *Abolition & the Underground Railroad in Vermont*. Charleston, SC: History Press, 2013.

Sherburne, Michelle Arnosky. *The St. Albans Raid: Confederate Attack on Vermont*. Charleston, SC: History Press, 2014.

Sixth Triennial Report of the Class of 1869 of Harvard College. Boston: Rockwell and Churchill, 1888.

Skinner, Henrietta Dana. *An Echo from Parnassus: Girlhood Memories of Longfellow and His Friends*. New York: J. H. Sears, 1928.

Solomon, Barbara Miller. *In the Company of Educated Women.* New Haven, CT: Yale University Press, 1985.

Spencer-Wood, Suzanne M. "A Survey of Domestic Reform Movement Sites in Boston and Cambridge, Ca. 1865–1905." *Historical Archaeology* 21, no. 2 (1987): 7–36.

Spitzer, John, ed. *American Orchestras in the Nineteenth Century.* Chicago: University of Chicago Press, 2012.

Stowe, Harriet Beecher. "A Model Village." *The Revolution* 1 (April 2, 1868): 1.

Strasser, Susan. *Never Done.* New York: Pantheon, 1982.

Tarver, Erin C., and Shannon Sullivan, eds. *Feminist Interpretations of William James.* University Park: Pennsylvania State University Press, 2015.

Thomas, Rose Fay. "The Chicago Amateur Musical Club." *Music* 1 (1892): 205.

Thomas, Rose Fay. *Memoirs of Theodore Thomas.* New York: Moffat, Yard, 1911; POD, Benediction Classics, 2009.

Thomas, Rose Fay. *Our Mountain Garden.* New York: Macmillan, 1904; POD, Forgotten Books, 2012.

Tolles, Bryant F., Jr. *Summer Cottages in the White Mountains: The Architecture of Leisure and Recreation, 1870 to 1930.* Lebanon, NH: University Press of New England, 2000.

Upton, George, ed. *Theodore Thomas: A Musical Autobiography.* New York: Da Capo, 1964.

Walker, Alan. "*Franz Liszt: The Final Years, 1861–1886.*" Ithaca, NY: Cornell University Press, 1997.

Ward, Lucile Parrish. *A Musical Legacy of 100 Years.* Greenville, SC: A Press, 1995.

Ward, Roger. *Peirce & Religion: Knowledge, Transformation and the Reality of God.* Lanham: Lexington Books, 2018.

Welter, Barbara. "The Cult of True Womanhood: 1820–1860." *American Quarterly* 18, no. 2, pt. 1 (Summer 1966): 151–74.

Williams, Kenneth. "International Students in Music: Crossing Boundaries." *College Music Symposium* 41 (2001): 43–56.

Wilson, Gregory C., ed. *Bethlehem New Hampshire: A Bicentennial History.* Littleton, NH: Bondcliff Books, 1999.

World Bank. *Women, Business and the Law 2024.* Washington, DC: World Bank, 2024. https://doi.org/10.1596/978-1-4648-2063-2.

World's Columbian Exposition. *Dedicatory and Opening Ceremonies of the World's Columbian Exposition.* Chicago: Stone, Kastler & Painter, 1893.

Index

Italicized page numbers indicate figures.

Andrea Friederici Ross is the author of *Edith: The Rogue Rockefeller McCormick* and *Let the Lions Roar! The Evolution of Brookfield Zoo*. Andrea has worked as the operations manager of the Chicago Symphony Orchestra, as assistant to the director of the Chicago Zoological Society, and at her local public school library. Most importantly, she is the proud mother of two incredible humans and the happy companion of two unruly rescue dogs. Andrea votes in every election, embodies none of the attributes of True Womanhood, and is grateful for the women who fought to make those options possible.